The Field Archaeology
of Exmoor

The Field Archaeology
of Exmoor

Hazel Riley and Robert Wilson-North

ENGLISH HERITAGE

Published by English Heritage at the National Monuments Record Centre,
Great Western Village, Kemble Drive, Swindon SN2 2GZ

Copyright © English Heritage 2001
Images (except as otherwise shown) © English Heritage
Applications for the reproduction of images should be made to the
National Monuments Record

First Published 2001

ISBN 1 873592 58 2

Product Code XA20019

British Library Cataloguing in Publication Data
A CIP catalogue record for this book is available from the British Library.

Edited and brought to press by David M Jones and Andrew McLaren,
    Publications, English Heritage
Indexed by Veronica Stebbing
Designed by Chuck Goodwin

Printed by Snoeck-Ducaju & Zoon, Ghent

Contents

Illustrations

Foreword

The National Parks, which include many of the best loved parts of the English landscape, are valued and enjoyed by large numbers of people – especially those from the surrounding area who often develop a particular affinity and affection for them.

Exmoor was defined and designated in the first round of national park creations. Between the wild open moors there are the narrow, hidden valleys so readily associated with R D Blackmore's romantic tale of *Lorna Doone*; to the north lies the rugged, scenic coastline sought out by the Romantic poets and, in their wake, by discriminating holiday-makers. Within these landscapes the archaeology of Exmoor has received little recognition, being seen as less dramatic than the more obvious remains on nearby Dartmoor; in consequence it has attracted less scholarly attention than it deserves. This book goes some way to rectifying that imbalance. The work that is presented here is the result of a systematic survey of the archaeology of the Park, undertaken by the Exeter staff of the former Royal Commission on the Historical Monuments of England (RCHME). It draws on a mass of newly discovered and newly illustrated material, setting all of this in its context so as to give a coherent and authoritative account of this fascinating aspect of the Park. A comprehensive study of the buildings on Exmoor was not attempted, although some complementary work on a selection of farmsteads is incorporated. This enriches the archaeological account of farms and field systems of the medieval and early modern periods, and also illustrates the great potential offered by the study of the buildings when they are seen within their landscape context.

Research has confirmed that the survival and condition of archaeological sites and monuments within National Parks is significantly better than that of comparable remains outside them. This is due, in no small part, to the knowledge, care and effective management afforded by the specialist staff of the National Park Authorities. Both the RCHME and English Heritage – since 1999 joined in a single body – have sought to support such effective management and to encourage its development. That determination was formally recognised in 1995 by the Joint Statement on Archaeology and the Historic Environment in National Parks, with its commitment to partnership and collaboration in research and survey, to which the organisations were signatories. It has also been recognised in practice by a wide range of surveys undertaken on a partnership basis in most of the English National Parks. Increasingly, too, these partnerships have allowed the results of research to be communicated to a wider public in an attractive and accessible way.

The aims and progress of this particular fieldwork project on Exmoor were warmly supported throughout by both the National Park Authority (ENPA), and by the National Trust. That co-operation has extended to this publication, which has been aided by substantial grants from the Park Authority and from the Trust, assistance that English Heritage is delighted to acknowledge. We all share a common desire to make the new information and enhanced understanding readily available to the local community and to visitors. The main credit for bringing the programme to a successful conclusion lies with the core team of field staff: Hazel Riley, Iain Sainsbury and Robert Wilson-North. Their enthusiasm, commitment and courtesy made many friends for the project along the way and have ensured that the archaeology of Exmoor is better known and understood, adding greatly to our appreciation and enjoyment of these very special landscapes.

Sir Neil Cossons
CHAIRMAN, ENGLISH HERITAGE

Humphrey Temperley
CHAIRMAN, EXMOOR NATIONAL PARK AUTHORITY

Acknowledgements

The fieldwork was carried out over a number of years by staff based at the Exeter Office of the RCHME. Hazel Riley, Iain Sainsbury and Rob Wilson-North undertook the fieldwork, with contributions from Martin Fletcher, Phil Newman, Paul Pattison, Simon Probert and Norman Quinnell. Jo Best, Jon Dempsey, Elaine Jamieson, Phil Marter and Cilla Wild also worked on the project. Nigel Fradgeley and Barry Jones carried out the farmstead survey. Phil Newman was responsible for the illustrations; Jane Brayne, Nigel Fradgeley and Elaine Jamieson also contributed material. The photographs were taken by Roger Featherstone, Damien Grady and Mike Hesketh-Roberts. Simon Crutchley, Carolyn Dyer and Helen Winton carried out air photographic transcription during the project.

Paul Everson, Veryan Heal, Mike Jones, Henrietta Quinnell, Brian Pearce, Isabel Richardson and Graham Wills kindly commented on the draft text. Professor Malcolm Todd and Ken Smith read the text for English Heritage. Abby Hunt and Liz Nickels helped with compiling and typing the text.

Many individuals and organisations were generous with their time and information. The authors would like to thank staff at the Devon and Somerset Sites and Monuments Records; the Somerset Studies Library; the West Country Studies Library; the Devon Record Office; the North Devon Record Office; the Somerset Archive and Record Service; the Somerset County Council Museums Service and the Museum of Barnstaple and North Devon. Peter Claughton, the late Hazel Eardley-Wilmot, Veryan Heal, Bob Higham, Mike Jones, Gill Juleff, Richard McDonnell, Ernest Mold, Norman Quinnell and Isabel Richardson all generously contributed material.

The authors would also like to express thanks to all the landowners who generously allowed access to sites, and often provided information unavailable elsewhere.

Summary

Exmoor, a remote upland area straddling North Devon and West Somerset, is now a National Park. The archaeology of Exmoor has been neglected in the past. Very little was known of this upland landscape, particularly when compared to the remains on Dartmoor and Bodmin Moor. There had been no structured fieldwork on Exmoor and the archaeological records reflected this lack of basic information.

This book describes the field archaeology of Exmoor from its earliest manifestations to the end of World War II. It is principally concerned with the field evidence, but also places the sites and monuments in their historical context. The book presents the results of a project whose main thrust was earthwork survey, but which also included air photographic transcription, air and ground photography and the recording of standing buildings. Several reconstruction drawings help to interpret the landscape. A gazetteer lists the principal sites considered, and a glossary explains the specialist terms used throughout the text.

The results of this work are presented in chronological order. The wide variety of archaeological remains are described and illustrated by numerous plans and photographs. Distribution maps show the extent of archaeological remains across Exmoor and detailed plans and earthwork surveys illustrate their form. A number of landscape studies consider the evidence in its wider context.

For the earlier prehistoric periods, Exmoor contains a wealth of intriguing stone monuments. The fragile stone settings preserved on the open moor are possibly a unique survival. Hundreds of Bronze Age barrows and cairns occur across the moor, giving one of the highest densities of these sites in England. For the first time, the evidence for later prehistoric enclosed settlements on Exmoor is presented. Detailed surveys of all of these sites have been carried out. Our perception of Roman Exmoor is changing with the discovery of new military and industrial sites in the last few years.

The relative lack of evidence for early medieval Exmoor contrasts with the wealth of sites and historical information for the time after the Norman Conquest. Detailed surveys of deserted villages and abandoned field systems have revealed the workings of the medieval landscape. Isolated farms are a characteristic feature of Exmoor's modern landscape, but this book draws together the evidence showing that these places often had a long history of development, from hamlet to farm. Nineteenth-century agricultural improvement had a huge impact on Exmoor, with the creation of model farms and the enclosure and drainage of tracts of open moor. In the 19th century, there was also the exploitation of Exmoor's minerals on a large scale. In World War II, Exmoor's remoteness made it suitable for military training. Intriguing survivals include testing ground for chemical weapons and tank training ranges.

This book draws together the archaeological evidence on Exmoor for the first time. It highlights both the fragility and the quality of the resource and provides the framework for future research.

Résumé

Exmoor, une région de hautes terres isolée, à cheval sur les comtés de North Devon et de West Somerset, bénéficie du statut de parc national. On a négligé l'archéologie d'Exmoor dans le passé. On connaissait très peu de choses sur ce paysage de hautes terres, en particulier si on le compare au patrimoine des landes de Dartmoor et de Bodmin Moor. On n'avait pas effectué de levés de terrains structurés à Exmoor et les archives archéologiques reflétaient ce manque de renseignements fondamentaux.

Ce livre décrit l'archéologie de terrain d'Exmoor depuis ses manifestations les plus anciennes jusqu'à la fin de la deuxième guerre mondiale. Il traite plus particulièrement des témoignages trouvés sur le terrain, mais il replace également dans leur contexte historique les sites et les monuments. Le livre présente les résultats d'une étude dont le moteur principal consistait en relevés de fossés et talus, mais qui comprenait également des transcriptions de photographies aériennes, des photographies aériennes et au sol, et le répertoriage des bâtiments debouts. Plusieurs croquis de reconstruction facilitent l'interprétation du paysage. Un répertoire fournit une liste des principaux sites et un glossaire explique les termes techniques utilisés tout au long du texte.

Les résultats de ces travaux sont présentés dans l'ordre chronologique. Les vestiges archéologiques y sont décrits dans toute leur diversité et ils sont illustrés par de nombreux plans et photographies. Des cartes mettent en évidence la répartition et l'étendue des vestiges archéologiques sur toute la lande d'Exmoor, tandis que des plans détaillés et des levés de fossés et talus illustrent leurs formes. Quelques des études de paysages examine ces témoignages dans le cadre plus vaste.

En ce qui concerne les périodes préhistoriques primitives, Exmoor recèle une riche collection de monuments de pierre mystérieux. Ces fragiles arrangements de pierres préservés sur la lande ouverte sont peut-être les seuls qui ont subsisté. On a découvert, partout sur la lande, des centaines de tumulus et de cairns de l'âge du bronze, ce qui constitue une des plus fortes densités de sites de ce type en Angleterre. On présente pour la première fois des témoignages d'occupations avec enclos de la préhistoire la plus tardive sur la lande d'Exmoor. Des études détaillées de toutes ces structures ont été effectuées sur tous ces sites. Notre perception d'Exmoor à l'époque romaine change à la suite de la découverte de nouveaux sites militaires et industriels au cours de ces dernières années.

Le relatif manque de témoignages en ce qui concerne le début de la période médiévale à Exmoor contraste avec sa richesse en sites et renseignements historiques relatifs à l'époque postérieure à la conquête normande. Des études détaillées de villages désertés et de systèmes de champs abandonnés ont révélé les rouages du paysage médiéval. Les fermes isolées sont un trait caractéristique du paysage moderne d'Exmoor, mais ce livre réunit les indices qui démontrent que le développement de ces endroits, de hameau à ferme isolée, constituait souvent une longue histoire. Les progrès de l'agriculture au dix-neuvième siècle eurent un énorme impact à Exmoor, avec la création de fermes modèles, l'introduction de clôtures et le drainage de la lande ouverte. Le 19ème siècle vit également l'exploitation des minéraux se développer sur une grande échelle. Quant à la seconde guerre mondiale, l'éloignement d'Exmoor en fit un lieu adapté aux manoeuvres militaires. Parmi ce patrimoine mystérieux, on compte un lieu d'expérimentation pour armes chimiques et des champs de manoeuvres pour tanks.

C'est la première fois qu'un livre rassemble tous les témoignages archéologiques d'Exmoor. Il souligne à la fois la fragilité et la qualité des ressources et fournit un cadre pour les recherches à venir.

Traduction: Annie Pritchard

Zusammenfassung

Exmoor, ein abseits hochländiges Gebiet auf North Devon und West Summerset liegend, ist ein National Park. Die Archäologie von Exmor wurde in der Vergangenheit vernachlässigt. Sehr wenig ist bekannt von diesem Hochland, besonders im Vergleich zu den Überresten auf Dartmoor und Bodmin Moor. Es fanden bisher keine struktukurierten Feldarbeiten auf Exmoor statt, und die archäologischen Urkunden machen das Fehlen von Basisinformationen deutlich.

Dieses Buch beschreibt die Feldarchäologie von Exmoor von seinen frühen Manifestierungen bis zum Ende des Zweiten Weltkrieges. Es beschäftigt sich vornehmlich mit Feldspuren, bringt jedoch die Standorte und deren Überreste in einen historischen Zusammenhang. Das Buch präsentiert die Resultate eines Projekts, dessen Hauptrichtung Erdwerkuntersuchung war. Es enthält aber auch Luftaufnahmenabschriften, Luft- und Bodenfotografie sowie die Katalogiesierung der noch stehenden Gebäude. Mehrere Rekonstruierungsskizzen helfen dem Beschreiben der Landschaft. Ein alphabetisches Ortsverzeichnes liefert eine Liste der Hauptstandorte, und ein Glossar erklärt die Spezialterminolgie im Text.

Die Ergebnisse dieser Arbeit werden in chronologischer Folge präsentiert. Die Vielzahl der archäologischen Überreste werden beschrieben und mit vielen Plänen und Fotografien illustriert. Verteilungskarten zeigen die Ausmaße der archäolgischen Überreste auf Exmoor und detaillierte Pläne und Erdwerksuntersuchungen stellen Ihre Formen dar. Eine Reihe von Landschaftstudien behandeln den Sachverhalt in seinem groesseren Umfeld.

Exmoor besitzt eine Vielzahl von faszinierenden Steinbauwerken aus früheren Zeitaltern. Wahrscheinlich einzigartig sind die fragilen Steinfassungen, welche in dem offenen Moorland überleben. Hunderte von Hügelgräbern und Steinhügeln aus dem Bronzezeitalter tauchen im Moor auf, eine der dichtesten Anhäufungen dieser Standorte in England. Beweise für die letzten prähistorischen geschlossenen Niederlassungen auf Exmoor werden zum ersten Mal präsentiert. Detaillierte Gutachten von allen diesen Standorten wurden erstellt. Unsere Auffassung vom Römischen Exmoor wird verändert mit der Entdeckung von militärischen und industriellen Standorten in den letzten Jahren.

Das relative Fehlen von Beweisen für das frühe mittelalterliche Exmoor steht im Widerspruch zu den vielen Standorten und den historischen Information aus der Zeit nach der Normannischen Eroberung. Detaillierte Untersuchungen von verlassenen Dörfern und aufgegebenen Feldsystemen überliefern die Arbeiten einer mittelalterlichen Landschaft. Isolierte Farmen sind charektaristisch für Exmoors moderne Landschaft. Dieses Buch zeigt jedoch, daß viele dieser Plätze eine lange Geschichte der Entwicklung haben, vom Weiler zur Farm. Landwirtschaftliche Verbesserungen im 19. Jahrhundert hatten einen immensen Einfluß auf die moderne Exmoorlandschaft mit dem Entstehen von Modellfarmen und dem Einzäunen und Trockenlegen des offenen Moors. Das 19. Jahrhundert sah die Ausbeutung von Exmoors Mineralien auf großangelegter Basis. Exmoors Abgelegenheit machten es ideal für militärisches Training im Zweiten Weltkrieg. Faszinierende Überreste beinhalten Testplätze für chemische Waffen und Panzertrainingsgelände.

Dieses Buch bringt die archäologischen Beweise von Exmoor zum ersten Mal zusammen. Es bringt die Anfälligkeit und Qualität der Ressourcen hervor, und liefert die Struktur für zukünftige Untersuchungen.

Übersetzung: Norman Behrend

AD	Post-medieval 1600-1900
	Later medieval 1066-1600
	Early medieval 410-1066
	Roman/Romano-British AD43-410
	Late Iron Age 100BC-AD43
	Middle Iron Age 400-100
	Early Iron Age 700-400
	Late Bronze Age 1000-700
	Middle Bronze Age 1500-1000
	Early Bronze Age 2000-1500
	Late Neolithic 3000-2000
	Early Neolithic 4000-3000
	Late Mesolithic 8000-4000
	Early Mesolithic 10,000- 8000
BC	Late Upper Palaeolithic 11,500-10,000
	Full Last Glacial 18,000-11,500
	Early Upper Palaeolithic Lower and Middle Palaeolithic ?500,000 - 18,000

Introduction

This book came into being as the result of the very limited knowledge of Exmoor's archaeology. Not only was there a minimal amount of reliable excavated material available, but even more basic information, such as the location of prehistoric barrows and field banks, was sadly lacking. It was to remedy this situation that the Royal Commission on the Historical Monuments of England (RCHME) Exmoor Project was set up. The project aimed to examine the archaeology of the whole of the Exmoor National Park, looking at archaeological field monuments and landscapes from all periods in time. This book presents the results of that extensive survey project. It is hoped that this publication will help to place the archaeology of Exmoor in its rightful place – not as Dartmoor's poor relation but its equal if very different partner.

This book is concerned with what survives in the landscape, not with buried remains for which there is no visible evidence: the paucity of modern excavation on Exmoor makes this a necessity. The precise dates of most sites on Exmoor, particularly for the earlier periods, are unknown. However, they can be placed within a broad chronological sequence by period, illustrated by the time-line (Fig i.1).

One of the main purposes of the project was the enhancement of the archaeological record. The detailed records produced during the course of the survey can be found in the National Monuments Record (NMR) at Swindon – now the archive of English Heritage. Distribution maps of archaeological sites form the basis of each chapter. A gazetteer linking each of these sites to the NMR can be found in the Appendices. These also contain a list of the detailed survey reports produced during the project and a list of radiocarbon dates referred to in the text. Dates are expressed in calibrated radiocarbon years or conventional years as appropriate. A glossary explains specialist terms used in the text.

The process of fieldwork was not one of instant revelations – new discoveries were not made every day. A painstaking and patient approach to the landscape was needed. Much of the fieldwork was carried out in the winter when the bracken had died back. Trudging the open moor on a wet February afternoon looking for the elusive remains of Bronze Age houses and fields or surveying fish weirs on the beach was part of that process. Without it, this book could not have been written.

Figure i.1
Time-line illustrating the archaeological periods and their approximate duration.

1
The Exmoor landscape

The natural environment

Early topographic writers saw Exmoor as a bleak, upland area: 'I see a spacious coarse barren and wild object, yielding little comfort by his rough complexion...It is Exemoore we are come unto...' (Westcote *c* 1630, quoted in Chanter and Worth 1905, 378). Exmoor today is an area of diverse and contrasting landscape, from the grass and heather moors of the Chains to the secretive wooded valleys of the rivers Exe and Barle. In the past, Exmoor was remote and isolated – much of it remains so.

Exmoor was designated a National Park in 1954. The area defined by the Exmoor National Park Authority (ENPA) boundary covers some 686 square kilometres. Two-thirds of Exmoor lies in Somerset, the remainder in Devon (Figs 1.1 and 1.2).

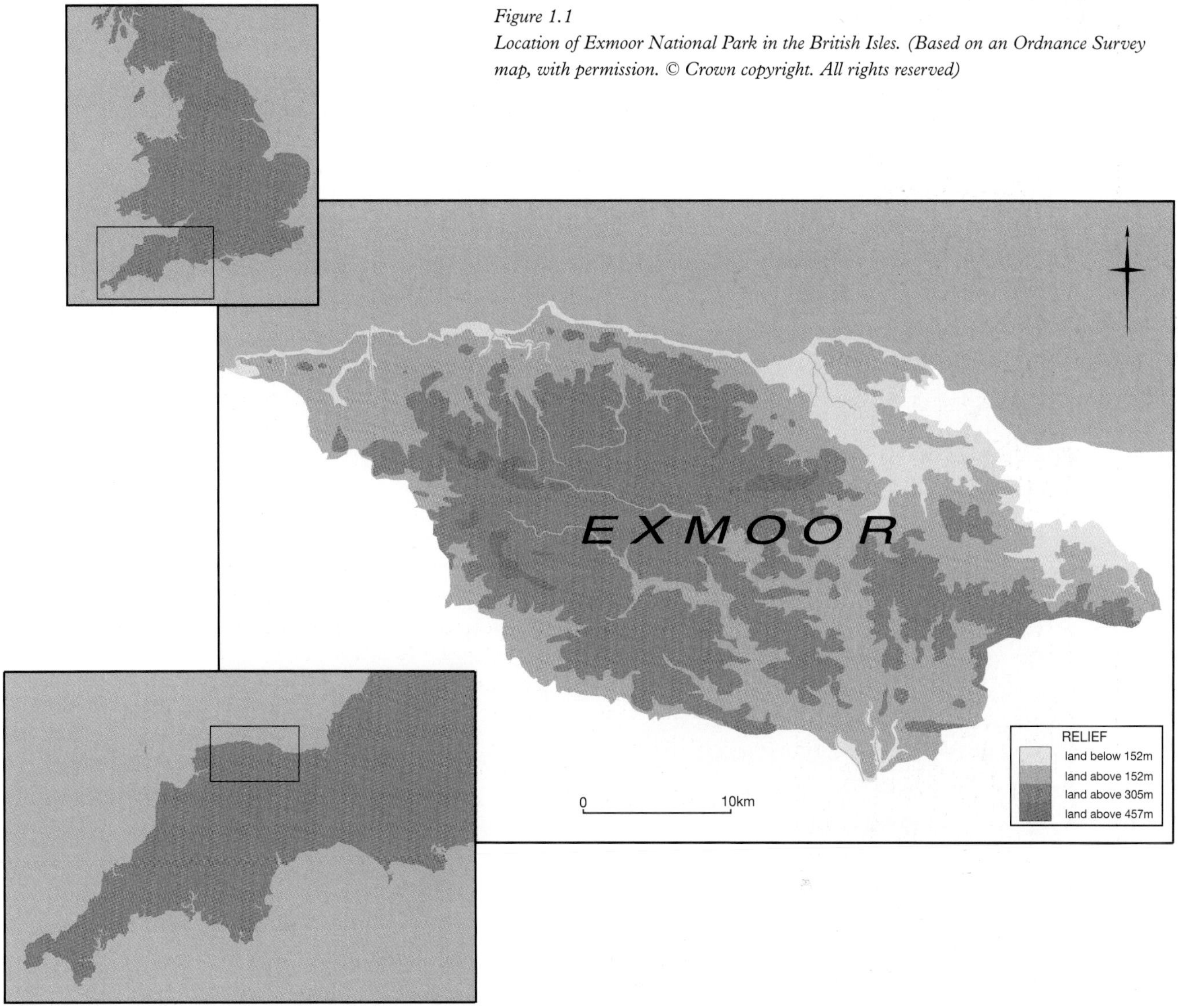

Figure 1.1
Location of Exmoor National Park in the British Isles. (Based on an Ordnance Survey map, with permission. © Crown copyright. All rights reserved)

EXMOOR

RELIEF	
	land below 152m
	land above 152m
	land above 305m
	land above 457m

0   10km

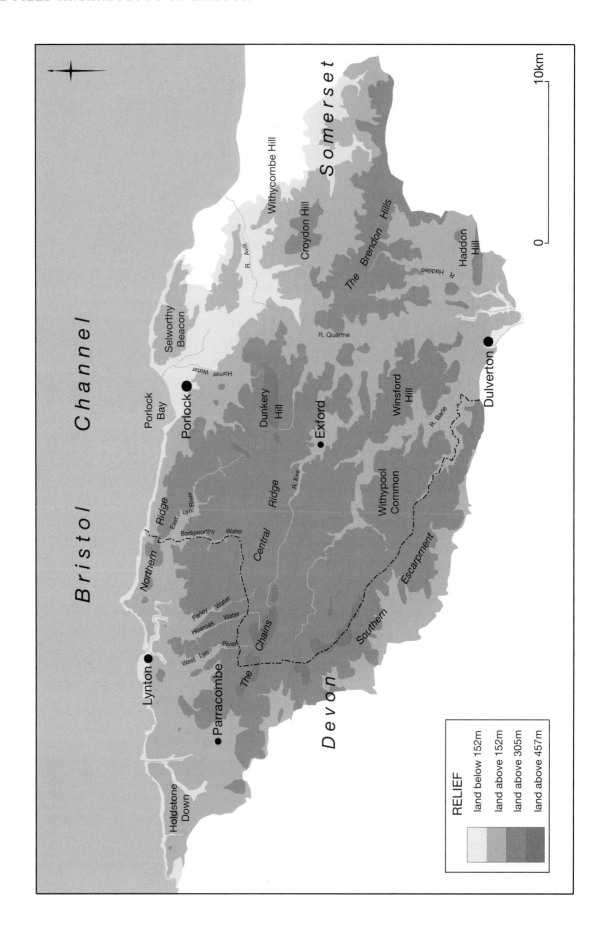

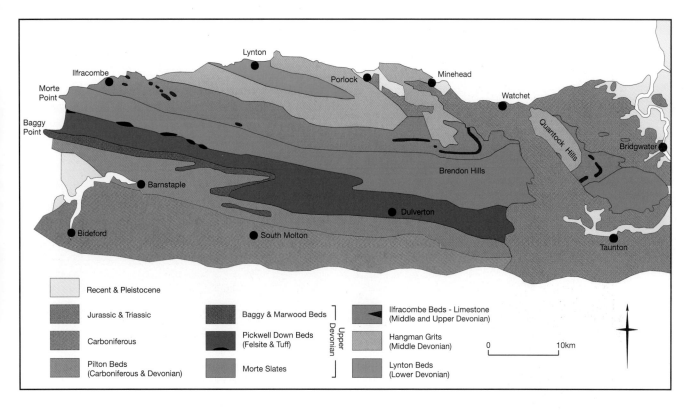

Topography and geology

Exmoor is dominated by three east–west ridges: the southern escarpment, which includes the commons of Molland and Anstey, the central ridge, encompassing the Chains and Dunkery Hill, and the northern ridge, taking in the coastal areas overlooking the Bristol Channel (Fig 1.2). More than half of Exmoor is above 300m in altitude. The highest peak is Dunkery Beacon at more than 500m, west of this the Chains lie at *c* 450m. This central ridge is the source of Exmoor's major rivers. The West and East Lyn are the major north flowing rivers. The Exe and Barle have cut deep, meandering valleys in the southern part of the Park. To the east, the Brendon Hills are the dominant landform, with the Vale of Porlock isolating the uplands centred on Selworthy Beacon.

The main mass of Exmoor is composed of Devonian rocks from all three of the major divisions of that geological time period (Fig 1.3). Exmoor's oldest rocks are the Lower Devonian Lynton Beds, grey slates and sandstones laid down 350 million years ago. These make up the majestic cliffs around Lynton. To their west and east, the Hangman Grits of the Middle Devonian period are responsible for Exmoor's characteristic coastal landforms on the northern escarpment (Fig 1.4). These ancient sandstones, resistant to erosion and

weathering, make up the highest parts of Exmoor: the Chains and the Dunkery massif form the central plateau, with Selworthy Beacon and Croydon Hill to the east. The Ilfracombe Beds of the Middle and Upper Devonian periods outcrop in a belt to the south around Simonsbath, Exford and Wheddon Cross. Within the slates of the Ilfracombe beds are small pockets of limestone, known as the Leigh Barton, Roadwater and Rodhuish Limestones. The Upper Devonian slates and sandstones – the Pickwell Down Beds and Morte Slates – form the country of Exmoor's southern escarpment: North Molton Ridge, West and East Anstey Commons and Haddon Hill. To the north, Withypool Common, Winsford Hill and the Brendon Hills are made up of these same rocks.

The north-eastern corner of Exmoor contains outcrops of very different, younger rocks, where the Vale of Porlock is composed of Permian, Triassic and Jurassic rocks. Around Wootton Courtenay and Beggearn Huish these rocks contain calcareous pebbles. Some of the most recent deposits are the peat of the high plateau and the alluvial material in the river valleys. Exmoor's foreshore is made up of rocky scree and water worn shingle, derived from rapid erosion during the Pleistocene (*see* Glossary) when Exmoor was subject to a periglacial (*see* Glossary) climate (Edmonds *et al* 1975).

Figure 1.3
Geological map of north Devon and west (After Edmonds et al 1975, fig 10) (Reproduced by permission of the British Geological Survey. © NERC. All rights reserved. IPR/18–9C)

Figure 1.2 (facing page) Exmoor: relief and topography. (Based on an Ordnance Survey map, with permission. © Crown copyright. All rights reserved)

Figure 1.4
The Exmoor coast: Butter
Hill and the Foreland rise
high above the steep cliffs
near Countisbury.
(AA00/0440)

Figure 1.5
Exmoor: land use map.
(Based on an Ordnance
Survey map, with permis-
sion. © Crown copyright.
All rights reserved.
Additional information
copyright ENPA)

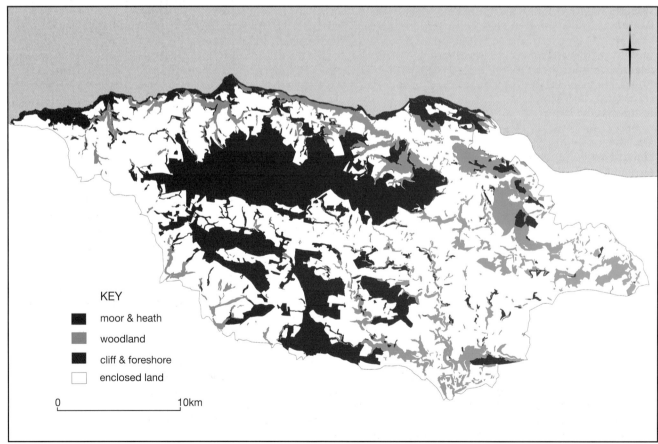

KEY

- moor & heath
- woodland
- cliff & foreshore
- enclosed land

0   10km

Vegetation and land use

Exmoor contains 16,000 hectares of moorland, dominated by purple moor grass and heather, with deer sedge, cotton grass, rushes and whortleberry (Fig 1.5). A great block of unenclosed moor and rough pasture stretches from Challacombe Common and the Chains in the west to Dunkery Hill in the east. It includes much of the former Royal Forest of Exmoor, together with some of the surrounding Commons (Fig 1.6). South of Exford and Simonsbath, the moorland is broken up by areas of enclosed land, but Molland and Anstey Commons and Winsford Hill are significant landscape features of the southern escarpment. Moving eastwards, isolated pockets of moor include Withycombe Hill, Rodhuish Common and Haddon Hill. Important but fragmented areas of coastal heath are scattered along Exmoor's rocky northern coast – from Holdstone Down in the west to Selworthy Beacon in the east (Sinclair 1972). Exmoor ponies, perhaps descendants of the native British hill pony, roam in free-living herds on the open moorland. Areas supporting Exmoor ponies include Dunkery Hill, Brendon Common, Winsford Hill, Molland Common and Haddon Hill (Baker 1993).

The rest of Exmoor's landscape is taken up with woodland and enclosed land. The latter is regularly improved for pasture or under arable cultivation, which is concentrated in the Vale of Porlock, once famous for its malting barley (*see* Fig 2.4).

Woodland covers one-tenth of Exmoor. On the coast, stands of coppiced oak clinging to the cliffs are a common feature around Culbone and Glenthorne. The river valleys contain some of Exmoor's oldest woodlands. In Horner Wood, the ancient pollards shelter colonies of bats and the woods are a refuge for lichens and ferns. The woodland margins provide an important habitat for red deer. The main herds live on Dunkery Hill, Ley Hill and Porlock Common. The Quarme, Exe and Barle valleys, together with the coastal heaths, also support significant numbers of red deer (Allen 1990).

On Exmoor's eastern fringes, plantations of conifers cover *c* 12,000 hectares on Croydon Hill and the Brendons. Exmoor, however, escaped the worst excesses of afforestation of the uplands. In the 1950s a proposal to lease land on the Chains to the Forestry Commission for deep ploughing

and planting with Sitka spruce was put forward. This provoked such an outcry that the proposal was dropped.

Exmoor's woods contain many exotic and deliberately planted trees. The walnut trees of the Vale of Porlock provided timber for gunstocks in the 18th century (*see* Fig 6.9). Sir Thomas Dyke Acland planted the great woods above Selworthy section by section, to commemorate the births of his children. The great English oaks of Nettlecombe Park not only enhance the landscape but also were a source of timber for the Navy. The beech hedges add an extra dimension to the post-medieval enclosure landscape of much of upland Exmoor (*see* Fig 3.25) (Miles 1972).

Figure 1.6
The heart of Exmoor: grass and heather moor on Hoaroak Hill. A circular sheep-fold lies close to the wall that marks the boundary of the former Royal Forest of Exmoor; to the right is Furzehill Common.
(NMR 15606/22)
(© Crown copyright.NMR)

Archaeological research on Exmoor

Antiquarians

The 13th-century documents describing the boundaries of the Royal Forest of Exmoor refer to some of Exmoor's finest barrows. They were obvious features in the medieval landscape to use as boundary markers. John Leland, crossing Exmoor between 1540–1542 during his journeys to salvage material from the monasteries following their recent dissolution, thought that the barrows were made for this purpose: 'for ther be Hillokes of Yerth cast up of auncient tyme for Markes and Limites betwixt Somersetshir and Devonshire. And here about is the Limes and Boundes of Exmore forest.' (Leland *c* 1540, quoted in Worth 1906, 62). Another early antiquarian and topographic writer was William Camden whose *Britannia* was first published in 1586. He recognised the existence of stone settings and stone circles (Chapter 2) on Exmoor: '. . . a filthy and barren ground named Exmore, neere unto Severne sea, a great part whereof is counted within Sommersetshire; and wherein there are seen certain monuments of anticke work, to wit, stones pitched in order, some triangle-wise, others in round circle . . .'(Camden 1610, quoted in Chanter and Worth 1905, 377).

A hollow in the centre of a barrow suggests that it has been opened at some time in the past. On Exmoor, numerous barrows show the marks of these early excavations. Several of the large barrows have a distinct trench around their perimeter, perhaps the remains of a deliberate attempt to look for a kerb (*see* Glossary). We lack records, however, as to when they were opened, who carried out the excavation and what was found. This was recognised nearly one hundred years ago when Captain Harold Fargus and the Reverend R W Oldham opened three barrows on Martinhoe Common. They found nothing apart from charcoal, but noted that 'all of the barrows in the neighbourhood had been opened before' (Worth 1907, 83).

The first antiquarian accounts of Exmoor are from the 17th century. Thomas Westcote recognised various stone monuments on Mattocks Down, and produced what appears to be the first depiction of Exmoor's field archaeology (reproduced from MSS in Chanter and Worth 1905, 379). In the middle of the 17th century James Boevey moved to Simonsbath (Chapter 5). He dug into several of the local barrows and purportedly found a number of urns containing Roman and Greek coins (Aubrey 1626–1697, 766–7). Westcote recounts the tale of the robbing of one of the barrows near Brockenbarrow Lane. A labourer was building a house and used the barrow as a quarry for stone. He found a 'stone oven' (probably a cist (*see* Glossary) or stone-lined grave) and an 'earthern pot'. On trying to seize the latter, the man heard the trampling of horses. At his third attempt, he took the urn, finding only ashes in it. Then the unfortunate man lost both his sight and his hearing – three months later he was dead (Westcote *c* 1630, quoted in Worth 1879, 149–50).

This tale illustrates two common aspects of the perception of archaeological sites. On the one hand, there is a lust for gain – treasure seeking – but on the other, the labourer is afraid of the dead and there is an association of the site with unworldly happenings. Magic and folklore is also woven into accounts of prehistoric sites. The standing stones on Mattocks Down were known as the 'Gyants Quoits.' Two large stone slabs on Porlock Common – the Whit Stones – are said to be the result of a contest between a giant and the devil hurling stones from Hurlstone Point. The devil also figures in the story of Tarr Steps – a stone clapper bridge spanning the River Barle. Legend has it that he built the bridge in a single night. An incidental result of the devil's labours was the creation of Mounsey Castle – an Iron Age hillfort – (Chapter 3) by the accidental dropping of a load of stones on the way to Tarr Steps (Grinsell 1970a, 158).

By the 18th century the antiquity of the stone monuments and burial mounds was beginning to be realised, although there was a definite propensity to attribute such works to the Druids. Thus Collinson, writing his *History and Antiquities of the County of Somerset* in 1791, recognises the later prehistoric enclosures and hillforts as 'assuredly vestiges of antiquity'. He does, however, suggest they were constructed in the early ages of Druidism, for the celebration of religious rites, or for 'feats of activity or athletick exhibitions' (Collinson 1791, II, 20). Early writers were often eager to fit prehistoric sites with known historical events. Phelps gives a good description of the later prehistoric enclosure and outworks (*see* Glossary) at Bury Castle, Selworthy but

PHOTOGRAPH OF THE CULBONE CIST *IN SITU*.

suggests that they are Danish works, the result of a raid on Porlock early in the 10th century AD (Phelps 1836).

Richard Fenton opened several barrows on Exmoor in the early years of the 19th century. His workmen dug into three of the Selworthy Beacon barrow group – finding only charcoal (Fenton 1811). In 1820 a cist was found in Langridge Wood when the surrounding cairn was removed for road material. The grave contained a skeleton, which was re-interred in Treborough churchyard. A remarkable discovery was made in 1896 by workmen quarrying for stone on the edge of Yenworthy Common (Elworthy 1896). They found a stone cist (known as the Culbone cist) concealing 'a grinning skull', several bones – the skeleton

of a young man – and a fine Beaker pot (*see* Glossary) (Figs 1.7 and 2.8).

An unpublished manuscript entitled *Some Account of the Fortified Hills in the County of Devon, whether British, Roman, Anglo-Saxon or Danish with plans of many of them*, written by Henry Woollcombe in 1839, contains some of our earliest depictions of Exmoor's field monuments. Although his plans owe more to the picturesque movement than the school of accurate plan-making (Fig 1.8), Woollcombe conveys the atmosphere at the remote hillfort of Shoulsbury as it was nearly two hundred years ago: 'The whole inclosure is a complete morass incapable of being walked on. Indeed the whole hill is a bog and marshy and requires great care even in this dry season to pick out your path.

Figure 1.7
The Culbone cist: this Bronze Age burial was discovered by a workman in 1896. (By courtesy of Somerset County Council Museums Service)

7

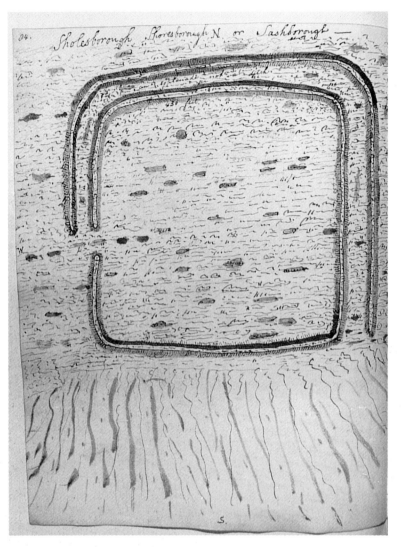

Figure 1.8
Shoulsbury Castle: depicted
by Henry Woollcombe in
1839. (By courtesy of
the Devon and Exeter
Institution Library)
(AA00/0387)

The parts with double ramparts was never a ditch, it was rather an esplanade for men to draw up on.'(Woollcombe 1839, 55).

Archaeological work in the 20th century

The Barrow Committee of the Devonshire Association, set up to 'collect and record facts relating to barrows in Devonshire, and to take steps, where possible, for their investigation' (Worth 1879, 146), are justly famous for their exertions on Dartmoor. These august Victorian and Edwardian gentlemen did not confine themselves to the granite moor: the Reverend J F Chanter and R H Worth conducted a certain amount of research and excavation on Exmoor. In fact it was Worth, at the end of the 19th century, who admirably summed up the situation: '...the antiquities of this district (Exmoor) have never received the

attention they deserve and the Forest may therefore be commended to the attention of zealous and discreet archaeologists.' (Chanter and Worth 1905, 375).

Chanter was the rector of Parracombe at the turn of the century. He investigated many of Exmoor's barrows on behalf of the Barrow Committee, and his reports of this work form the first reliable accounts of excavations and recording of Exmoor's field archaeology (Worth 1905; 1906; 1907; 1913). Chanter dug a total of eight large barrows; he also described and recognised the importance of Setta Barrow and Five Barrows. His most thorough investigations appear to have been at Brockenbarrow, where a group of three barrows were excavated. One of these was the barrow opened in the 17th century by the terrified workman – Chanter found post-medieval pottery in one disturbed mound. In another, a large cordoned urn (see Glossary) containing a cremation was found in a cist. The urn was recovered in several pieces and was further damaged when dropped by a drunken porter at the North Devon Atheneaum in 1914 or 1915 (see Fig 2.9).

While Chanter and Worth were examining barrows, they also encountered Exmoor's stone monument (Chapter 2). At first these were considered as mere adjuncts to the barrow groups, but Chanter and Worth soon realised that they were an important group of monuments in their own right. The results of their fieldwork, including plans and descriptions of 25 stone monuments, were published in two important papers: *The rude stone monuments of Exmoor and its borders I* and *II* (Chanter and Worth 1905; 1906). St George Gray carried on with this work of survey and record, detailing both of Exmoor's stone circles and a complex stone setting discovered as late as 1931 (Gray 1906; 1928; 1931a).

Only two sites on Exmoor have been the subject of large-scale excavations. These are the Roman fortlets on the coast at Martinhoe and Old Burrow, until recently the only known Roman sites on Exmoor (Chapter 3). St George Gray carried out a small-scale investigation at Old Burrow in 1911 (Fig 1.9). Aileen Fox and William Ravenhill excavated both sites on a larger scale between 1960 and 1963 (Gray and Tapp 1912; Fox and Ravenhill 1966). Perhaps the lack of things Roman on Exmoor contributed to its neglect in terms of excavation during the middle years of the 20th century. The first comprehensive thematic surveys of Exmoor's archaeology

by systematic fieldwork, however, were made in the 1950s and 1960s. Leslie Grinsell covered the ground as part of his county by county record of barrows. The fieldwork is published as part of the county lists for Somerset and Devon (Grinsell 1969; 1970b). Grinsell's *The Archaeology of Exmoor* published in 1970 remains the standard reference work, although its net is cast wide – it is subtitled 'Bideford to Bridgwater'. Also published in 1970 was *Antiquary's Exmoor*, a slim volume summarising existing knowledge (Whybrow 1970). Several amateur archaeologists have worked on Exmoor, notably Hazel Eardley-Wilmot, who discovered several significant prehistoric sites and published accounts of her research (Eardley-Wilmot 1983; 1990).

In 1977 a survey to look at all of Exmoor's archaeology began. This was carried out by an examination of air photographs, and all archaeological features were plotted onto a base map. Some fieldwork was also carried out. The results of this survey showed that Exmoor had a far greater number of archaeological sites than was previously realised (McDonnell 1985a). The vulnerability of Exmoor's stone monuments, particularly the stone settings, has long been known. Between 1988 and 1992, the RCHME undertook a project to accurately locate and record each of these sites (Quinnell and Dunn 1992). An archaeologist for the Exmoor National Park was appointed in 1991 and it was soon realised that a programme of extensive fieldwork and survey was necessary for the management and conservation of the Park's archaeological resource.

Figure 1.9
Old Burrow Roman fortlet:
St George Gray directed
excavations in 1911 at Old
Burrow, one of a handful of
sites excavated on Exmoor.
(BB72/1043)

Landscape Study 1 Antiquarian investigations at the Chapman Barrows and Wood Barrow

Figure 1.10
The Chapman Barrows linear barrow cemetery: these large Bronze Age burial mounds lie on the western edge of the moor. They have been a focus for antiquarian and later excavation work, but none have been examined using modern techniques.
(NMR 18307/15)

The Chapman Barrows, climbing the grassy slopes up towards the Chains, are some of the finest on Exmoor (Fig 1.10). Beyond lie Longstone Barrow and Wood Barrow. They have been recognised for hundreds of years as ancient burial places with a mysterious past. Thomas Westcote, writing in 1630, recalls how 'fiery dragons have been seen flying and lighting on them'. He also sets down one of the earliest recorded barrow openings on Exmoor (quoted in full by Worth (1879, 159–60). Wood Barrow, a convenient marker of the county boundary and the Royal Forest of Exmoor, was probably the subject of this

strange tale (Fig 1.11). A certain gentleman informed his friends that the barrow contained a 'great brass pan and therein much treasure both silver and gold' (Worth 1879, 159). He managed to convince two of his acquaintances that he would protect them from the powers of evil if they opened the barrow and shared the treasure with him. The barrow was duly dug into and a brass pan, covered with a large stone, was found. After a certain amount of fainting, the stone was removed but there was no treasure – 'the bottom where the treasure should have been was very bright and clean, the rest all eaten with cankered rust' (Worth 1879, 160) – perhaps the remains of a bronze vessel.

John Frederick Chanter, rector of Parracombe at the turn of the century, heard that one of Chapman Barrows had been opened in 1885. He sought out the culprit, a Mr Thomas Antell of Parracombe, who was made to tell all. Antell had been directed by a farmer to remove stones from a barrow for the hedge bank they were building. He found what purported to be a stone kerb and a pottery vessel, covered with a flat stone. The stone slab was 2ft (0.6m) square and the pot stood an impressive 2ft (0.6m) high and 1ft 6in (0.45m) wide. The pot broke soon after it was found. Mr Antell was sure that the bones from this vessel were from sheep – the remains of mutton stew overlooked by the builders of the barrow.

The Reverend Chanter himself opened another of the Chapman Barrows in 1905. A long narrow trench was dug towards the centre, and eventually the central burial was found. Chanter identified a kerb around the base of the mound, and a stone cairn, placed above the burial pit (Fig 1.12). The burial in this pit was covered with stone slabs and some bones and teeth were identifiable in the cremated material. The material that made up the mound was turf and soil – individual turves could be recognised – and a lot of charcoal was noted.

These three accounts of barrow openings, which span nearly 300 years, illustrate our changing perceptions and expectations of antiquity. In the 17th century, the barrow was seen as a source of treasure but also as a feared object – there was a price to be paid for tampering with the dead. The 19th century account suggests a more pragmatic view,

using the barrow material for a hedge, with apparently no compunction at interfering with the remains of the ancestors. Chanter, in 1905, sought facts, and carefully drew and recorded his findings. His account of bones and teeth in the cremation and turves in the burial mound indicates the potential contained within Exmoor's prehistoric sites.

The study of the human remains and the grave-goods buried alongside them will tell us much about the people who lived on Exmoor in the Bronze Age. The examination of the mound, the soil buried under it, and the flora and fauna preserved in these, will give us information about the environment in which these people lived.

Figure 1.11
Wood Barrow: this fine Bronze Age barrow lies to the east of the Chapman Barrows, on the edge of the Chains. Its prominent position led to its use in the medieval period as a boundary mark of the Royal Forest of Exmoor. (AA00/0378)

Figure 1.12
Sections of one of the Chapman Barrows (top) and Roe Barrow (bottom), recorded during Chanter's excavations in 1905. (Worth 1905, plate IV, opp p 93) (By permission of the Devonshire Association)

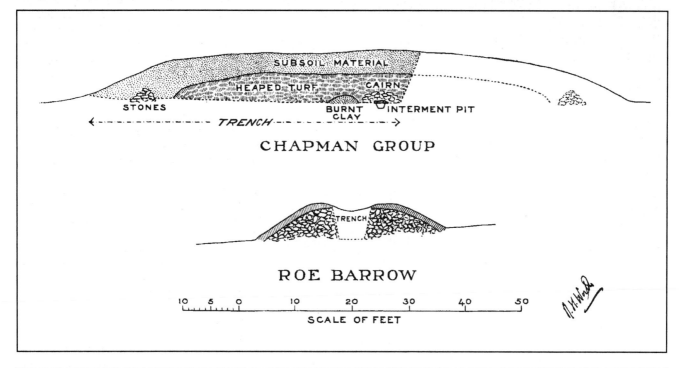

The RCHME Exmoor Project

The successful management, presentation and preservation of Exmoor's historic landscape is reliant on a sound background of information. This body of data is contained locally in the county Sites and Monuments Records (SMRs - *see* Glossary) and nationally in the National Monuments Record (NMR - *see* Glossary). The process of surveying and recording is an important part of the compilation of these databases. As was noted above, our knowledge of the archaeology of Exmoor was limited. The RCHME Exmoor Project was initiated in 1993 as a response to the need for a programme of archaeological survey work and record enhancement on Exmoor. The aim of the project was to improve the archaeological records for Exmoor, looking at sites of all periods – ranging from Neolithic and Bronze Age stone monuments to the military buildings of World War II. Two people carried out the fieldwork over a period of six years, working from west to east across the moor. The survey results were put into the NMR during the course of the project, making them available to the public and to the ENPA.

Fieldwork: survey and record

The Ordnance Survey 1:10 000 map sheets were used as the base map for the survey. Their coverage of Exmoor is shown on Fig 1.13. Some 43 full or partial sheets were used in conjunction with the records contained in the NMR and the Devon and Somerset SMRs. The air photographic transcription (*see* Glossary) work carried out in 1985 was also used. An examination of this material led to an assessment of which sites should be visited. Some sites, in particular the stone settings and several barrow groups, had been investigated by the RCHME very recently. Apart from these, every recorded prehistoric site was visited and surveyed onto the National Grid at a scale of 1:2 500. A full description of each monument was made and its condition noted. These descriptions form the basis of the records input to the NMR.

Exmoor's unenclosed moorland and rough pastures are the best places for the survival of prehistoric archaeology. For this reason, the unenclosed areas of Exmoor were carefully reconnoitred for new sites. Areas of moor recently swaled (burnt for

*Figure 1.13
Exmoor: coverage of the area by the Ordnance Survey 1:10 000 map sheets. (Based on an Ordnance Survey map, with permission. © Crown copyright. All rights reserved)*

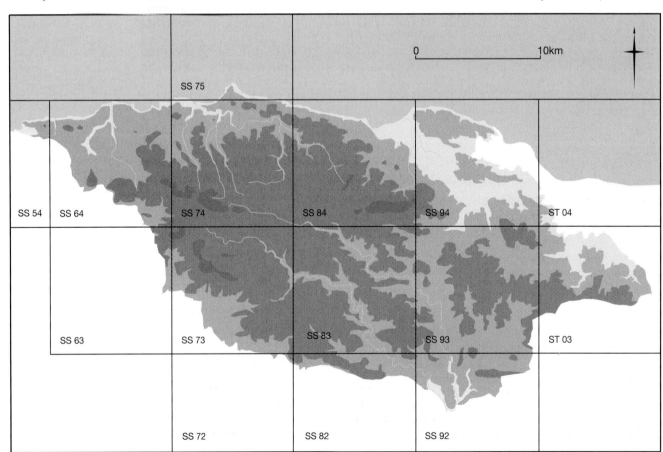

Figure 1.14
Robin How, Dunkery Hill:
instrumental survey of a
Bronze Age cairn.
(AA00/0951)

vegetation management) were also targeted as much as was logistically possible. Instrumental survey – using a total station theodolite or global positioning system (GPS) survey equipment – was used to map the sites on open moorland (Figs 1.14 and 5.33). Such survey techniques have made it possible to map the large areas of prehistoric field systems and ritual landscapes for the first time on Exmoor (Chapter 2). The foreshore was also considered and GPS survey proved invaluable for recording sites in this difficult landscape (Chapter 5).

During the course of the project, it became apparent that very few of Exmoor's field monuments had been adequately planned. Exmoor has had no tradition of plan-making of its archaeological sites. The first accurate plans are those made by the Ordnance Survey on the first large-scale maps of the country. These were carried out at a scale of 1:2 500 in the late 19th century. During the 1950s and 1960s the Ordnance Survey Archaeology Division revised these plans, and these small-scale plans were the only record of such complex earthworks as Bat's Castle and Holwell Castle. For this reason, a certain amount of time was set aside for large-scale survey of sites considered to require it. These included Iron Age hillforts and enclosures, Roman forts (Chapter 3), deserted medieval villages and motte and bailey castles (Chapter 4).

At the request of the ENPA archaeologist, large-scale surveys of several sites were undertaken to deal with specific management issues during the project. A popular footpath crosses Cow Castle, a hillfort near Simonsbath. A large-scale survey of this site shows exactly where the path crosses the Iron Age bank and ditch, enabling an assessment of erosion (Chapter 3). Fieldwork was planned to co-ordinate with the Early Ironworking Project, set up by the ENPA and the National Trust (Chapter 6) (Juleff 1997). The RCHME project also encompassed detailed recording of various blocks of land owned by the ENPA. The National Park Authority needs to know the extent and location of the archaeological resource before it can be managed appropriately. On the moorland of Haddon Hill several new cairns were discovered; on North Hill the remains of World War II buildings were recorded (Chapter 6) (Appendix 3).

Photography

Exmoor's archaeological record was particularly deficient in photography. A photographer from the RCHME carried out a programme of ground photography during the course of the project. Sites recorded included World War II buildings, farm buildings, industrial remains and sites distinctive of Exmoor (Fig 1.15).

Figure 1.15
Woolhanger Music Room: this ornate octagonal room contained a steam-powered organ, dating from the 19th century. Surviving features include two Bath Stone fireplaces and mullioned windows. A series of detailed photographs is an effective way of quickly recording such sites. (AA97/1346)
(© Crown copyright.NMR)

Figure 1.16
Exmoor: areas covered by RCHME air photographic transcription. (Based on an Ordnance Survey map, with permission. © Crown copyright. All rights reserved)

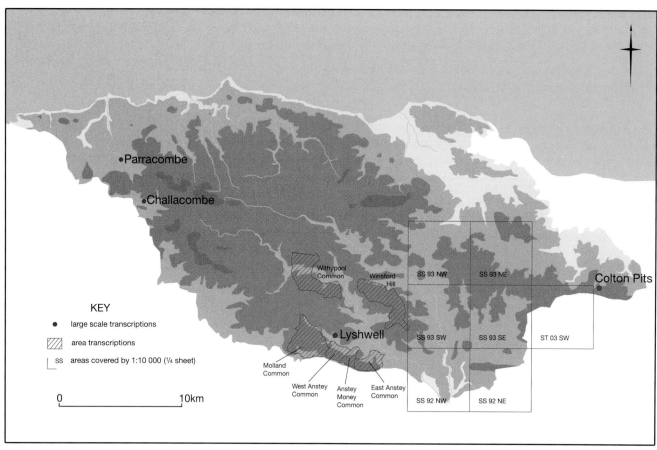

The RCHME also carried out several seasons of air photography over Exmoor, specifically for archaeological purposes. More than 1,500 air photographs have been taken during the course of the project, both of individual sites and wider landscapes.

Some parts of Exmoor are difficult to assess by ground survey – either because of thick vegetation or through enclosure and subsequent land improvement. Several areas were singled out as in need of air photographic transcription as fieldwork progressed. In all, more than 12,000 hectares have been examined in this way (Fig 1.16). These included the commons on the south and east of the former Royal Forest that contain large areas of complex field systems (Chapter 5) and the western part of the Brendon Hills – a landscape of enclosure and land improvement. Air photographic transcription was also used in conjunction with ground survey, to record the whole archaeological landscape – as at Parracombe and the Dane's Brook Valley (Chapters 4 and 5).

Building recording

The study of Exmoor's vernacular architecture was outside the scope of the current project. It was recognised, however, that the study of Exmoor's deserted medieval and post-medieval farmsteads would be aided by an assessment of Exmoor's working farms. To this end, in consultation with the ENPA Historic Environment Team, several sites were chosen for investigation by architectural historians of the RCHME (Chapter 5).

The National Monuments Record

The results of all of the survey work are in the NMR. Descriptions and grid references of all of the sites investigated are contained in the computerised database. The survey drawings, reports, air and ground photographs are also at the NMR. The sites mentioned in the text and shown on the distribution maps are linked to these records by the site gazetteer (Appendix 1). Individual site or area reports are listed in Appendix 3.

2
The earlier prehistoric period

Introduction and chronology

The Palaeolithic
(?500,000–10,000 BC)

Conventional radiocarbon dates (*see* Glossary) are not reliable any earlier than about 60,000 years ago. The Lower and Middle Palaeolithic periods are therefore fixed by correlation with comparable Pleistocene sequences, dated by geological methods and by a range of other scientific techniques. Later Palaeolithic sites, where deposits are found stratified in caves or sealed under peat, alluvium or colluvium, can be dated by radiocarbon determinations of organic material such as bone or wood (Wymer 1981; Barton 1997).

The very earliest evidence of the presence of man on Exmoor is a fragment of a stone handaxe, found near Porlock (Fig 2.1). This was made and used during the Lower Palaeolithic period, perhaps as early as 300,000 years ago. The context of this find is unclear (Roe 1968), but it was probably from river gravels exposed at the coast, so the handaxe might have been transported some distance from its place of manufacture and use.

The last major ice age began more than 30,000 years ago. During its early phases modern humans moved into much of Britain and northern Europe – then still a single landmass. Early Upper Palaeolithic sites such as Kent's Cavern, Torquay, were occupied at this time. Between *c* 18,000 and 11,500 BC the ice age was at its peak and Britain was

Figure 2.1
Exmoor: distribution of Palaeolithic and Mesolithic artefacts. (Based on an Ordnance Survey map, with permission.

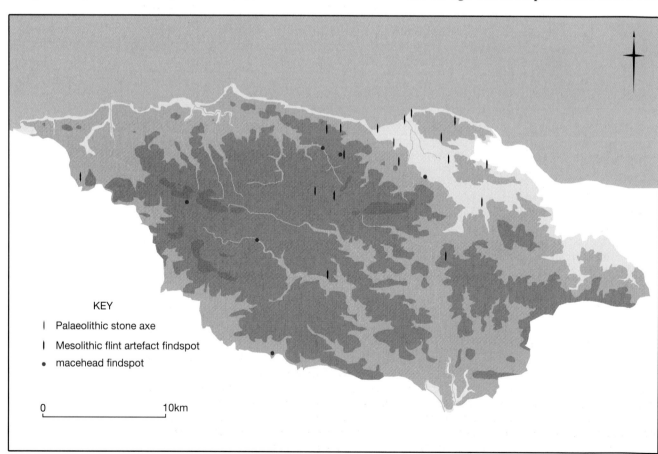

KEY

| Palaeolithic stone axe

| Mesolithic flint artefact findspot

• macehead findspot

0 ———————— 10km

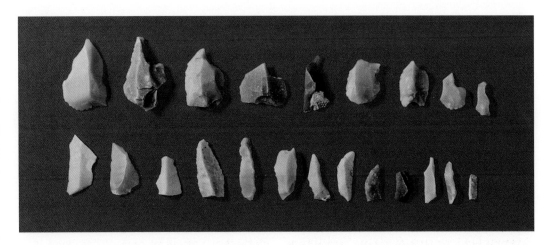

Figure 2.2
Later Mesolithic worked
flints from Hawkcombe
Head: microburins (top)
and microliths (bottom).
The microliths are
c 20–30mm long.
(By courtesy of Somerset
County Council Museums
Service) (AA99/07938)

unsuitable for human settlement. As the ice retreated, hunting communities of the Later Upper Palaeolithic period returned to Britain. There is little evidence of these communities from the south-west and none from Exmoor.

The Mesolithic period (10,000–4000 BC)

The most common evidence of Mesolithic activity on Exmoor is in the form of assemblages of flint tools. These are found as surface scatters, so that radiocarbon dates cannot usually be obtained. These artefacts are dated by comparison with other flint assemblages whose dates are known by either absolute or relative means. Most of the flint assemblages from Exmoor have not been studied in enough detail to assign them positively to particular prehistoric periods, although that from Hawkcombe Head does appear to be Late Mesolithic in date (Norman 1982). The flints from Kentisbury Down are a good example of this problem, where Mesolithic, Neolithic and Bronze Age material has been collected from a small area (Miles 1976).

The Early Mesolithic period (10,000–8000 BC)

A major environmental change took place in Britain between 10,000 and 8000 BC, when extensive areas of tundra were gradually replaced by mixed woodlands, as temperatures rose. The ice sheets continued to melt and the sea level rose. The range of food available for people to exploit widened and new types of stone tools developed for hunting small mammals and catching fish. Early Mesolithic flint assemblages are characterised by small flint tools – broad blade microliths (*see* Glossary) – used for the tips of arrows and spears. There are no Early Mesolithic sites recorded from Exmoor, reflecting the paucity of such sites from the south-west peninsula generally. The potential for finding such sites exists: under peaty soils or alluvial deposits and in old assemblages of artefacts, which might contain unrecognised earlier components.

The Late Mesolithic period (8000–4000 BC)

About 8,000 years ago, as a result of the continuing rise in sea level, Britain became an island. On Exmoor, we see the first real evidence of human occupation, in the form of the narrow blade microliths used by Late Mesolithic hunter-gatherer communities. These are tiny flint tools (Fig 2.2), some so small that they were not used singly, but hafted together on wooden handles to make harpoons or spears.

Late Mesolithic flint tools have been found on Exmoor during the past one hundred years. They are often not accurately located and their distribution can reflect the activity of a single collector (Fig 2.1). This might be the case for the sites west of Minehead, where A V Cornish and Miss M Hatch-Barnwell were keen collectors. Between 1966 and 1968 the Reverend W G Eyre, Rector of Kentisbury, collected more than 600 worked flints from a field on Kentisbury Down, which had been recently ploughed for the first time. Some microliths were found, together with Neolithic and Early Bronze Age arrowheads. A prehistoric enclosure of the 1st millennium BC lies close by, highlighting the evidence for human activity on Exmoor through many millennia. Seven maceheads (*see* Glossary) have been discovered as chance finds on Exmoor; these artefacts probably date from the later Mesolithic period.

Landscape Study 2 Porlock Bay and Hawkcombe Head: Mesolithic hunter-gatherers in upland and coastal landscapes

The distribution of known Late Mesolithic material shows a concentration on the coast of West Somerset, particularly around Porlock. Mesolithic flints have been found in a field behind the shingle ridge at the eastern end of Porlock Bay and finds of flint tools have been made on the cliffs at Hurlstone Point, across Bossington Hill and North Hill. A quantity of Mesolithic material, including a stone macehead, has been reported from Ash Farm, west of Hawkcombe Head. A flint-working site lies at Hawkcombe Head itself, on the open moor above Porlock. A L Wedlake discovered the site in 1942, where the peaty soil was disturbed by deeply rutted tracks. Several hundred pieces of worked flint have been collected from this site during the past 50 years, making it the largest assemblage of microliths from Exmoor (Figs 2.2 and 2.3).

The people who used these tools probably collected the raw material – flint pebbles – from the beach at Porlock Bay. The material probably represents the remains of the hunting camps of four or five small family groups who spent the summer months based at Hawkcombe Head. The surrounding country, mostly covered with oak woods, was rich in food resources including aurochs (*see* Glossary), elk, red and roe deer.

Porlock Bay lies 3km to the north-east of Hawkcombe Head. It provides one of only a handful of access points to the foreshore and sea along Exmoor's precipitous coast. Porlock Marsh is an area of low-lying land behind the foreshore, protected by a huge shingle ridge (Fig 2.4). The marsh, together with the foreshore and sea beyond, contained important food resources. Hunter-gatherers could choose from wildfowl overwintering on the salt marsh; crabs or limpets from the rocky beach and fish from the sea. The groups who hunted in the upland forests during the summer months had only to move a few miles down the valley to survive the winter. Traces of such

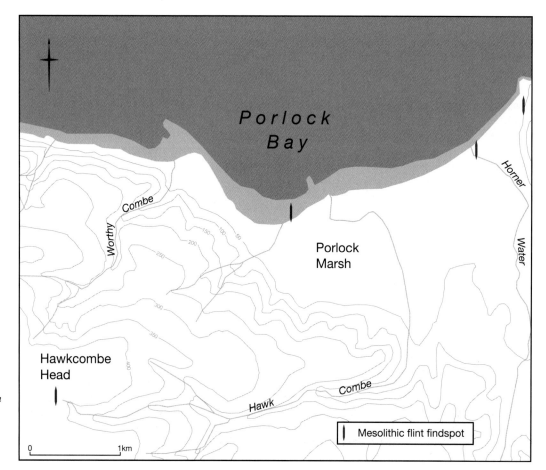

Figure 2.3
Mesolithic finds in the Porlock area. (Based on an Ordnance Survey map, with permission.
© Crown copyright.
All rights reserved)

Figure 2.4
Porlock Bay from the air: the Mesolithic site at Hawkcombe Head lies at the head of the wooded combe (top left). Mesolithic flints have been found near Horner Water (foreground) and under the peat exposed at low tide near Porlock Weir harbour.
(NMR 18017/12)
(© Crown copyright.NMR)

Figure 2.5
Porlock Bay: layer of peat exposed at low tide. Mesolithic material was found sealed underneath this peat layer in the 19th century. (Hazel Riley, English Heritage)

groups were found on the beach in Porlock Bay. The rise in sea level has submerged part of the coast, which once could support forest. At Porlock, tree stumps 5,000 years old and areas of peat can be seen at low tide in among the shingle (Fig 2.5). Mesolithic flints were found underneath this submerged forest. In the autumn of 1869, Mr Boyd Dawkins and the Reverend Winwood dug through the submerged forest to examine the material sealed beneath it. Several pieces of worked flint were found, including some Mesolithic material (Boyd Dawkins 1872).

The Neolithic (4000–2000 BC)

The beginnings of agriculture in Britain took place in the Neolithic period and, by necessity, brought a more settled way of life. There is little evidence of the settlements of these early farmers, but from the Late Neolithic period the spectacular stone houses of Skara Brae in the Orkneys survive. There is more evidence for ritual and ceremony from this time. The dead were buried in massive long barrows or megalithic tombs (*see* Glossary). The distinctive causewayed enclosures and, later, henge monuments (*see* Glossary) were the foci for ritual and ceremony during this time.

There is no evidence of actual Neolithic settlement on Exmoor, but through the years chance finds of Neolithic artefacts have occurred. Several flint axes, of the kind used for felling trees, have been found on Exmoor. A finely worked discoidal flint knife (*see* Glossary) was found among a large scatter of worked flints on Kentisbury Down (Fig 2.6). We also know that Neolithic communities were using Exmoor as a hunting ground: more than a dozen characteristic leaf-shaped and transverse and triangular arrowheads (*see* Glossary) have been found on Exmoor. Although many of these

do not have a precise location, there is a particular concentration in the area around Selworthy Beacon (Fig 2.7). A few greenstone axes (*see* Glossary) have also been found on and around Exmoor. Both the greenstone and the flint were brought to Exmoor. The greenstone probably originated from Cornwall, the flint from Wessex and the south Devon coast. Such items would therefore have had a value beyond that of the utilitarian.

The fragile stone settings, elusive stone rows and stone circles are the earliest traces of human impact on Exmoor's landscape. Unfortunately, the chronology of Exmoor's earlier prehistoric field archaeology is not dated by absolute means. Exmoor lacks a sequence of radiocarbon dates from secure contexts on excavated sites. Similarly, there are no large assemblages of prehistoric pottery from sites on Exmoor that can be compared with well-dated examples from other parts of southern England, particularly Cornwall and Wessex. As there has been so little excavation on Exmoor, we have to rely on analogy with similar sites from Cornwall, Devon, Somerset and South Wales. Like Exmoor, both Dartmoor and Bodmin Moor have few recent excavations with radiocarbon sequences (Quinnell 1994a, 49; Johnson and

Figure 2.6
Late Neolithic discoidal flint knife, c 90mm wide, from Kentisbury Common. (By courtesy of the Museum of Barnstaple and North Devon) (BB99/10341)

Rose 1994, 4). The stone monuments – circles, rows and settings – are generally placed in the Late Neolithic–Early Bronze Age, although no firm radiocarbon chronology exists for these types of monument.

The Bronze Age (2000–700 BC)

The Bronze Age is marked by the introduction of new metal-working technology, important for display and prestige as well as for more utilitarian uses. The landscape is dominated by monuments to the dead – the great barrow cemeteries of Wessex, for example. On Dartmoor, the remarkable reave systems of the Middle Bronze Age are enduring survivals of people's need to control large areas of the landscape.

Cairns and barrows are better studied than the stone monuments. Radiocarbon dates and pottery typology show that the major period for the construction of cairns and barrows in many parts of Britain is between 2000 and 1500 BC. A study of radiocarbon dates from such sites in Cornwall showed that 25 of 29 sites were in the range of 2200 to 1500 BC (Christie 1988). A recent review of 16 dates from Devon and Cornwall showed a concentration about 1800 BC. A ring cairn at Shallowmead on the southern edge of Exmoor, and a small burial cairn on Bratton Down, just outside the western edge of Exmoor, both have radiocarbon dates that are late in the date range, at c 1500–900 BC (Quinnell 1988; 1997) (Appendix 2).

Artefacts from excavated barrows and cairns are rare from Exmoor. There is very little identifiable pottery that is well provenanced. The Culbone cist – a Bronze Age burial found on the edge of Yenworthy Common – contained a finely decorated Beaker pot (Fig 2.8). This type of pottery now has a date range of between 2600 and 1800 BC from a programme of country-wide radiocarbon dating (Kinnes et al 1991). A large cordoned urn of Early Bronze Age date was found in one of the Brockenbarrow group of round barrows (Fig 2.9).

There have been no recent excavations on any of Exmoor's prehistoric field systems or hut circles, and there are no records of any artefacts associated with them. In the southwest generally, such sites are dated to the 2nd millennium BC. On Dartmoor, much of the prehistoric moorland settlement is dated to the later part of the 2nd millennium BC, based on pottery groups and limited radiocarbon determinations (Quinnell 1994b, 76).

Figure 2.7
Leaf-shaped Early Neolithic arrowheads (right) and barbed and tanged Early Bronze Age arrowheads (left) found in the Selworthy area. The barbed and tanged arrowheads are c 20mm high. (By courtesy of Somerset County Council Museums Service) (AA99/07932)

Figure 2.8
The Culbone Beaker: found in 1896, accompanying a Bronze Age burial in a stone cist on the edge of Yenworthy Common. The pot is c 150mm high. (By courtesy of Somerset County Council Museums Service) (AA99/07934)

Several objects that were in use during the Bronze Age have been found, by chance, on Exmoor. Flint tools were still utilised for subsistence activities such as farming and hunting. Two stone axe-hammers of Early Bronze age date, one from Tippacott and one, perhaps of Cornish stone, from Challacombe, are recorded from Exmoor. The finely worked barbed and tanged flint arrowheads (*see* Glossary), also Early Bronze Age date, from Kentisbury Down and around Selworthy Beacon (Fig 2.7) might also have conveyed an element of prestige to their owners. Likewise, the beautiful bronze bracelet of Middle Bronze Age date, found in the Roadwater area in the 19th century (Fig 2.10) (Gray 1931b; Pearce 1983, nos 700 a–c; 701). At Hayne, near Roadwater, an Early Bronze Age copper flat axe, together with two bronze palstaves (*see* Glossary) and a socketed bronze axe, all of later Bronze Age date, were found in the 19th century. This range of dates suggests a hoard of scrap metal, carefully gathered and hidden.

Palaeoenvironmental evidence
(*see* Glossary)

Upland areas such as Exmoor contain a record of past environments. Organic materials such as plant remains, pollen, insects and bones can be preserved under the appropriate conditions. The uplands of Exmoor have some areas of blanket peat and valley mire that have been studied in some detail. The dynamic coastal environment of Porlock Bay provides an opportunity for the study of an evolving salt marsh. The earlier research on the peats of upland Exmoor concentrated on the question of dating the onset of peat formation. In this work, the field monuments were seen as an aid to the research, not as part of the problem (Merryfield and Moore 1974). More recent work has tried to integrate palaeoenvironmental studies with archaeological sites, with varying degrees of success (Francis 1986; Francis and Slater 1990; 1992; Canti *et al* 1995). It appears that peat formation on Exmoor began at different times according to local topographic and climatic factors. Hence, peat began to form on the Chains plateau about the beginning of the 3rd millennium BC and during the 1st millennium BC on Codsend Moors (Straker and Crabtree 1995, 45). The activities of human communities might have contributed towards the onset of peat formation, as forest clearance and grazing the

Figure 2.9
The Brockenbarrow Urn: Bronze Age cordoned urn, c 300mm high, excavated from one of the Brockenbarrow group in 1906. (By courtesy of the Museum of Barnstaple and North Devon) (BB99/10347)

Figure 2.10
Middle Bronze Age bronze bracelet, c 70mm in diameter, found near Roadwater in the 19th century. (By courtesy of Somerset County Council Museums Service) (AA99/07935)

The need for modern excavation to give a firm chronology for both Exmoor's and Dartmoor's prehistoric field monuments was highlighted recently. At Gold Park on the eastern edge of Dartmoor, a presumed Bronze Age house platform produced radiocarbon dates and pottery placing it in the later Iron Age (Gibson 1992).

moor can have a deleterious effect on the mineral soil, but this is hard to quantify (Francis and Slater 1990, 22). Some evidence has been recovered to help our understanding of the way of life of the Neolithic and Bronze Age communities who visited and lived on Exmoor. Plant species indicative of arable cultivation and stock grazing are preserved in the pollen record from Hoar Moor (Francis and Slater 1990, 19). The impression of a barley grain on the Culbone Beaker also shows that some cereals were being grown at this time (Helbaek 1952, 199; 226). The partial skeleton of an aurochs, the ancestor of our domestic cattle, found under the shingle ridge at Porlock, has been dated to the Early Bronze Age (McDonnell 1998).

The fossil pollen record provides us with details of the actual trees that grew on Exmoor. At the end of the last glaciation, improving climatic conditions led to dwarf willow and birch replacing the arctic tundra of periglacial Exmoor. As the climate ameliorated further, larger birches, Scots pine and hazel dominated the uplands, with willow and alder on the lower land and oak and lime in the combes. By the beginning of the Neolithic period, some 6,000 years ago, oak, alder, lime and elm were well established. The remains of such trees are occasionally found preserved in the peats of upland Exmoor. An oak tree, found in a bog on Halscombe Allotment, was dated to the Neolithic period, and some prehistoric tree stumps preserved below peat at Warren Farm are tangible reminders of Exmoor's past tree cover (V Heal, personal communication; McDonnell 1985b).

The Neolithic and Bronze Age: stone monuments

Stone monuments are the earliest man-made structures on Exmoor. Although not precisely dated, they are generally attributed to the Late Neolithic and Early Bronze Age (Todd 1987, 103), following a tradition of megalith building that probably originated in the major stone circles and avenues of Wessex (Burl 1993, 23). The dating relies on analogy with similar sites elsewhere in England rather than on direct dating evidence from the Exmoor examples themselves.

The stone monuments have long been recognised both by early topographers visiting Exmoor and by the local community. Camden, writing in the early 17th century, mentioned stone circles and stones set in a triangle (Chapter 1), and subsequent visitors reiterated and echoed him. Chanter and Worth began to map the stone settings systematically in 1905, but were led by the presumption that all were laid out to a specific (usually geometric) pattern. This was only partly true: Camden's stone triangles, identified and surveyed by Chanter and Worth, are in reality only the fragmentary remains of more complex settings. The process of discovery and recording, initiated by Chanter and Worth, was carried on by St George Gray. He surveyed the stone circle on Withypool Hill in 1905 and that on Porlock Allotment in 1928 (Gray 1906; 1928). More recently, discoveries have included the location of the subtle White Ladder stone row in 1975 by Hazel Eardley-Wilmot (1983, 4). The first comprehensive mapping of Exmoor's stone monuments was carried out between 1988 and 1992 by staff of the RCHME (Quinnell and Dunn 1992), but to date no synthetic study of Exmoor's earliest landscapes, putting the stone monuments in their context, has been attempted.

The stone monuments fall into four broad categories: stone circles, stone rows, stone settings and solitary (or paired) standing stones. The majority of these terms have a resonance with other south-western moorlands where comparable sites exist, although stone settings occur only on Exmoor. The distribution and precise form of the remains, however, is locally distinctive and laboured comparison with elsewhere is not helpful. In the following, selected examples are used to illustrate and characterise the monuments. Their distribution, relationship with topography and association with other archaeological monuments is also examined.

The stone monuments are made from the local sandstone and slate, and are almost always less than 0.5m high. They have been described as 'minilithic' rather than megalithic (Burl 1993, 88): tiny stone shafts, lost in tussocks of reed and moor grass. The fragility of these monuments means that they are always vulnerable. The RCHME noted that 10% of Exmoor's stone monuments had been totally destroyed during this century, and many more were less complete than when originally described (Quinnell and Dunn 1992, 4), yet their insubstantial form belies their importance in understanding the beginnings of settled communities on the moor.

Siting and distribution

Nearly all of Exmoor's stone monuments survive on moorland outside the limits of medieval and later agricultural improvement. The distribution is therefore largely confined to the western half of Exmoor National Park, with particular concentrations within the area of the former Royal Forest (Fig 2.11). Even the extensive commons that surrounded the Royal Forest are largely devoid of these sites – they also have evidence of medieval cultivation. The distribution of surviving stone settings on Exmoor is not a reliable indicator of their original extent. Nevertheless, it is surprising that outlying blocks of moorland, such as Selworthy Beacon and the extreme eastern end of Dunkery Hill, do not contain the remnants of any stone monuments.

Within the areas of survival, stone settings show a marked concentration around the headwaters of valleys. Here they usually occupy crest positions on the edges of spurs overlooking minor tributaries of the major valleys. Most are on the northern escarpment overlooking tributaries of the West Lyn River, Hoaroak Water, Farley Water, Badgworthy Water, Chalk Water, Weir Water and Chetsford Water. Some have been noted on the south flowing rivers: River Quarme, River Exe, River Barle and the Dane's Brook, although here they are scarce perhaps due to the intensity of agricultural improvement on the southern escarpments.

Some of the stone rows occupy ridges or traverse slopes leading up to ridges on which other monuments such as barrows and cairns are placed. There appears to be no direct association between stone rows and stone settings, nor between major barrows and stone settings. Exceptional associations do occur: a fine stone setting lies just to the south of the Chapman Barrow. There is a very strong association between small cairns and stone settings, with many stone settings having cairns of less than 6m in diameter adjacent to them.

Stone settings occur close to many of the prehistoric settlements. This fact, combined with the extensive number of them, suggests that they might have played a greater role in the day to day life of these communities than the rarer rows and circles, although it should be stressed that it is not clear whether they are contemporary.

Stone circles

Two stone circles are known on Exmoor, Withypool Hill and Porlock (Figs 2.12 and 2.13). The former was discovered in 1898 when Mr Archibald Hamilton's horse stumbled over one of its stones (Gray 1906, 42), and the latter in the years before 1928 (Gray 1928, 71). The circles are 36m and 24.5m in diameter respectively and are no longer complete. That on Withypool Hill lies in isolation on gentle north facing slopes, while that at Porlock is part of a complex that includes a short stone row and a cairn. St George Gray carried out limited excavation at Porlock but nothing of archaeological interest was discovered. Both stone circles are comparable to the larger circles on Dartmoor (Todd 1987, 100; Butler 1997, 152), which are generally assumed to date from the Late Neolithic to Early Bronze Age.

Stone rows

There are eight stone rows on Exmoor: Culbone, Cheriton Ridge, Furzehill, Madacombe, Porlock, Thornworthy Little Common, White Ladder and Wilmersham. They fall into two distinct categories on the basis of length. Three are long: between 280m and 420m, and the remaining five are short: between 12m and 68m. Five are certainly single rows, two are double rows, while one, the Wilmersham stone row, seems to be a combination of a single and double row.

Within the rows the stones are set at close intervals, usually about 2m apart. One third of the stones in the White Ladder stone row are blocks of local quartz (Fig 2.14). The stones are therefore very low with the 'tallest' being only 0.1m high. The use of quartz in a stone row is very unusual. Most of the stone rows form part of monument complexes with the longest three having direct topographic associations with major barrows or barrow groups. Of the short stone rows, Thornworthy Little Common lies near a possible prehistoric field system, Cheriton lies on a ridge with other stone settings and a ring cairn (Fig 2.15), while Porlock is part of a complex that includes a stone circle and cairn, although the stone row is aligned on neither (Fig 2.12). The Wilmersham stone row lies close to a prehistoric field system, and has at times been misinterpreted as a field bank (Eardley-Wilmot 1983, 32).

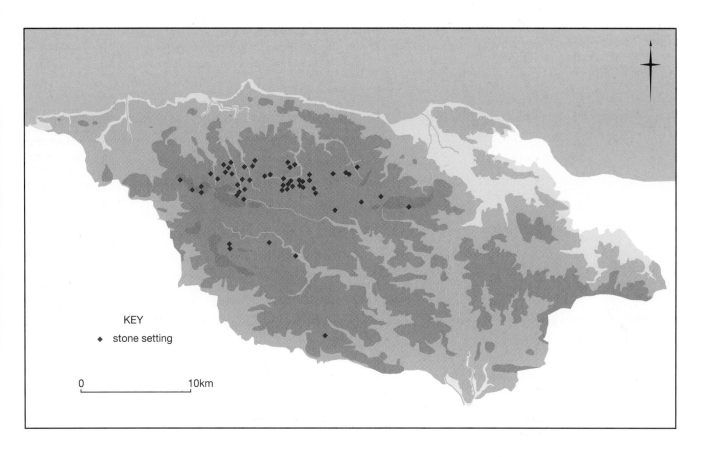

KEY

◆ stone setting

0   10km

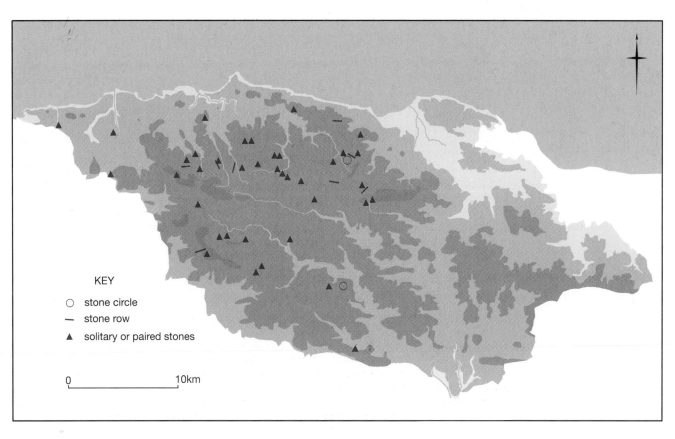

KEY

○ stone circle

— stone row

▲ solitary or paired stones

0   10km

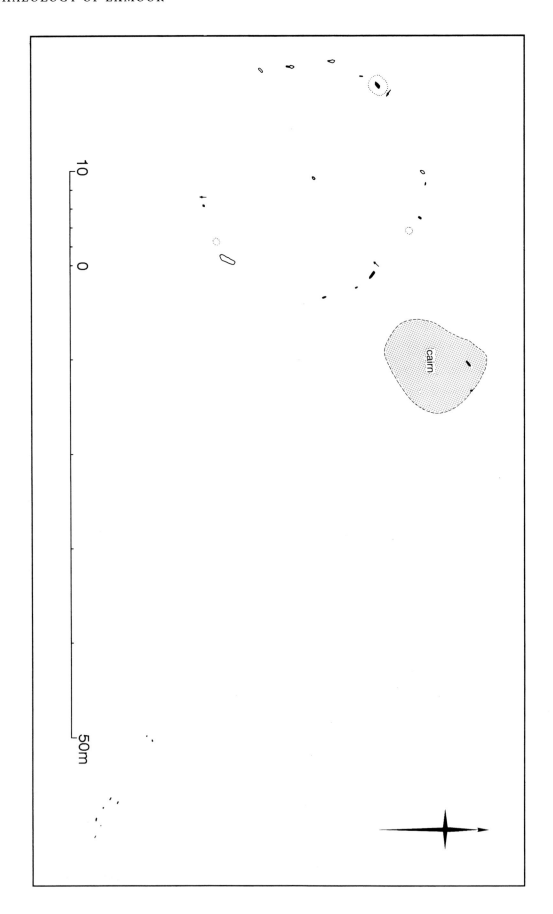

Figure 2.12
The Porlock stone circle,
stone row and cairn.
For key see Fig 2.16.

cairn

10

0

50m

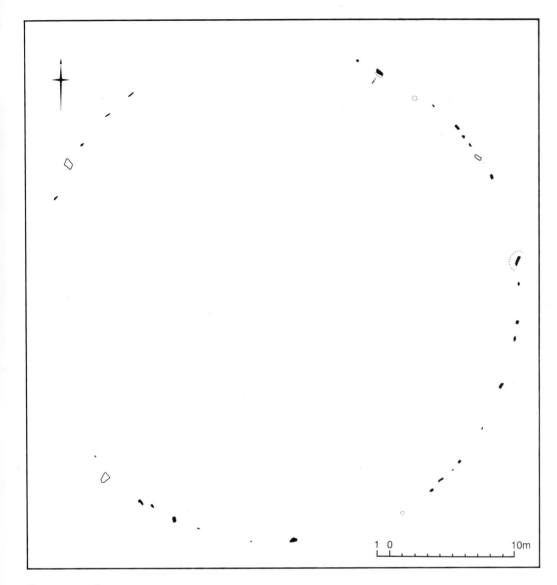

Figure 2.13
The Withypool stone circle:
an almost perfect circle,
made of very small stones.
For key see Fig 2.16.

Stone settings

Stone settings are arrangements of upright stones placed in roughly geometric patterns or apparently randomly, they are 'almost without parallel in Britain and Ireland' (Burl 1993, 89) (Figs 2.16 and 2.17). They are by far the most common stone monument on Exmoor. Fifty-seven can be conclusively identified, while a large number are known to have been destroyed. As early as 1905 the practice of removing standing stones for walling, field gutters, drains and gate posts was well attested (Chanter and Worth 1905, 376), and others would have been removed by cultivation of the moor in the 19th century. It is likely that some of the paired standing stones, or even the solitary ones, are the last remnants of stone settings. Even the loss of a single stone from a stone setting can obscure the original arrangement of the stones.

The majority of the stone settings are incomplete so that their original 'design' cannot be recognised; either that or they were constructed in a way that today appears random. Ten are rectangular in shape, however. These are distinctly different from stone rows and Burl has described them as 'boxes' (1993, 90). Four are quincunxes – five stones in all: four marking the corners of a square with a single central stone. At least seven form a roughly linear arrangement with alignments between some of the stones. Stones seem to have been placed with care. In rectangular settings, for example, the long sides of the individual stones are parallel with the rows themselves (Fig 2.16).

Figure 2.14 (right)
The White Ladder stone
row. The Devon/Somerset
county boundary closely
follows its course.

Figure 2.15 (far right)
The short stone row on
Cheriton Ridge.
For key see Fig 2.16.

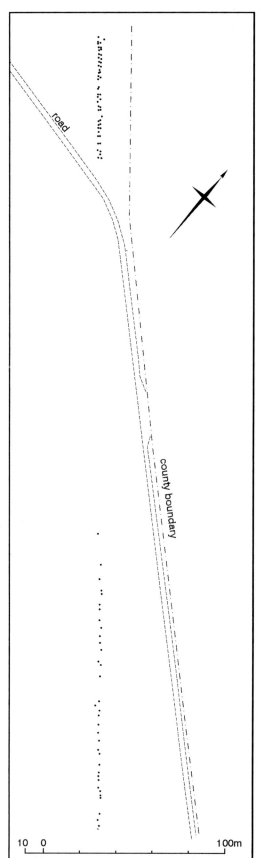

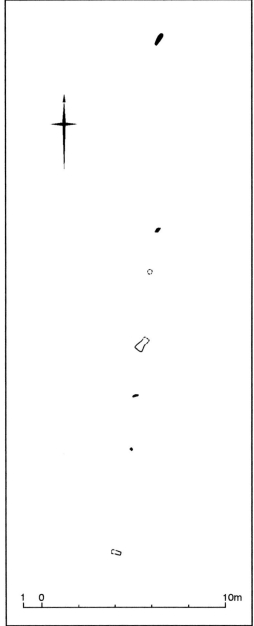

Figure 2.16 (facing page)
Stone settings: the Chapman Barrows stone setting,
a quincunx; East Pinford, a rectangular setting; Pig Hill 1,
a stone setting that appears random; Kittuck, a linear stone
setting with a cairn at its north-east end; Almsworthy
Common, a stone setting that, although not a precise
geometric shape, has significant alignments between some
of the stones.

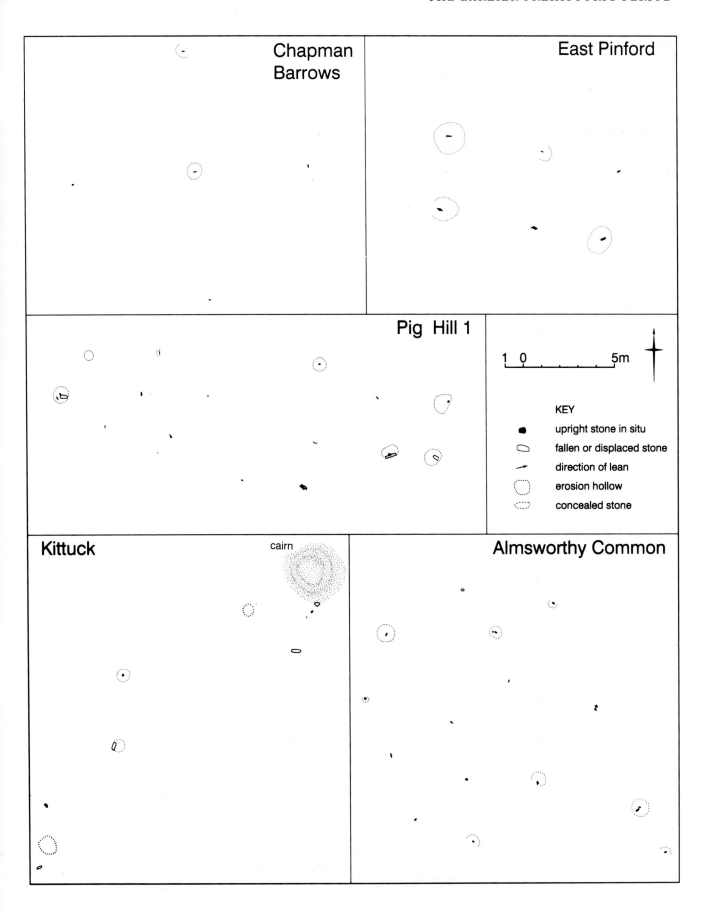

Solitary and paired stones

Perhaps the most evocative of all of Exmoor's stone monuments is the Long Stone near Challacombe. It is exceptional in size, a sliver of slate 3m high, 'a dark finger thrusting up from the sullen earth' (Bourne 1991, 89), standing within a saddle looking south-westwards out from the moor (Fig 2.18). There are other isolated stones on the moor. That on Anstey Common occupies a very similar position at the head of a narrow combe, and is only 1.3m high. Others are in less dramatic and distinctive locations. In many cases it is impossible to be sure whether these stones are prehistoric or whether they were erected later as rubbing posts for sheep or as markers.

A large number of standing stones on Exmoor are paired. This is a phenomenon widely recognised across the west of the United Kingdom, and excavations have revealed evidence of cremations and other rituals beneath and around the stones (Burl 1993, 182–3), although on Exmoor no excavation has taken place. Some of these paired stones are no doubt the fragmentary remains of once more extensive stone settings.

Landscape Study 3 Stone settings around the upper reaches of Badgworthy Water

This is a solitary and wild landscape of undulating grass moorland with long spurs and plateaux segmented by narrow deep combes. Later farming has had little influence here except for the construction of some enclosure fences in the 19th century.

Badgworthy Water runs northwards out of the moor before joining the East Lyn River and thence flowing to the sea at Lynmouth. The river catchment is the eastern half of Brendon Common, Lanacombe, Trout Hill, Pinford and Larkbarrow. Tributary streams flow between these areas to join the main river. Prehistoric monuments cluster along the spurs above the tributary streams (Fig 2.19). While some prehistoric settlement and farming is represented by the hut circle, enclosures and field banks, and burial by the presence of cairns and barrows, by far the most common monument type is the stone setting.

There are 16 stone settings. Most overlook the tributary streams, and occupy either spur end or crest positions. Many of the stone settings are close to small cairns, which might echo the relationship between Dartmoor's stone rows and its small cairns. The stone settings occur in areas where there are traces of prehistoric settlement and field systems although it is unclear both whether they are contemporary and whether there is any relationship. The larger cairns tend to occupy ridge top positions and as a result are away from the other monuments.

The purpose of the stone settings is unknown, but their frequency on Exmoor and their close relationship with small cairns suggests that they were part of the ritual or spiritual life of those who lived and farmed there at the beginning of the Bronze Age. The proximity of these sites to prehistoric field boundaries and settlements also suggests that they were part of the regular spiritual life of isolated communities, rather than remote sites used only occasionally.

Figure 2.17 (facing, top) The Clannon Ball stone setting is perched on the lip of the valley of Farley Water. (© Copyright Jane Brayne)

Figure 2.18 (facing, bottom) The Long Stone with Longstone Barrow in the background. (AA00/0365)

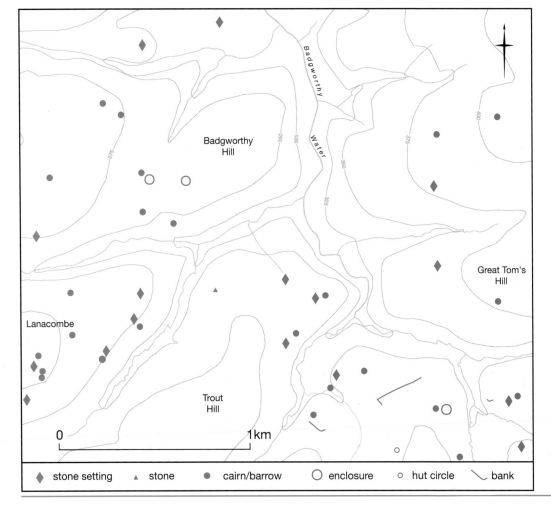

Figure 2.19 Stone settings and other prehistoric monuments around the upper reaches of Badgworthy Water. (Based on an Ordnance Survey map, with permission. © Crown copyright. All rights reserved)

Barrows and cairns

Nowhere is the distinctiveness of Exmoor's landscape more closely intertwined with the monuments of its ancient past than in the ever-present skyline barrows – the massive, circular burial mounds of the Bronze Age. They are by far the most common prehistoric monument on Exmoor: more than 370 have been found, varying in size from 2m to 35m in diameter. The greatest and most obvious barrows are in a sense the tip of the iceberg. Many more smaller ones occupy less prominent locations, and no doubt yet more await discovery. They punctuate the landscape and are found in isolation, in small groups, in linear straggles along the skyline; sometimes they occur close to stone settings, stone rows, hut circles and field systems.

The name barrow is said to derive from the Old English *beorg*, a mound. But on Exmoor many natural mounds have barrow suffixes, such as Flexbarrow near Cow Castle, so the barrow element in a place-name cannot be equated with the existence of a burial mound.

Antiquarian work

Barrows have always been the object of people's fascination and speculation, partly because they are so visible, partly because of what they might contain, but most of all because they have long been known as the burial grounds of ancient peoples:

> *But here, upon this desolate spot, which perhaps never experienced the labours of the industrious husbandmen; but has remained the same for a long succession of many thousand years; the eye of reflection sees stand uninterrupted a number of simple sepulchres of departed souls, whether of warriors, priests or kings it matters not; their names have long been buried with their persons in the dust of oblivion, and their memories have perished with their mouldering urns. A morsel of earth now damps in silence the eclat of noisy warriors, and the green turf serves as a sufficient shroud for kings!*
> (Collinson 1791, II, 20)

The earliest records of them are due to their practical use as markers of boundaries in a landscape devoid of other recognisable features, and it is for this reason that so many are named: Chapman Barrows, Wambarrows, Black Barrow, Alderman's Barrow. There is good reason to believe that they were being used as such as early as the 13th century. By the 1500s barrows were so associated with boundary markers in people's minds that Leland formalised the myth that they were actually constructed as markers of the Royal Forest. They regularly occur in the Perambulations of the Royal Forest in the 17th century (Grinsell 1970b, 103). Since the late 19th century the Ordnance Survey have used many of these vantage points for triangulation stations, and a few barrow names seem to originate from this time when the surveyors needed to identify a point by name; Wiveliscombe Barrow is an example.

Many of Exmoor's barrows show signs of robbing: the digging of a pit into the top of the mound in the hope of finding grave goods or more prosaically robbing stone for field walls. The earliest such event to be recorded was the opening of one of the Brockenbarrow group before 1630, when the farmer was interrupted by the constant sound of the thundering hooves of ghostly horses. In about 1670, John Aubrey mentions that James Boevey, the owner of the Royal Forest during the Commonwealth, opened several barrows on Exmoor. During the early part of the 19th century Richard Fenton dug into several of the barrows around Dunkery Hill, and sent his men to open barrows on Selworthy Beacon (Chapter 1).

In the late 19th century the Devonshire Association set up its Barrow Committee and the flurry of activity that followed provides the only information about the contents of major barrows within Exmoor National Park. Although the archaeological record is poor it seems clear that a common feature of Exmoor's barrows is a primary cremation burial over which the barrow was constructed. While rich grave goods have not been recorded from the moor, the area around Exmoor has yielded a number of prestigious artefacts (Todd 1987, 146), and it is almost certain that some of Exmoor's barrows contain such items. They might also contain secondary burials spanning several centuries.

Distribution and siting in the landscape

Exmoor's ridges and summits are usually occupied by one or more barrows (Fig 2.20). The three east–west ridges that cross the moor – the southern escarpment, the central ridge and the northern ridge – all have large concentrations of barrows, including some of the largest monuments. Their distribution is not constant. Sometimes there are linear clusters, such as the Chapman Barrows, elsewhere there are groups of one, two or three

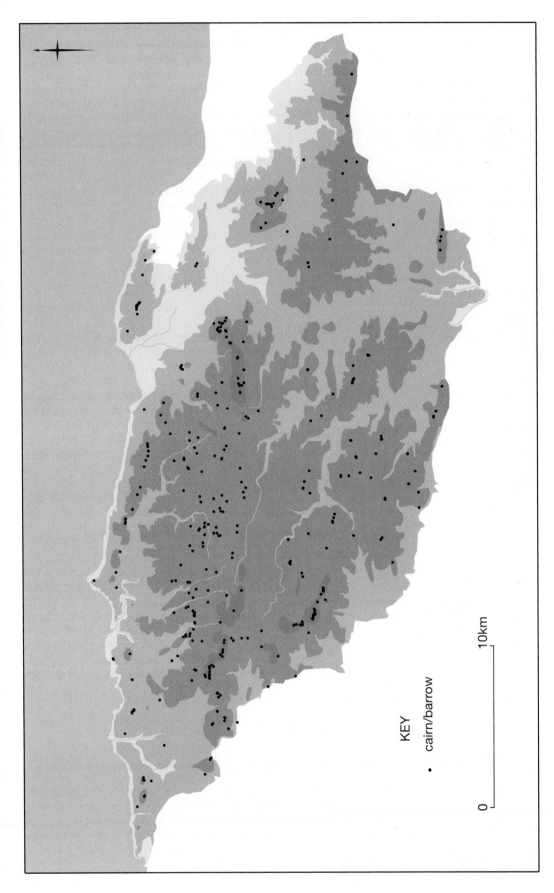

Figure 2.20
Exmoor: distribution of
barrows and cairns.
(Based on an Ordnance
Survey map, with permis-
sion. © Crown copyright.
All rights reserved)

KEY

• cairn/barrow

10km

0

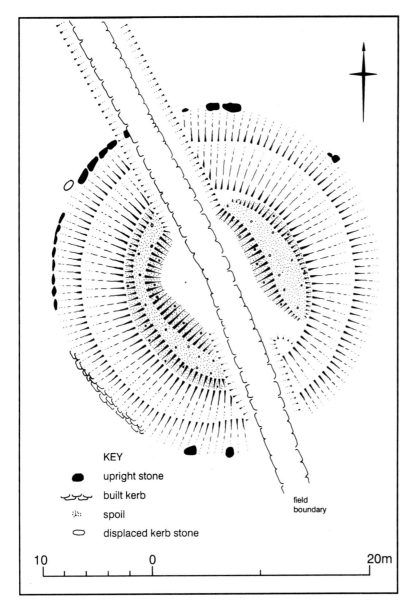

KEY

⬛ upright stone

〰 built kerb

∷ spoil

⬭ displaced kerb stone

field
boundary

10   0   20m

Figure 2.21
Setta Barrow has an
elaborate kerb of edge-set
blocks, upright stones and
coursed walling.

stone rows all lead up towards ridges on which are major barrows or barrow groups. Does this suggest that they are prestige barrows, perhaps predating many of the others?

Holwell Barrow, Longstone Barrow and Wood Barrow are prominently sited on ridges, but at dramatic locations, apparently deliberately chosen close to the steep valley heads. The nine barrows that make up the Five Barrows group are most prominent when seen from the south of Exmoor. Even 20km away they are clearly distinguishable on the southern escarpment, and yet closer in, are completely obscured by the rising ground. Some barrows, for example on The Foreland and one of the Trentishoe barrow group, look northwards over the sea, rising ground obscures views inland.

Dating

The chronology of Exmoor's barrows is uncertain. A chronic lack of full scale, modern excavation means that none of the major barrows are securely dated. Neither do archaeologists understand for how long the barrows were used. Traditionally they are considered to date from *c* 2000 BC to 1500 BC (Todd 1987, 140), although recent work elsewhere in the country has shown that some originate in the Neolithic (Quinnell 1994a, 52). The truth is that the archaeological evidence to prove this on Exmoor does not exist. The closest modern dating evidence comes from an 8m diameter barrow on Bratton Down (just outside Exmoor National Park) excavated by Charles Whybrow in 1971 and this yielded a radiocarbon date with a range from the late 2nd to early 1st millennium BC (Quinnell 1997). Long barrows and henges, the archetypal Neolithic monuments found elsewhere in southern England, do not occur on Exmoor. The suggested henge near Woolhanger Farm is more likely to be a tree ring enclosure (*see* Glossary) of the 18th or early 19th century.

Physical characteristics

Exmoor's barrows are constructed either from stone or a mixture of earth and stone. This has lead to the use of the term barrow for predominantly earthen mounds and cairn for mounds constructed mainly of stone (Grinsell 1984, 5). In reality the monuments are the same. They are nearly always circular, and comprise either a pudding basin mound (a cone with the top shaved off) or a low mound with a wide summit (more like a platform). These categories were recognised by

barrows together, in other instances there are irregular clusters (as around Robin and Joaney How). The minor ridges usually have barrows on them as well; for example, Ilkerton Ridge has a line of barrows along it, and on the end of Barcombe Down, a minor ridge running south-west from the moor, a well-preserved cairn was recently discovered only 20m from the main road.

While the distribution concentrates on the ridges and summits, there are individual barrows and groups on lower lying ground and on hillslopes. At Madacombe, the distribution might be partly related to the source of streams (Field 1999, 6–7). Barrows have also been noted close to many prehistoric settlements, for example Wilmersham Common. The association of small cairns and stone settings has already been mentioned. The long

Colt Hoare in Wessex in the early 19th century and were described by him as cone barrows and broad barrows respectively (McOmish *et al* forthcoming). Some barrows have an encircling ditch, or more rarely construction quarries. On Exmoor the external appearance of the barrows has nearly always proved, when they are excavated, to conceal a much more complex interior. Any sub-classification based on appearance alone could, therefore, be highly misleading. Rather it is useful to cite instances where external appearance does reveal structural information, and obviously examples where archaeological intervention has yielded evidence.

Kerbs

The mound of the barrow was often retained with a kerb, that is a wall of upright stone slabs or laid stones placed in a ring around its base. Kerbs or possible kerbs are visible on 21 of Exmoor's barrows, varying from a single upright stone remaining at the base of the mound to the well-preserved example of Setta Barrow (Figs 2.21 and 2.22). On several more, a marked change in the profile of the barrow might mark the position of a kerb that has been engulfed in slippage as the mound eroded through the centuries. It is likely that many more barrows had a kerb than the field evidence alone suggests.

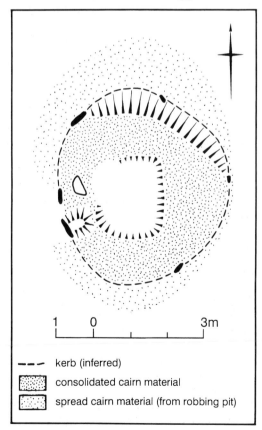

1   0   3m

- - - kerb (inferred)

▦ consolidated cairn material

▢ spread cairn material (from robbing pit)

Cists

Cists are small chambers in which burials or cremations were inserted. They usually occur within barrows, but sometimes can be found freestanding, such as the possible example at Clannon Ball. On Exmoor, seven cists are documented, either through antiquarian excavation or through the process of robbing, usually for road construction in the 19th century. One certain cist is still visible, at Langridge Wood, Roadwater (Fig 2.23). It comprises a massive rectangular grave lined with enormous stone slabs, and originally closed by a capstone 2m across. The barrow material formerly covering the cist was removed before 1839, but traces of the barrow survive. A second example is the possible cist on Clannon Ball (Fig 2.23). It is difficult to categorise but is closer in form to a cist than to any other of Exmoor's monuments.

Ring cairns

Ring cairns – circular banks of earth and stone – have a wide distribution in south-west England (Johnson and Rose 1994, 40; Butler 1997, 188–95; Turner 1990, 27–86). The recognition of ring cairns on Exmoor is problematic, reflecting their recent recognition as a monument type generally. The first ring cairn discovered on Exmoor was probably one of the Chapman Barrows opened by the Reverend Chanter in 1905, although it was not recognised as such at the time. His section drawing and description seems to show that the barrow was in fact an infilled ring cairn, the structure of the ring lost beneath the enormous mound constructed over it (Fig 1.12). Similar occurrences have been recognised elsewhere in south-west England (for example, Miles 1975, 57).

One ring cairn on Exmoor, Shallowmead, was excavated in the 1970s. Initially it was believed to be a hut circle, but excavation proved this to be wrong (Quinnell 1997) (Fig 2.24). It was 8.5m in diameter and comprised an encircling stony bank with an outer face of laid slabs and an inner face of upright stones. Tantalisingly, no cremations were found. It was in use sometime during the period 1500–1100 BC. Strikingly similar to the Shallowmead ring cairn is the most impressive surviving example on the moor: that on Cheriton Ridge (Fig 2.25). Although damaged, it still has intact sections of a compact encircling bank of rubble, with an internal face of upright stones. It occupies a dramatic position on the saddle of the ridge. In some cases it is not possible to distinguish confidently

Figure 2.22
The small cairn on Pig Hill has an incomplete kerb of six stones.

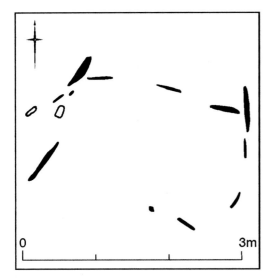

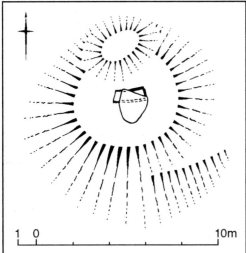

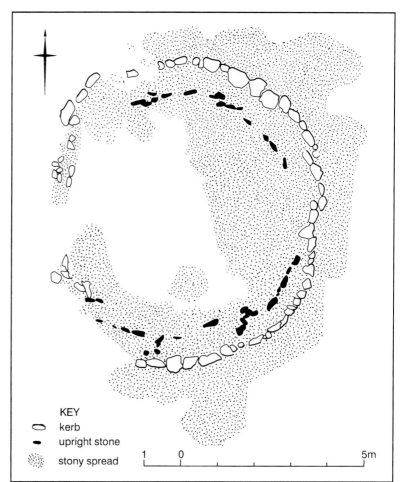

KEY

⬭ kerb

━ upright stone

⣿ stony spread

Figure 2.23 (above) Cists: the enigmatic stone 'box' on Clannon Ball might be a free-standing cist (top). The cist in Langridge Wood is at the centre of a flattened barrow (bottom).

Figure 2.24 (above right) Shallowmead ring cairn: excavation showed that this ring cairn had an outer face of laid stones and an inner face of standing stones. The excavation was carried out by H Quinnell in 1977 and the plan is reproduced with her permission and that of the Devon Archaeological Society. (© Copyright Henrietta Quinnell and the Devon Archaeological Society)

Figure 2.25 (right) The Cheriton Ridge ring cairn has a damaged bank of earth and stone, faced with upright stones on the inside.

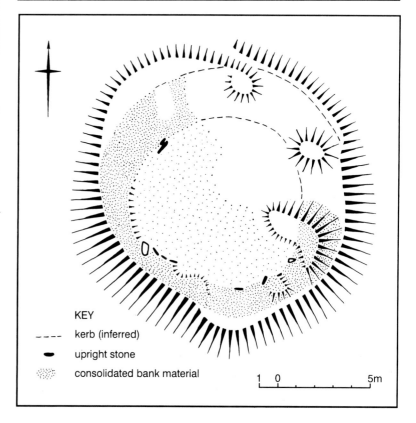

KEY

╌╌ kerb (inferred)

━ upright stone

⣿ consolidated bank material

between ring cairns and hut circles, examples of this occur on Thorn Hill.

Other cairns and barrows

A number of Exmoor's barrows and cairns display features that enable them to be distinguished from simple barrows and ring cairns. These features might be part of the original construction of the barrow, but might also occur because of later interference with its form due to antiquarian digging or robbing. A farmer looking for large stones suitable for gateposts might have dug a trench around the foot of the barrow hoping to encounter the kerb stones. This robbing trench might today look like an integral part of the site.

One of the Five Barrows group has a particularly complex form, which includes a slightly domed mound, encircling ditch and outer bank (Fig 2.26). The top of the mound is reached by a break in the ditch and outer bank. A newly discovered barrow to the north-east of Picked Stones Farm might well be a similar platform cairn, but if so it is the biggest so far recorded on Exmoor, being 35m in diameter. One of the Chapman Barrows has a well-marked ledge or berm (*see Glossary*) around its base, but this might be the result of antiquarian digging. On Exmoor such examples might hint at different forms of construction, but until more of these visually more complex barrows are excavated, understanding them fully from the surface evidence is impossible.

Ditches and quarries

The presence of encircling ditches either for quarry material or as an integral part of the monument have been widely noted, such as at Anstey Barrows, Lype Hill and the Chapman Barrows. Sometimes the ditches have silted up and can only be recognised by the presence of a band of rushes around the base of the barrow. On Dunkery Beacon and Robin and Joaney How are stone quarries specifically for the construction of the barrows (Fig 2.27).

Other features

The use of quartz in prehistoric stone monuments has been discussed above. On Exmoor, its use in barrows has also been noted. At Lype Hill the largest barrow has a 'necklace' of quartz running around the edge of the summit – to its builders, this glittering band of white would have dramatically emphasised the mound. It emphasises to us how important the appearance of the barrow must have been, and shows us that the original construction would not have included a covering of turf.

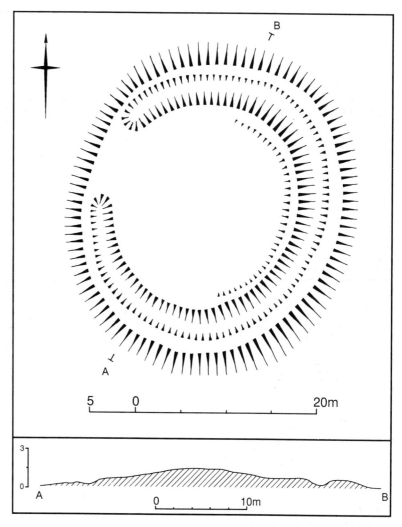

5 0   20m

3
0
A   0   10m   B

Figure 2.26 (above)
The most easterly of the Five Barrows has a complex form, comprising an encircling ditch and outer bank. The barrow has a slightly domed mound, visible on the detailed profile.

Figure 2.27 (below)
Robin How: the quarry ditch on the eastern edge of the massive summit cairn provided the material for the stony mound.

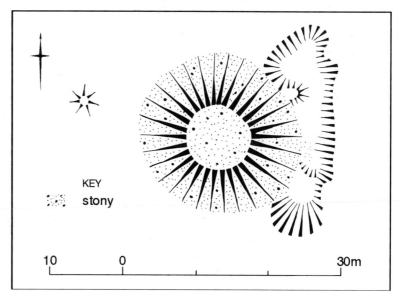

KEY
stony

10   0   30m

Landscape Study 4 Bronze Age barrows in the landscape

Towards the west end of the prominent west–east ridge that forms the central spine of Exmoor are the Chapman Barrows: a line of enormous barrows, nine of which are more than 20m in diameter, and certainly the most dramatic on the moor (Fig 2.28). They look southwards to Dartmoor, north to the Black Mountains of South Wales, and on a clear day both Lundy Island and Bodmin Moor can be glimpsed. The group is positioned between lower ground to the west and the high plateau of The Chains to the east, which gives the visitor a dramatic experience of ascending through the barrow group. The biggest barrows occupy the highest ground at the eastern end. Their close arrangement in a linear cemetery is highly unusual on Exmoor, where the barrows tend to be more loosely grouped or evenly distributed. Most of the Chapman Barrows, however, lie on a west–east axis. At some distance to the east is a second cemetery. It is dominated by Longstone Barrow, which lies at the west end and by Wood Barrow at the east end, both are huge burial mounds, and both are sited towards the end of the highest point on the ridge with the same breathtaking aspect. Wood Barrow in particular seems to be sited close to the dramatic Woodbarrow Hangings (Figs 2.29 and 6.11).

At the eastern end of the Dunkery massif, at a point where the central ridge ends, are two great cairns called Robin and Joaney How,

Figure 2.28 (facing page) The Chapman Barrows looking west along the linear cemetery. (© Copyright Jane Brayne)

Figure 2.29 Chapman Barrows: location of the barrow cemeteries. (Based on an Ordnance Survey map, with permission. © Crown copyright. All rights reserved)

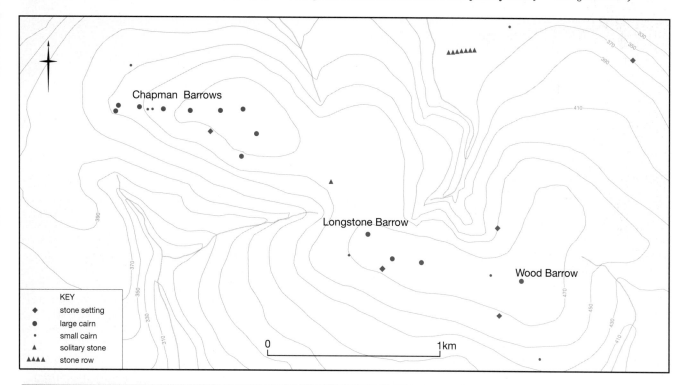

KEY
- ◆ stone setting
- ● large cairn
- · small cairn
- ▲ solitary stone
- ▲▲▲▲ stone row

Chapman Barrows

Longstone Barrow

Wood Barrow

0   1km

Figure 2.30 Robin and Joaney How. (AA00/0953)

Figure 2.31
Robin and Joaney How,
two summit cairns on the
eastern end of the Dunkery
ridge, have a cluster of
smaller cairns around
them. (Based on an
Ordnance Survey map,
with permission.
© Crown copyright.
All rights reserved)

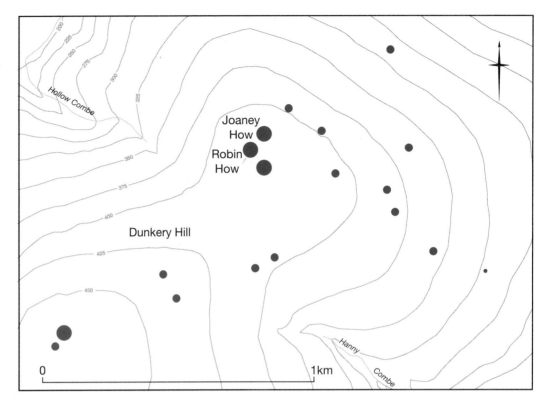

allegedly named after Robin Hood and Little John (Fig 2.30). They occupy the broad flat end of the Dunkery Ridge, and below them are a series of natural terraces containing smaller cairns, many occupying the false crests of the terraces (Fig 2.31). These seem to cluster around the major cairns. They provide one of the best examples of a major barrow group – prestige barrows – with satellite barrows, perhaps later in date, clustering around.

Bronze Age settlement and agriculture

Prehistoric field systems are generally divided into two types. Irregular or aggregate field systems are laid out in a piecemeal fashion. Cohesive field systems have a regular, planned layout. They might be coaxial, with the fields arranged along a main axis, or they might consist of blocks of rectangular fields. The evidence from the south-west peninsula suggests that the irregular field systems are earlier in date than the cohesive field systems. On Dartmoor these irregular fields are often incorporated into a more planned landscape (Fleming 1988, 101). On Exmoor, however, there is no fixed chronology for the field systems, and the following account is based on field observation and analogy with other areas in the south-west.

The Bronze Age landscape of Dartmoor is well known: planned field systems range across the moors; impressive hut circles, constructed from granite slabs, are placed within the fields, or lie close by. When Lesley Grinsell considered the archaeology of Exmoor in 1970 he was only able to locate a few possible earlier prehistoric field systems and hut circles on Exmoor (Grinsell 1970a, 50–51). It was clear that a programme of fieldwork on Exmoor was needed. In 1980 a major study of air photographs located several potential areas of prehistoric field system and settlement on Exmoor (McDonnell 1985a). The results of this, combined with the current survey, mean that we now have a far more coherent and comprehensive picture than that available to Grinsell in 1970, although the scope for new discoveries remains.

The distribution of field systems and settlements

The distribution map (Fig 2.32) shows a scatter of prehistoric field systems and unenclosed settlement sites across Exmoor, with a focus on the unimproved central area,

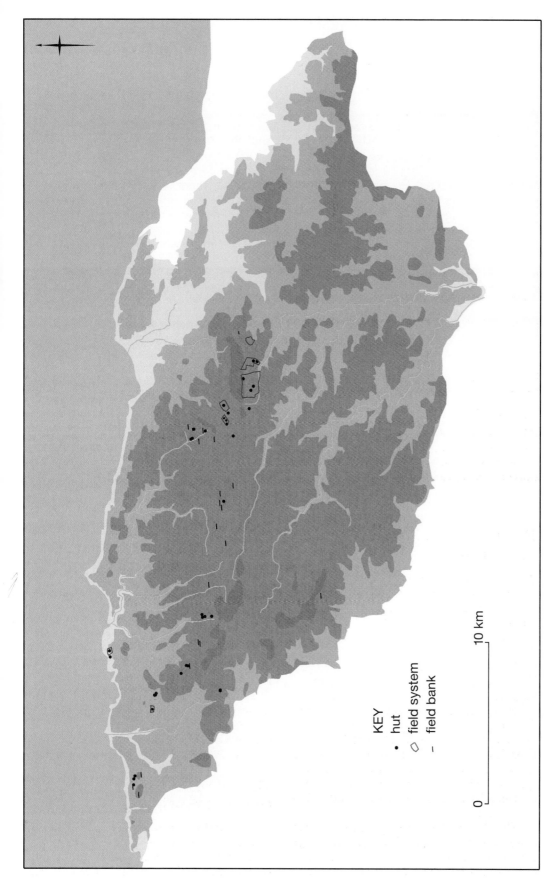

Figure 2.32
Exmoor: distribution of
Bronze Age settlement and
agriculture. (Based on an
Ordnance Survey map,
with permission.
© Crown copyright.
All rights reserved)

KEY
• hut
◇ field system
– field bank

10 km

0

Figure 2.33
Porlock Allotment: this prehistoric enclosure contains a single stance for a hut (see Fig 2.40). The traces of peat cutting, carried out over large areas of the Commons in the post-medieval period, can be seen in the right of the photograph. This would effectively remove slight traces of prehistoric field banks. (NMR 1459/291) (© Crown copyright.NMR)

but also on the commons where enclosure was late and agriculture has remained non-intensive. Even in these areas of high potential for the survival of prehistoric remains, the map shows that the pattern on Exmoor is very different from that of other south-western uplands. Both Dartmoor and Bodmin Moor have evidence for extensive settlement in the 2nd millennium BC (Fleming 1988; Johnson and Rose 1994), whereas on Exmoor only 10 prehistoric field systems, 20 fragmentary prehistoric field banks and 45 hut circles or house platforms are currently known.

This distribution can be explained by a number of factors. The first is the nature of the underlying geology. There is little readily available freestone on Exmoor, unlike Dartmoor, where granite clitter litters the surface. This lack of suitable stone means that houses were likely to be constructed of materials that leave little trace in the archaeological record, such as timber and thatch. It also suggests that the initial phase of clearance for enclosure and/or ploughing would result in only small amounts of stone cleared to form the field edges, with a hedge or sturdy timber fence forming the barrier. A second factor influencing the distribution is that of destruction of sites by later agricultural activity. There are only a few large areas of unenclosed moor left on Exmoor.

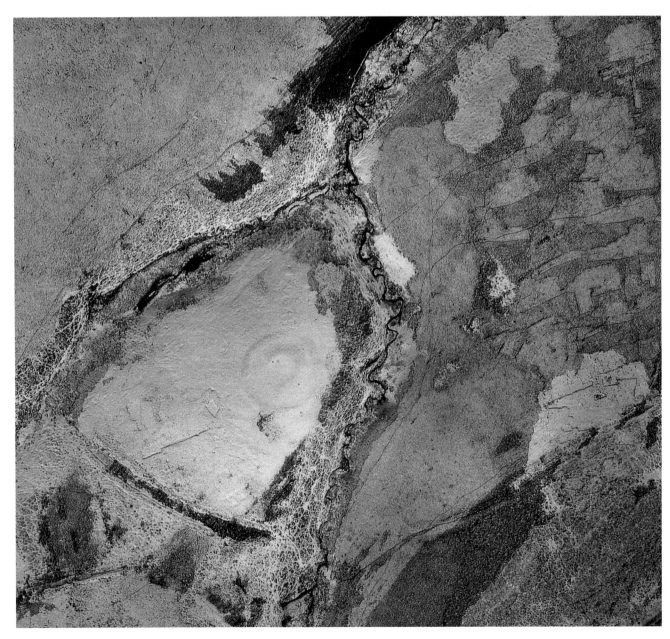

Outside the former Royal Forest, there was extensive enclosure and improvement throughout the medieval and post-medieval periods. In the 19th century the Knight family worked on enclosing and improving the Forest itself (Chapter 5). The current vegetation of many areas can be a problem, particularly as the practice of swaling has become less common. The slight banks of prehistoric field systems might be masked by vegetation, such as heather, gorse and bilberry, or by blanket peat that has been forming on the high, wet parts of the moor as early as the 3rd millennium BC. Peat cutting, documented on Exmoor since the 13th century (Hallam 1978) and still carried out today, might have disturbed or destroyed slight fragments of field bank or clearance heaps (Fig 2.33). Stone robbing of archaeological sites, particularly in the 19th century when enclosure of the moor with stone-faced banks was common, is evident on many areas of Exmoor. Finally, although the present project has sought to tackle this, there has been little systematic fieldwork on Exmoor, so that new sites must still await discovery.

The morphology of field systems

The earliest traces of human domestic life on Exmoor can be seen in the remains of houses – hut circles and house platforms – and of farming – fields and field systems. Most common are the very fragmentary remains of field banks, often with clearance cairns (see Glossary) nearby. These banks are constructed of earth and stones, and might be the result of small-scale field clearance for arable plots. They occur right across the central portion of Exmoor, from Holdstone Down and Trentishoe Down in the west to Porlock Allotment and the eastern flanks of Dunkery in the east. The remains lie on what is now open moor, at altitudes of between 300m and 420m. These slight banks occur in association with hut circles, such as on Holdstone Down and Porlock Allotment, or they can be isolated features, as at Lanacombe. Their form suggests we are looking at the remains of a few fields, perhaps an individual farmstead. Other structures such as shelters, stores and stock enclosures, made of timber and hedging, have long since vanished from the landscape. On Holdstone Down, high on the coast of north Devon, a hut circle, a single plot of land marked by some intermittent stony banks and several heaps of stones,

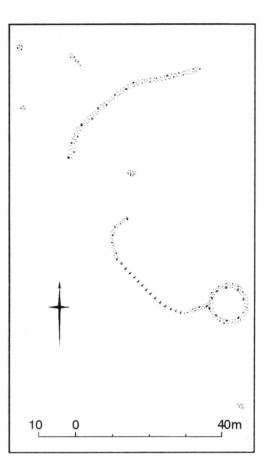

Figure 2.34
Prehistoric field banks, clearance cairns and hut circle on Holdstone Down.

10 0 40m

cleared in advance of cultivation, are all that remain of the early farmers who lived on Exmoor (Fig 2.34).

Larger areas of prehistoric field systems are concentrated in the central part of the moor, with a small western outlier on Martinhoe Common. All of the field systems have been discovered in the past 30 years, as a result of examining air photographs and field work. Most of Exmoor's field systems are cohesive in plan. At the Valley of Rocks, long, rectangular strip fields survive on steep slopes on a pocket of coastal heath (Fig 2.35). Two field systems on opposing sides of Chetsford Water are both laid out in a regular fashion. On Honeycombe Hill, small rectangular fields are laid out along a main north–east/south–west axis. On Great Hill one of the large rectangular fields is divided into small strips (Fig 2.36). The prehistoric field systems on Codsend Moors, Hoar Moor and Mansley Combe are a remarkable survival on enclosed land (Fig 2.37). The area was enclosed in the 19th century but remains as rough pasture. Five areas of prehistoric field system survive on the southern flanks of the Dunkery massif. This complex displays all of the

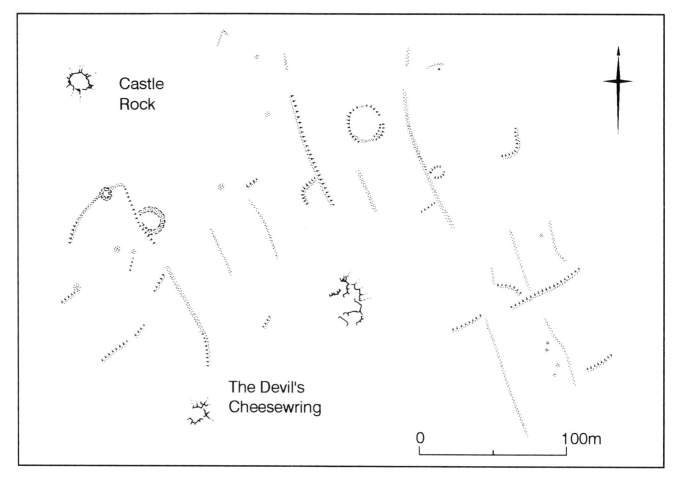

Castle
Rock

The Devil's
Cheesewring

0   100m

Figure 2.35
Valley of Rocks: this exten-
sive prehistoric field system
survives in a pocket of
coast and heathland, close
to the town of Lynton. The
remains of cairns, hut
circles and enclosures lie
within the fields.
For key see Fig 2.36.

Figure 2.36 (facing page)
Bronze Age field systems:
Great Hill (top) and
Honeycombe Hill (bottom).

elements described above. Hut circles with fragments of field banks and clearance cairns lie on the northern edge and small, irregular fields with clearance cairns survive to the west. Two areas of regular, rectangular fields survive in the centre of the complex, with another at Mansley Combe. The remains are difficult to interpret as they are slight, fragmentary and occur in long grass and marsh. There is evidence of later agriculture: medieval lynchets (*see* Glossary) overlie the prehistoric fields at Mansley Combe and long, parallel fields of medieval or post-medieval date slight part of the central complex.

Hut circles and house platforms

There are 45 unenclosed prehistoric hut circles or house platforms known on Exmoor. They are spread across the moor and are often associated with both the fragmentary and planned field systems described above. The huts and houses occur singly or in small groups of two or three and range in size from between 4 and 12m in diameter (internally). The hut circles are stony rings of earth and stone banks, with a level interior. Evidence of actual walling, in the form of edge set stone slabs, is rare on Exmoor with only four hut circles exhibiting this. These are on Porlock Allotment, where two of the three hut circles show the remains of walling (Fig 2.38a), at Holdstone Down and at the Valley of Rocks. This lack of walling suggests that the structures themselves were made of turf, timber or timber and stone. Even on Dartmoor, where freestone is abundant, excavation has shown that timber structures are often present, both as predecessors to stone hut circles and as independent buildings with no stone component (Todd 1987, 119). The entrances, where present, are set away from the prevailing weather and are marked by a gap in the bank, perhaps flanked by large stones as on Porlock Allotment. House platforms are less common than hut circles on Exmoor. They contain much less stone than hut circles, and are probably the stances for timber buildings. Two good examples lie on Porlock Allotment overlooking the headwaters of Weir Water.

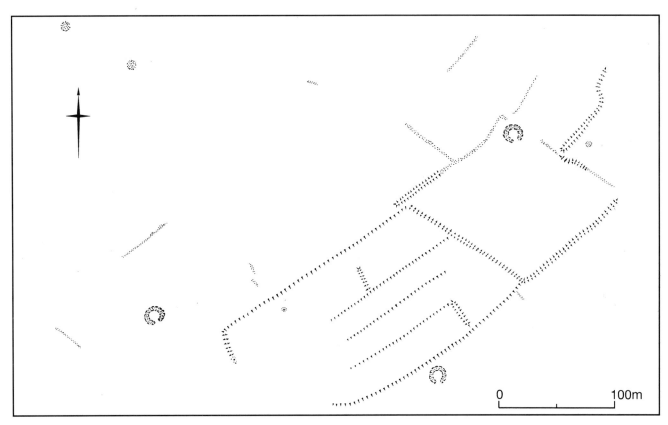

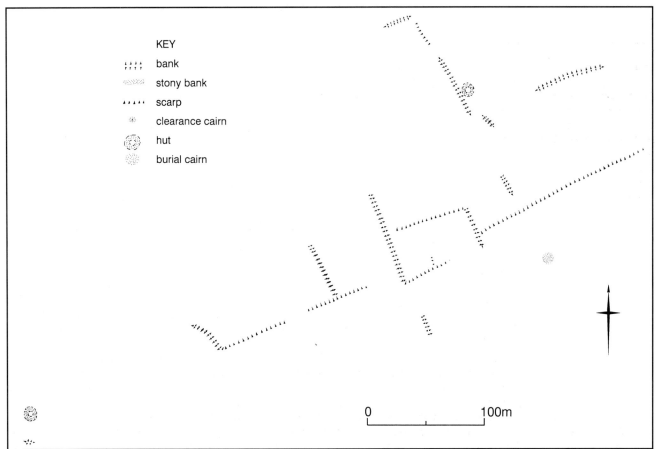

KEY

ǂǂǂǂ	bank
⠂⠒⠂	stony bank
▴▴▴▴▴	scarp
⊛	clearance cairn
◉	hut
⦿	burial cairn

Figure 2.37
Air photograph of Codsend and Hoar Moors, February 1999. The snow highlights the slight field banks of the prehistoric field system, with later fields on a different alignment overlying them (right). The circular enclosure, one of the latest prehistoric elements, is visible as a dark circle (centre). The regular rectangular fields currently in use are a result of 19th-century enclosure. (NMR 18256/06)
(© Crown copyright. NMR)

Here, level platforms have been created by the constructon of circular scoops on a steep slope (Fig 2.38b).

Settlements and field systems

Nearly all of the hut circles are directly associated with, or are close to, prehistoric field systems. Those associated with the cohesive field systems tend to be on the edge of, or just outside, the field system itself. At Great Hill one hut circle is situated in the corner of a field, the other two lie outside the southern and north-western edges of the field system (Fig 2.36). The remains on Great Hill represent the home and farm of perhaps three families, or an extended family group, who lived by farming what is

now open moorland. The farm was mixed: the small strip fields divided by lynchets show that arable farming was practised. The surrounding land would have been a mixture of woodland with some clearings, supporting grassland and heath. This would provide good grazing for cattle and sheep. It would also harbour wild animals to supplement the home-produced food (Fig 2.39). Although we have no excavated evidence from the Exmoor sites, a prehistoric quern was found close to the Valley of Rocks, and a tiny flint scraper of the type commonly used in the early part of the 2nd millennium BC, was recently found near Great Hill. There is little cereal pollen from this period in the fossil record for Exmoor. Weeds of arable cultivation are present in the pollen

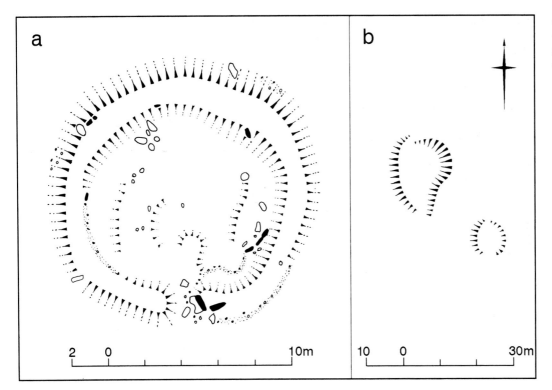

a

b

2   0   10m

10   0   30m

Figure 2.38
Hut circle (a) and house platforms (b) on Porlock Allotment.

record for the 2nd and 1st millennium BC from Hoar Moor and an impression of a barley grain was found on the Culbone Beaker. The excavated evidence from similar sites on Dartmoor suggests a way of life dominated by stock-rearing, with small-scale cultivation of cereals and beans (Todd 1987).

The beginning of enclosed settlement

Several of the earlier prehistoric field systems on Exmoor are associated with circular or sub-rectangular enclosures, quite different from the fields themselves. At the Valley of Rocks, two such enclosures occur within the field system, although the precise relationship of them to the field banks is unclear. One of these enclosures contains one or two prehistoric house platforms (Fig 2.35). Similarly, at Codsend two enclosures occur within the earlier prehistoric field systems, although they contain no evidence for house platforms. At South Common, on land brought into cultivation in the 19th century, are two enclosures. One contains a hut circle, the other a house platform; close by are two unenclosed hut circles (Fig 2.40a). These sites are not associated with prehistoric field systems, although the narrow ridge and furrow (*see* Glossary) visible here might have destroyed

such slight features. A similar site on Porlock Allotment, close to the line of the Porlock–Simonsbath railway, lies close to two unenclosed house platforms. The nearby field bank could be associated with any of these settlement sites (Fig 2.40b). Across the valley an enclosure containing a single house platform is situated on a spur overlooking the headwaters of Weir Water. There is no associated field system: here the surrounding land has been heavily disturbed by peat cutting (Figs 2.40c and 2.33).

In the south-west generally, it appears that the end of the 2nd millennium BC was a time of change. Notwithstanding our lack of a firm chronology, it seems that the large, planned field systems on Dartmoor fell into disuse. During the 1st millennium BC defended settlements or hillforts were built on the fringes of the upland areas (Silvester 1979; Quinnell 1994b). On Bodmin Moor defended enclosures of the 1st millennium BC occur away from the moor (Johnson and Rose 1994, fig 50). This suggests a time of stress, whether from pressure on the land due to climate deterioration, or from the introduction of the new technology of iron working. On Exmoor we might be seeing the beginning of this change at sites such as Valley of Rocks and Codsend, where the need for an enclosed farmstead was met by adapting existing settlements.

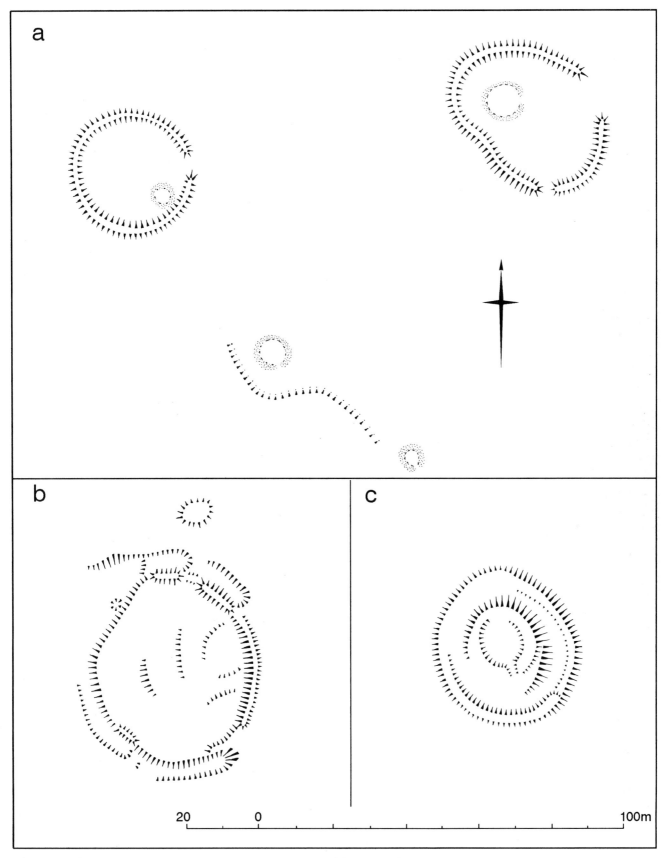

Figure 2.39 (left)
Great Hill: Bronze Age landscape. (© Copyright Jane Brayne)

Figure 2.40 (above)
Enclosed settlement: South Common (a) and Porlock Allotment (b and c).

Landscape Study 5 Prehistoric fields and 19th-century enclosure on Codsend Moors, Hoar Moor and Mansley Combe

Codsend and Hoar Moors lie on the south-western flank of Dunkery Hill, between 280m and 480m. The land is enclosed, but is mainly rough pasture on fairly steep, south-facing slopes (Fig 2.41). The prehistoric sites that lie on these moors were discovered during the 1980s and 1990s through examining air photographs and field survey. The prehistoric features lie in five groups across an area of 4 hectares (Fig 2.42). Originally they might have covered a greater area as the edges of features have been robbed for stone, disturbed by ploughing or extend into areas of marsh or peat. One of the earliest elements of the site might be the hut circles and clearance cairns close to the limit of 19th-century enclosure. Another early element of the site lies to the west, where small, irregular fields and clearance heaps are visible. The regular, rectangular strip fields of the central areas are more typical of the planned fields of the 2nd millennium BC. The eastern edge of Codsend Moors displays characteristics of both earlier and later field systems. Small, irregular fields appear to be laid out on a long axis, and a large circular enclosure, characteristic of the 1st millennium BC, is situated within these fields. A similar enclosure also lies inside planned rectangular fields in the central complex. Only excavation can unravel this complicated sequence.

The communities living and working here in the 2nd millennium BC grew crops. The pollen grains from weeds of arable agriculture were found fossilised in peaty soil on Hoar Moor. The presence of clearance cairns also suggests arable cultivation. The Bronze Age farmers grazed cattle and sheep on the open grassy heaths nearby. The great burial mounds of earlier generations were still very much in evidence up on Dunkery

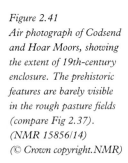

Figure 2.41
Air photograph of Codsend and Hoar Moors, showing the extent of 19th-century enclosure. The prehistoric features are barely visible in the rough pasture fields (compare Fig 2.37).
(NMR 15856/14)
(© Crown copyright.NMR)

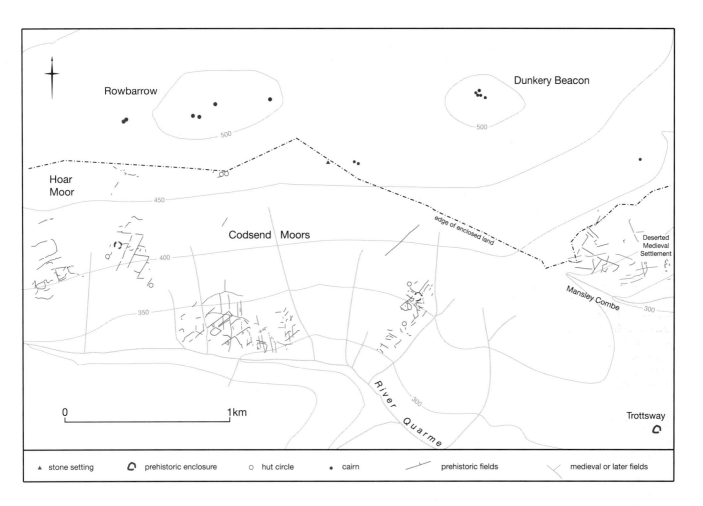

| ▲ stone setting | ⌂ prehistoric enclosure | ○ hut circle | • cairn | ⟋ prehistoric fields | ⤬ medieval or later fields |

Hill and Rowbarrow. Links with the past are also evident in the survival of a stone setting to the north of the fields. These monuments, earlier than the planned fields, might have had a territorial function. The communities who lived on Codsend and Hoar Moors in the 2nd millennium BC respected the monuments of their ancestors. If this stone setting did perform a territorial function, it is pertinent to note that, in the 19th century, an enclosure wall chose the same area to use as a boundary – in fact the wall has chopped the stone setting in two.

Overlying parts of this 4,000-year-old landscape are more fields – on a different alignment. These fields might be medieval or post-medieval in date. They do not reflect any of the later documented activity here. A deserted medieval settlement occupies a site at the head of Mansley Combe, where its fields overlie those of prehistoric date (Chapter 4). Before enclosure, at about the beginning of the 19th century, Codsend and

Figure 2.42
Prehistoric landscape, Codsend Moors, Hoar Moor and Mansley Combe. On the southern slopes of Dunkery lies the most extensive area of prehistoric field systems on Exmoor. At least three phases of enclosure and cultivation have taken place on this hillside. About 3,500 years ago, Bronze Age farmers cleared the land and made small fields, with huts nearby. About 1,000–500 years ago, the people who lived in the hamlets and isolated farms of the Quarme Valley cultivated these slopes to provide arable crops or winter fodder. In the 19th century the hillside was made into several large fields, now used for grazing stock.
(Based on an Ordnance Survey map, with permission.
© Crown copyright. All rights reserved)

Hoar Moors provided common pasture and turbary rights for several farms in the parishes of Exford and Cutcombe. An elaborate scheme for the enclosure of Codsend Moors in 1804 was never fully implemented. By 1842, as shown on tithe maps, the landscape appeared much as it does today.

The Neolithic and Bronze Age landscapes

The earliest evidence of humans on Exmoor provides a particularly partial and scant record, but by the end of the Bronze Age the archaeological evidence represents a range of human activities, based on agricultural subsistence. For the first time in Exmoor's evolution we have the opportunity to glimpse settled communities, to see their farms and homes, to raise questions about their beliefs and to look at the monuments of their dead. It is our first chance to see all these as elements of a wider landscape.

Before speculating too far, it is important to understand the limitations of the evidence. Firstly, the study of the early prehistoric period on Exmoor has been hampered by a lack of archaeological fieldwork. The present survey has gone some way to improving this situation. For the first time the entire landscape has been mapped so that sites of this period can be seen together. The remains are so fragmentary, however, that they are often difficult to identify, and there is a pressing need for more fieldwork. The discovery of sites might only be possible in times of drought when the peat shrinks and stony banks emerge through the turf, or when an area has been swaled giving the opportunity for very close ground inspection.

Secondly, what survives is only a partial picture – it is only the tip of the iceberg. Some aspects of the prehistoric landscape might simply not survive as surface archaeology. The lack of hut circles, for example, does not mean that Exmoor was thinly settled in the Bronze Age. Field systems without settlement evidence prove this not to be the case. The paucity of hut circles shows that we are only able to identify a few: the flimsier wooden or turf buildings might leave no visible trace at all.

Thirdly, the chronology is uncertain. Hardly any modern excavation has taken place on Exmoor, so dating is by analogy with similar sites elsewhere. There is an urgent need to fit Exmoor's field monuments into a more precise chronological framework, which only modern excavation could provide.

What is certain is that by the end of the Bronze Age, Exmoor was not the wilderness, the 'filthy barren ground' found by Camden (quoted in Chanter and Worth 1905, 377) nearly 2,000 years later. Rather it was a landscape of settled people in extended family groups or individual farms. These were pockets of agriculture on the gentle slopes above the combes – little fields carved out of the waste in a land of wooded valleys, heaths and areas of scrub. On the ridges and sometimes near to the houses and fields were barrow cemeteries, some recent and some already many hundreds of years old. The stone monuments, perhaps already old, were never far away from these settlements, and although not dramatically visible in the landscape, were perhaps an indicator of a continuing spiritual tradition.

Landscape Study 6   The earlier prehistoric landscape on Porlock Allotment and Honeycombe Hill

The north–east to south–west ridge, which includes Luccott Moor, separates the two valleys of Weir Water and Chetsford Water. Both valleys are joined by a series of minor tributary valleys. The resulting landscape is one of gently sloping ridges out of which run short spurs separated by deep combes. Most of the archaeology tends to occupy these spurs. It cannot be overstated how this topography determines the distribution of archaeological sites (Fig 2.43).

Eight hut circles are visible on the slopes above Weir Water. They cluster in twos or threes, on generally south or west facing slopes, although one group occupies nearly level ground close to the valley bottom – a sheltered natural terrace. These small groupings are typical of Exmoor and seem to represent individual farms or extended family groups. The huts vary in construction from stone rings with facing stones to earthen platforms. It seems likely that all would have supported buildings of timber possibly roofed with heather or straw thatch. Around the huts are fragmentary field banks, all that remains of a loose collection of cleared areas for growing the few crops required. These fields developed in a piecemeal way, perhaps after sporadic clearance of woodland and scrub. They were isolated pockets of agriculture. Elsewhere fragmentary field banks survive without hut circles implying that some timber buildings leave no surface footprint for archaeologists to find.

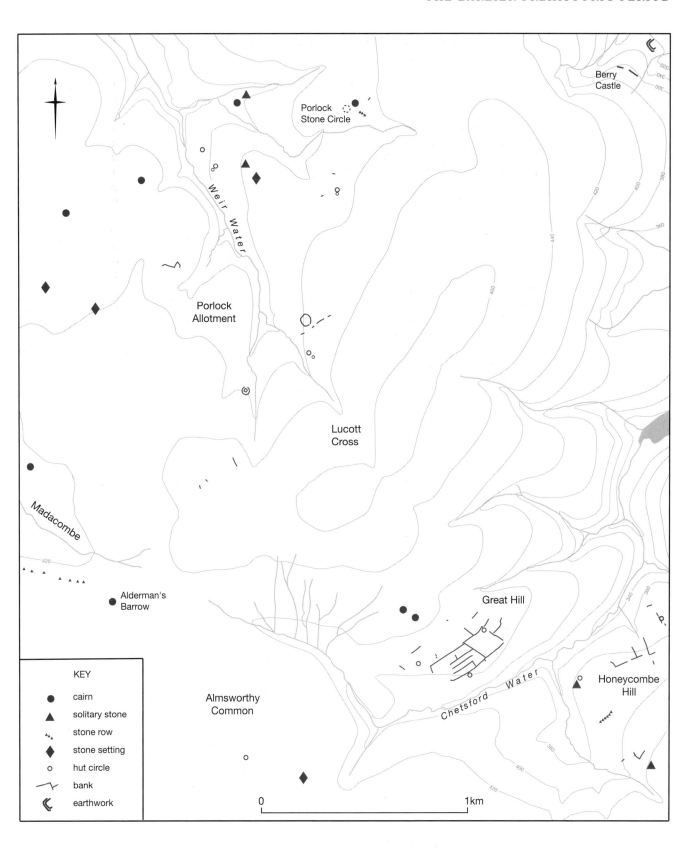

Figure 2.43
The earlier prehistoric landscape on Porlock Allotment, Luccott Moor and Honeycombe Hill.
(Based on an Ordnance Survey map, with permission. © Crown copyright. All rights reserved)

Figure 2.44
Looking north along Chetsford Water in the snow.
The Great Hill prehistoric settlement and field system is in
the middle foreground, and Honeycombe Hill is centre left.
(NMR 18256/19) (© Crown copyright.NMR)

Not far away on the western edge of Porlock Allotment are two stone settings. Some cairns occur in this landscape and close by is the Porlock stone circle, with its stone row and cairn.

South of Weir Water the high ridge of Luccott Moor did not seem to favour settlement, except perhaps for the strangely sited hut on Almsworthy Common. Its entrance is on the south-west, which on an exposed ridge at an altitude of 425m, must suggest that when it was used it lay in an area of woodland. The watershed of Almsworthy Common is topped by the great Alderman's Barrow, which overlooks the three valleys of Madacombe, Allcombe Water and Chetsford Water. The Madacombe stone row leads out of the valley itself towards this high ground, and the slopes of the valley have a sprinkling of barrows.

Around Chetsford Water the hut circles lie within more developed and planned field systems (Fig 2.44). That at Great Hill is highly regular, with lynchetted banks separating narrow strip fields. The three hut circles are spaced across the system and are sited economically at the edges of or outside the fields. Two large burial cairns are visible on the slope above. A similar though more fragmentary field system is visible on Honeycombe Hill, although it might originally have been much more extensive. Here only two huts could be found. One of them is sited against a field bank, presumably at the edge of a field, the other is poorly preserved and lies on the crest of the steep valley slope. The fields are regular and some are terraced strongly into the natural slope, but the plan is partly dictated by the topography. These planned field systems never stretched further than the spur on which they were laid out. Nearby the Wilmersham stone row is close to the field system, and perhaps its survival demonstrates a sense of continuity in the landscape.

3
The later prehistoric and Roman periods

Introduction and chronology

The Iron Age (700 BC–AD 43)

The Iron Age traditionally covers the period 700 BC to AD 43 (Cunliffe 1995, 27), but it is not possible to identify so neatly the cultural changes that mark the transition from Bronze Age to Iron Age. Neither was it an abrupt event, rather it was the culmination of a number of processes. The ultimate effect, however, was to change dramatically the way in which the landscape was peopled.

The terms suggest technological change, but undoubtedly the most powerful factor in this transition was the environment. What we know of the environment derives from cores taken through the peat deposits on Exmoor. Very few have been done, but they are invaluable in understanding Iron Age Exmoor. The pollen cores chart the steady and rapid decline of tree cover on the moor during the 1st millennium BC. This gives a general picture of the disappearance of woodland and the emergence of acid grassland and the accumulation of peat. Locally the picture is undoubtedly more complex, with parts of the landscape remaining tree covered. In some cases the inception of peat growth might not occur until the second half of the 1st millennium BC (Straker and Crabtree 1995, 43–51).

Traditionally this period has been seen as one of retreat from the high moors. On Dartmoor only a handful of sites are known from the high moor while a scatter of hillforts ring its margins (Gerrard 1997, 66). They are interpreted as marking a shift from settled communities practising a mixed economy to more pastoral activities on the sheltered drier slopes around the moor. On Exmoor the picture is rather different. There are seven hillforts on and around the moor, but there are many other smaller enclosures, conventionally termed hill-slope enclosures, scattered across all but the highest parts.

Exmoor's Iron Age field monuments could be seen against the background of the south-west at a time when 'unity did not become even a formal reality'; rather it was a fragmented landscape – 'a multitude of small fiefdoms' (Todd 1987, 167). The implication of hierarchy between hillforts and hill-slope enclosures is intriguing but so far none have been excavated to enable them to be measured against such social structure and organisation. What is also clear is that this was a time when greater emphasis seems to have been placed on land ownership and territories (Cunliffe 1993, 193).

The cultural material associated with this period is sparse. No Early Iron Age pottery has been conclusively identified on the moor, which is unsurprising when viewed against the rest of south-west England where there is scant and uncertain evidence in the ceramic record during the transition from Bronze Age to Iron Age. This is followed by the appearance of a series of distinctive regional types, South-Western Decorated Ware or Glastonbury Ware (see Glossary). These emerge in the 4th century BC, the Middle Iron Age, and continue until the 1st century BC, at which time it is argued that Devon became aceramic (see Glossary); but some of the Glastonbury forms might have continued in use until the Roman period (Cunliffe 1991, 84–5; Quinnell 1994b, 78). The pottery represents a distinct regional style, although it came from several production centres throughout the region at different times, which implies a sense of local distinctiveness, but not uniformity (Cunliffe 1991, 85). Excavation of the hillforts and hill-slope enclosures might be expected to yield such assemblages, which would greatly assist our understanding of settlement around Exmoor at this time.

There is hardly any evidence for Iron Age metalwork. The most notable find from the area is the remarkable bronze bowl from Rose Ash just outside Exmoor National Park (Fox 1961). But this is an isolated find, possibly even a votive offering at a time when the association of high status metalwork and rivers, springs and streams is well attested (Cunliffe 1993, 198). Other finds are difficult to date and include spindle whorls and several quern stones, hinting at various domestic activities, although none of these artefacts come from archaeological contexts.

By the Roman period, a tribe named the Dumnonii had emerged, probably covering the whole of Cornwall, Devon and much of west Somerset and presumably representing the amalgamation of various fiefdoms. The Dumnonii were an isolated tribe, preferring to barter than to strike their own currency – there is no Dumnonian coinage – and their origins are shrouded in mystery, as is the nature of their political and socio-economic structure (Costen 1992). The scarcity of hill-forts in Devon and west Somerset is in marked contrast to elsewhere in southern England, where elaborate hillforts dominate the Iron Age landscape. On Exmoor few hillforts are found, and these are usually simple enclo-sures. On Exmoor we are close to the eastern edge of Dumnonian territory, which was around the Parret Valley, east of the Quantock Hills. This has obvious, but so far unexplored, implications for the cultural evidence.

The Romano-British and Roman period (AD 43–410)

Evidence of specific native Roman activity on Exmoor is limited, although culturally it would be hard to distinguish it from the preceding centuries. It is reasonable to assume that the hillforts and other enclosures were used by the Dumnonii into the Roman period, but the conquering power itself is distinctly represented by a thin network of extant military sites: two fortlets and one probable fort, although more forts ring Exmoor from slightly farther afield.

Several isolated finds on Exmoor can be attributed to the Roman period. A Roman lamp was found in the Lyn river, and coin hoards have been found at Withiel Florey and at Bat's Castle, the latter concealed within the hillfort rampart. A number of smaller Roman coin hoards and stray coins have been found across the moor, several of these are associated with suggested Roman iron mining or smelting activity, but in only one case, at Dulverton, can this be stated with certainty. The largest assemblage of Roman material, both native and military, however, comes from the excavations at the two Roman fortlets of Old Burrow and Martinhoe. The value of this material is that it is from a dated archaeological context. It has also been suggested that these military fortifications were trading freely with the native Roman population. It is ironic that so far the only native pottery of the later prehis-toric period comes, not from a native settle-ment, but from the fortifications of the conquering power, with whom the local people were trading.

Hillforts

The hillforts of Exmoor are easily distin-guished from the mass of other Iron Age earthwork enclosures by their size: they all enclose an area of at least 1ha. Hill-slope enclosures, smaller in size and with less substantial earthworks, are discussed below. A hillfort is an impressive enclosure, usually on a hilltop. Substantial artificial earthworks, often cleverly combined with topographic features, define such enclosures. Hillforts generally date from the later part of the 1st millennium BC, and are the most striking of Iron Age monuments, often influencing subsequent patterns of land division and use.

There has been very little study of Exmoor's hillforts: there are no recorded excavations or geophysical surveys. They do not seem to have been considered as a group, distinct from the hill-slope enclosures. Rather, elaborate classification schemes have confused the issue (Whybrow 1967; Grinsell 1970a, 78–9). In the past, hillforts have been considered mainly in terms of defence, with great emphasis placed on their morphology. The function of a hillfort was seen in terms of the stronghold of a tribal group or clan chieftain. More recent approaches to the study of hilllforts, combined with an ever-increasing quantity of good quality excavated data, have focussed on different interpreta-tions. Hillforts are now seen as central places in the landscape – a focus for the community – but also as places where access is restricted. The earthworks can be seen as barriers designed to impress and to exclude certain groups of people from particular areas. Following on from this, one interpretation is that some hillforts might have played a similar role to the ritual complexes of earlier prehistory (Chapter 2).

Distribution and siting of hillforts

The seven hillforts on Exmoor exhibit a striking distribution. The majority lie on the margins of the moor, commanding the major river valleys (Fig 3.1). Shoulsbury Castle dominates the western approaches to the moor. Brooding and isolated, it overlooks the upper reaches of the Bray (Fig 3.2) and at more than 450m ranks as one of the

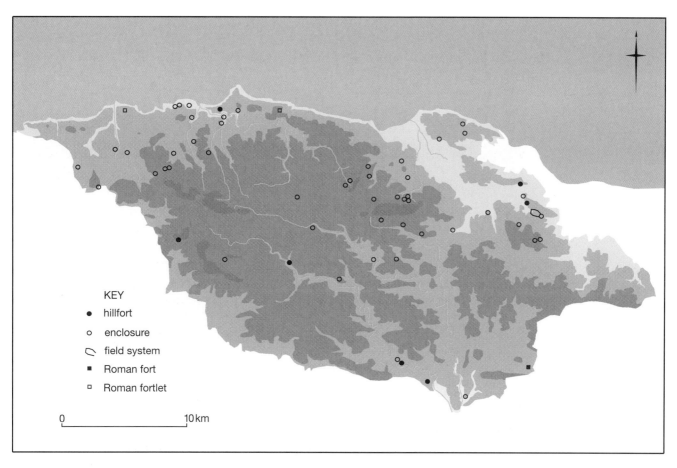

KEY

- ● hillfort
- ○ enclosure
- ⌓ field system
- ■ Roman fort
- □ Roman fortlet

0　　　　　　　　10 km

Figure 3.1
Exmoor: distribution of
hillforts, later prehistoric
enclosures, field systems
and Roman forts. (Based
on an Ordnance Survey
map, with permission.
© Crown copyright.
All rights reserved)

Figure 3.2
Looking east across
Exmoor. The hillfort of
Shoulsbury Castle lies in
the foreground. The fields,
commons and moors of
Exmoor unfold beyond.
(NMR 18528/36)

Figure 3.3
Air photograph of Wind Hill: the long and impressive earthwork creates an enormous enclosed area high above the Lyn Gorge. Medieval strip lynchets can be seen across much of the interior. (NMR 15329/04) (© Crown copyright. NMR)

Figure 3.3
Air photograph of Wind Hill: the long and impressive earthwork creates an enormous enclosed area high above the Lyn Gorge. Medieval strip lynchets can be seen across much of the interior. (NMR 15329/04) (© Crown copyright. NMR)

Figure 3.4
The upper Barle Valley: the hillfort of Cow Castle lies in the foreground at the junction of the River Barle and White Water. (NMR 18243/31) (© Crown copyright. NMR)

highest hillforts in England (Forde-Johnston 1976, 54). Wind Hill dominates the eastern side of the Lyn Gorge, with several small Iron Age enclosures below it, and enjoys unbroken views across the Bristol Channel to Wales (Fig 3.3). Similarly positioned on the north-eastern edge of Exmoor are Bat's Castle and Grabbist Hill, close to the coast yet within site of the Avill Valley. Finally, a group of three hillforts dominate the middle and lower reaches of the Barle Valley. Oldberry Castle and Mounsey Castle lie on promontories, high above the Barle at Dulverton. Cow Castle sits in splendid isolation on a valley floor knoll within the former Royal Forest (Fig 3.4).

Morphology of hillforts

Classification, size and shape

Most of Exmoor's hillforts are univallate (a single bank and ditch; *see also* Glossary); where a second bank exists it takes the form of a counterscarp (a bank on the outer lip of the ditch; *see also* Glossary). The exceptions are Bat's Castle, where the counterscarp bank is large enough to function as a second rampart and Shoulsbury Castle, which has an outer rampart and ditch. The areas enclosed range in size from 1 to 2 hectares. The exception is the promontory fort of Wind Hill, which encloses an area of 35 hectares (Fig 3.5).

The hillforts vary in shape according to their topographic setting. Cow Castle, Mounsey Castle and Oldberry Castle are

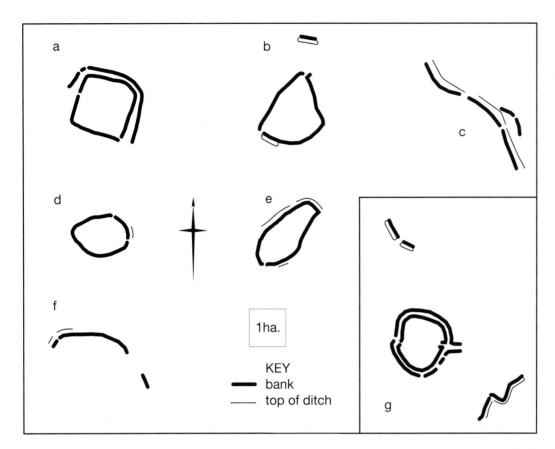

Figure 3.5
Exmoor hillfort morphology:
Shoulsbury Castle (a);
Mounsey Castle (b);
Wind Hill (c); Cow Castle
(d); Oldberry Castle (e);
Grabbist Hill (f) and Bat's
Castle (g).

a

b

c

d

e

f

1ha.

KEY
━━ bank
── top of ditch

g

examples of contour forts, where the earth-works follow the contour of the hillside to cut off the upper part of the hill from the ground below them; their ovoid shapes reflect the shape of the hilltops that they enclose. Wind Hill is a classic promontory fort: a high rampart and ditch cut off the gentlest approach to a promontory of land defined by steep natural slopes. Grabbist Hill makes clever use of both a steep hillside and earth-works. Again, the promontories define the shape of these enclosures. Shoulsbury Castle lies on the edge of a steep scarp, just below the plateau of Shoulsbarrow Common, and falls into the hill-slope category of hillforts (Forde-Johnston 1976, 7–8).

Hillfort earthworks

The construction of a hillfort represented a massive undertaking, a great investment of labour for communities who practised what was essentially a subsistence economy. Before the hillfort was constructed, the initial posi-tion of the earthworks on the hill was directed by a low marking-out bank, usually detected through excavation. At Shoulsbury Castle, however, the low bank of the outer earthwork might be the marking-out bank for a second line of earthworks that was never finished (Fig 3.3) (Silvester and Quinnell 1993, 28).

An external ditch provided both the material for the rampart and also an extra earthwork element. The problem of slippage of material back into the ditch was solved in two ways. One was to construct a box rampart (see Glossary), with a timber frame and earthern core. This type of timber framing is recognised through excavating a rampart and is generally the earlier of the two construction methods (Cunliffe 1991).

Figure 3.6
Shoulsbury Castle from the air, showing the incomplete nature of the outer bank (foreground) and the cairn that lies inside the hillfort. (NMR 18528/30)

A box rampart often had a berm or level area between the rampart base and the ditch top – this can be recognised in field monuments. The inner rampart at Bat's Castle might be separated from its ditch by a berm, but stone robbing has caused a lot of disturbance to the rampart (Fig 3.7). The second way to stop the rampart falling into the ditch was to build a glacis or dump rampart (*see* Glossary). This was a much simpler rampart, where successive dumps of soil created a continuous slope from the ditch bottom to the rampart top. Most of Exmoor's hillforts appear to have had this type of construction. A stone revetment wall would help to strengthen the rampart. Remarkably, remains of these walls can still be seen at Cow Castle, in the south-eastern rampart, and at Mounsey Castle, close to the south-western entrance where 12m of stone wall is visible in the rampart face (Fig 3.8). An internal quarry ditch, providing extra rampart material, is a common feature of Exmoor's hillforts. At Cow Castle and Mounsey Castle, internal quarry ditches, rock-cut in places, provide rampart material. At both of these sites an external ditch is only present close to the entrances (Figs 3.9 and 3.10).

Hillfort entrances

The most common type of entrance to a hillfort is a simple gap. This consists of a break in the rampart, with a corresponding causeway over the ditch. Good examples of simple gaps are exhibited at Grabbist Hill and the western entrance to Bat's Castle (Fig 3.7). The narrow corridor through the

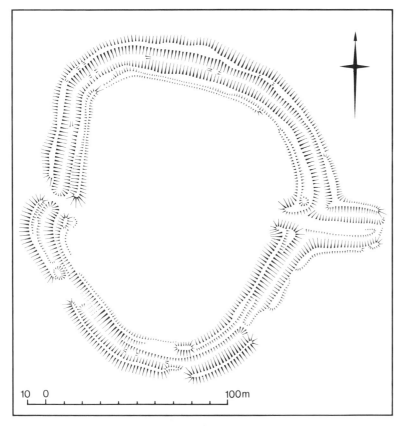

Figure 3.7 (above)
Earthwork survey of Bat's Castle, showing the complex form of the eastern entrance.

Figure 3.8 (right)
Mounsey Castle: detail of revetment wall by the south-western entrance. (Hazel Riley, English Heritage)

Figure 3.9 (facing, top)
Earthwork survey of Cow Castle, showing the internal quarry scarp and hut platforms close to the eastern entrance.

Figure 3.10 (facing, bottom)
Earthwork survey of Mounsey Castle, the ruined charcoal-burner's hut lies in the south-eastern corner of the hillfort.

rampart and ditch might be lengthened by thickening or turning the ends of the rampart, so making it more elaborate and impressive. Both of the entrances to Cow Castle are slightly in-turned and heightened, while the south-western entrance to Mounsey Castle has one out-turned and one in-turned rampart end, creating a long, embanked corridor through the ramparts. At Shoulsbury Castle, the outer rampart and ditch turn out as they approach both entrances, but the unfinished nature of the earthworks makes it difficult to imagine how the entrance ways functioned (Fig 3.6). The eastern entrance to Bat's Castle is the most complex on Exmoor. Not only do the inner ramparts thicken and turn inwards, but the ditch and counterscarp bank turn outwards to create an embanked corridor 65m long (Fig 3.7). Only excavation can give us a full understanding of how such an entrance worked. There might have been two or three strong timber gates and a series of wooden palisades on the rampart tops. Excavation of hillfort entrances often reveals complex sequences of timber features (Cunliffe 1991).

Outworks

There are three hillfort outworks on Exmoor, two were recognised only recently. At Mounsey Castle, a short length of rampart and ditch lie across the gentle northern approach (Fig 3.10). Two impressive earthworks lie to the south-east and north-west of Bat's Castle. These outworks are some distance from the hillfort and are formidable barriers in their own right (Fig 3.5). They might have functioned as elements that controlled access to the area in and around Bat's Castle, as well as being statements of control and dominance over the landscape.

Internal features

Shoulsbury Castle, Cow Castle and Bat's Castle, all on open moorland, have the potential for the identification of house platforms in their interiors. Unfortunately, Bat's Castle has ridging right across its interior (Fig 3.7), perhaps dating from World War II when it was used for growing potatoes. A Bronze Age barrow, Shoulsbarrow, lies in the north-east angle of Shoulsbury Castle. This was excavated sometime before 1906, but nothing, apparently, was found (*VCH Devon* I, 596). The interior of Cow Castle contains three or four slight platforms – probably the location of settlement sites, contemporary with the hillfort (Fig 3.9).

Mounsey Castle, within the lower, wooded part of the Barle Valley, has a tumbledown charcoal burners' hut inside it (Fig 3.10).

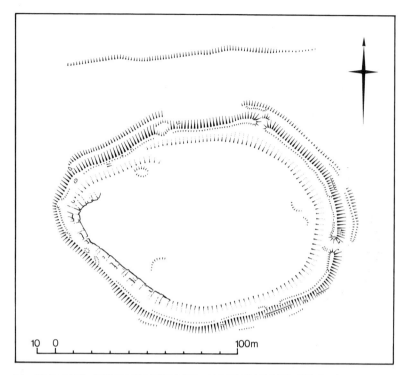

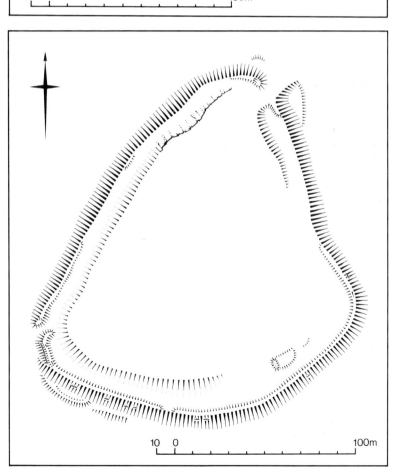

The interior of Grabbist Hill contains plough ridges, and Oldberry Castle has been converted into several pasture fields, with the defences becoming field boundaries. The interior of Wind Hill now contains 12 pasture fields, the main A39 trunk road, steep cliffs and coastal heath. A series of strip fields, more recent than the defensive work but still probably more than 500 years old, are revealed in air photographs (Fig 3.3).

Function

Our ideas about the functions of hillforts have changed through the years and their interpretation has moved away from the strictly defensive towards that of landscape foci. The consideration of hillforts must also be set within what is known about the structure and organisation of social groups in the 1st millennium BC. At this time we see the emergence of a distinct hierarchy in southern England, where a plethora of excavated evidence has shown that the elite of society lived in elaborate hillforts, presumably with some form of control over the surrounding landscape, its resources and inhabitants. It has been suggested that the south-west peninsula, isolated from these developments, remained a more traditional society, based on family groups, with a less hierarchical structure (Cunliffe 1995).

Exmoor appears to display features of both of these models. The very existence of hillforts on Exmoor suggests a hierarchical society. The small number of such sites could suggest that by this time society and the land were very tightly controlled by a small number of elite groups. The existence of so many smaller, hill-slope enclosures, however, is more indicative of a society based on individual family groups. The lack of a chronology for the Iron Age settlements on Exmoor, however, prevents further speculation, as we do not know when such sites were occupied.

Hillforts could have had several different functions, not all mutually exclusive. The traditional explanation was that a hillfort was for defence, suggesting an unstable society with many conflicts. Hillforts were seen as the stronghold of a chief or clan, functioning as places of refuge for the wider community in times of crisis. The outworks and additional enclosures were interpreted as stock enclosures. Exca-

vation and geophysical survey, however, have shown that many hillforts were occupied on a permanent basis. Excavations at Danebury in Hampshire showed a busy, organised settlement inside the defences. Numerous round houses, storage pits and raised granaries all suggest permanent occupation (Cunliffe 1993). Geophysical survey of the interior of Ham Hill in south Somerset, a hillfort about twice the size of Wind Hill, showed that both houses and field systems were enclosed within the massive defences, although the chronology of these features is uncertain (Dunn 1997).

Excavation at Danebury and South Cadbury has shown that they contained shrines, leading to the idea that hillforts could have functioned as awe-inspiring places in the landscape – places for ritual and religion rather than residence. The exclusion of certain groups of people by barriers in the landscape – the outworks and hillfort earthworks – is seen as part of this function.

Danebury, Ham Hill and South Cadbury, however, lie in landscapes quite different from those of Exmoor. We have seen that Exmoor's economy was predominantly pastoral in the Bronze Age and, as the climate deteriorated during the 1st millennium BC, there is every reason to suppose that it remained so. The evidence for later prehistoric field systems on Exmoor is restricted to a single area on the very eastern edge of the moor at Withycombe Hill.

The hillforts on the edge of the moor, like Oldberry Castle and Bat's Castle, might have been occupied throughout the year. They could have functioned as focal points in the landscape, providing a place for the trade and storage of goods. The complex arrangements at Bat's Castle could suggest a ritual function, particularly when seen in the context of other later prehistoric settlement in the area. Wind Hill could have accommodated several families and their livestock, or its very size could suggest a high status site with a specialised function. Shoulsbury Castle and Cow Castle, one at high altitude, the other in the heart of the former Royal Forest of Exmoor, are unlikely to have been occupied permanently. Their propinquity to upland pasture for summer grazing and to easily worked iron ore deposits might hold the key to their function.

Figure 3.11 (facing, top) The Barle Valley at Dulverton: the hillfort of Oldberry Castle can be clearly seen high above the town (foreground). Mounsey Castle and Brewer's Castle lie further up the river, both hidden in the thickly wooded valley. (NMR 18620/19)

Figure 3.12 (facing, bottom) Location of Oldberry Castle, Mounsey Castle and Brewer's Castle. (Based on an Ordnance Survey map, with permission. © Crown copyright. All rights reserved)

Landscape Study 7 Hillforts in the Barle Valley

Hillforts are some of the most striking prehistoric works on Exmoor. Whether used primarily for defence or as focal points for the community, they commanded areas of landscape in a way no field monuments had done before. The deeply incised valley of the River Barle acts as a gateway to Exmoor. The steep, wooded promontories high above the river provided the ideal locations for hillforts. The woods themselves have preserved stretches of these prehistoric earthworks. Within a few miles of Dulverton lie the hillforts of Oldberry Castle, Mounsey Castle and the smaller prehistoric enclosure known as Brewer's Castle (Figs 3.11 and 3.12). Oldberry Castle now only survives as an earthwork in Burridge Wood. The rest of the enclosure is fossilised by the present day field pattern of hedge banks – in existence since at least the 18th century (Fig 3.13). The tithe map for the parish of Dulverton, drawn in 1838, shows that the interior of the hillfort – then called Little Castle Close – was under arable cultivation.

Mounsey Castle, named from the ancient Monceaux family, now lies completely in woodland. The Dulverton tithe map depicts the site in some detail (Fig 3.14). It was divided into two parcels of land. The central portion, bearing the legend 'Mounsey Castle', was used for timber.

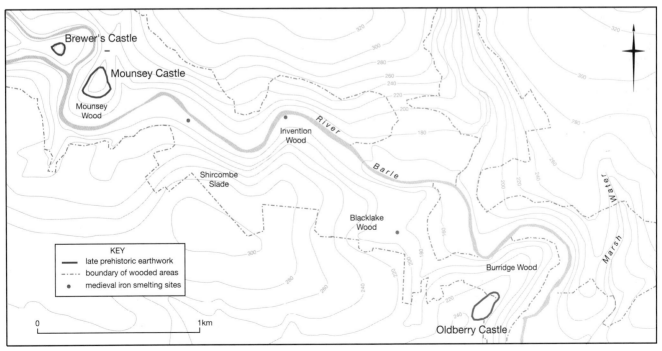

KEY
—— late prehistoric earthwork
—·—· boundary of wooded areas
• medieval iron smelting sites

Brewer's Castle

Mounsey Castle

Mounsey Wood

Invention Wood

River

Barle

Shircombe Slade

Blacklake Wood

Burridge Wood

Marsh Water

Oldberry Castle

0   1km

*Figure 3.13
Detail of Oldberry Castle
from the air. The form of
the hillfort is preserved by
the post-medieval fields.
The Iron Age bank and
ditch is picked out by snow
in Burridge Wood.
(NMR 18620/23)*

*Figure 3.14 (bottom)
Dulverton tithe map
(1838) shows the outline of
Mounsey Castle and
coppiced woodland inside
the hillfort (enhanced for
clarity). (By courtesy of
Somerset Archive and
Record Service)*

The outer portion was named Mounsey Wood and was a coppice wood. The trees on the tithe map are drawn as individual coppice stools. Charcoal burners used it during the historic period, leaving behind a tumble-down shelter and several working platforms. The charcoal was used nearby: on the valley floor at New Invention, Shircombe Slade and Blacklake Wood are iron-smelting sites, known to be of medieval date (Chapter 4). A visitor to Mounsey Castle in the 19th century describes the condition of the site well:

It is impossible to make accurate measurements, as the whole enclosure is thickly overgrown with bracken and trees. The latter are covered with long gray lichen, which give them a peculiarly eldritch appearance, particularly in the gloaming,

when, bearded with moss and in garments green, indistinct in the twilight, they induce a melancholy feeling, which is not lessened by the mournful voice of the river, two hundred feet beneath.

(Page 1893, 86).

Within shouting distance of Mounsey Castle, across the river, is Brewer's Castle. Three house platforms make use of the shelter afforded by its rocky interior. We do not know if Mounsey Castle and Brewer's Castle were occupied at the same time in prehistory. Brewer's Castle, like Mounsey Castle, has a tale to tell. Tradition associates the site with William Brewer, a Warden of the Royal Forest from 1216–1225, who had specific permission to hunt the king's deer. The stone foundations of a rectangular building are tucked just below the enclosure bank – identified by some as William Brewer's hunting lodge.

These three sites illustrate the potential for the study of the later prehistoric period on Exmoor. Two large hillforts lie close to each other, yet we do not know if they were in use at the same time. At Oldberry, the prehistoric earthwork enclosure is fossilised by the post-medieval field pattern. Iron Age deposits must still lie under the hedge banks and whole stretches of bank and ditch are preserved in Burridge Wood. Mounsey Castle lies a little farther up the River Barle. Shrouded in woodland, the hillfort appears to have survived virtually intact. The charcoal burners appear to have caused little damage to the prehistoric site they chose to live and work in. The good preservation of the archaeological deposits is shown by the presence of lengths of revetment wall visible in the ramparts (Fig 3.8).

Brewer's Castle, too, lies in the woods. The presence of possible prehistoric hut platforms surviving as earthworks is important, and deserves further study, as does the question of the contemporaneity of all three sites. An intriguing rectangular building at the base of the Iron Age ramparts also requires further work to ascertain its date and function. The presence of early medieval iron-working sites down on the valley floor and the Roman iron slag from Dulverton beg questions as to whether the prehistoric sites might have been re-used or occupied into the historic period. The wealth of available evidence for the historic period, together with the actual form of the woodland itself, has great potential for the study of the sites in their woodland landscape during this time.

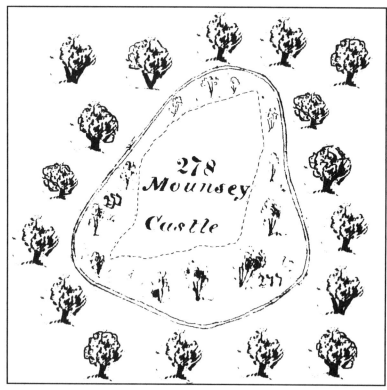

278
*Mounsey
Castle*

Hill-slope enclosures

Hill-slope enclosures are the main body of evidence for the Iron Age on Exmoor. We move from the varied monuments of the earlier prehistoric period reflecting a range of social and economic activities to the comparatively narrow range of evidence of later prehistory. This change seems striking now, but in reality it is the product of a prolonged evolution.

Hill-slope enclosures were first categorised by Lady Aileen Fox more than 40 years ago (Fox 1952). Despite their name, they occur on every type of ground, not just hill slopes, although they do favour sheltered, valley side locations. They can be distinguished from hillforts by their size – they are smaller and usually less well defended. Fox saw them as representing the shift to pastoral farming in the face of deteriorating climatic conditions. The reality is almost certainly more complicated than that, and might relate to fiefdoms, or territories within territories, and the production of iron. In other words, were they just farms or did they represent the centre of a local community?

What do these hill-slope enclosures represent? Without excavation or geophysical survey it is often difficult to answer even the most basic questions, such as whether they were farms or compounds for animals. At present most are assumed to have been settlements; their precise dating awaits the results of excavations, and is one of the central questions in our understanding of Exmoor's historic landscape. At their earliest we can see them emerging from the unenclosed settlements of the Bronze Age – they represent the formalization of settlement into ordered groups. Elsewhere, in rare examples, continuity into the early medieval period can be inferred. Hill-slope enclosures might be only one strand of settlement form for this period, the evidence for unenclosed settlements simply not surviving or evident in the landscape.

Morphology

It would be wrong to think that hill-slope enclosures are a tightly defined group of sites. The more impressive ones have been confused with hillforts, the slighter ones overlooked completely. In reality they encompass a range of monuments, perhaps of varying dates. Their essential characteristics are an area of ground enclosed by a bank, through which is almost always a simple, single entrance. They are usually between 50m and 80m across, although enclosures as small as 25m across have been found. They vary in shape from circular to rectangular, although the most common shape is ovoid (Figs 3.15 and 3.16). The presence or absence of settlement within the enclosures is often hard to prove from the surface evidence alone. Forty-eight enclosures have been identified on Exmoor as upstanding earthworks. Ploughing has undoubtedly flattened many more as air photography suggests. It seems likely that more enclosures will be located, since in the last five years two such sites have been discovered: the impressive rectangular enclosure at Timberscombe and the spur end enclosure on Ley Hill overlooking Horner Water (Fig 3.16).

From the form of these enclosures we can conclude that they were constructed or adapted for different purposes – some are more defensive than others. The banks that enclose them are sometimes substantial barriers, elsewhere they can be very slight. Equally some enclosures occupy highly defensible spur ends, others sit on open hillsides and seem vulnerable. It is most likely that some enclosures were built with defence and ostentation more in mind, while others were not.

Roborough Castle near Lynton is a typical hill-slope enclosure (Fig 3.17). It is an irregular oval with a bank and ditch enclosing an area 70m by 64m A simple gap through the bank on the south-west side marks the former entrance. The air photograph clearly shows at least one platform within the enclosure – the site of a circular building. Typically the site does not sit within or have an obvious associated field system. In fact the hedged lane dodges around the earthwork, suggesting that the enclosure is earlier than the road and the fields in which it now sits.

Five of Exmoor's hill-slope enclosures have additional outworks (Fig 3.18). Three have a single extra element – Berry Castle, Porlock, Voley Castle and Myrtleberry North (Fig 3.19). Two enclosures have multiple outworks marking two additional areas: Bury Castle, Selworthy and Staddon Hill Camp (Fig 3.20). In most of these cases the main enclosure occupies a spur end, and it could be argued that the outworks are later additions, and could even be defensive. Their purpose is uncertain, but common suggestions include stock corrals.

Figure 3.15
Hill-slope enclosures on
Exmoor: morphology.

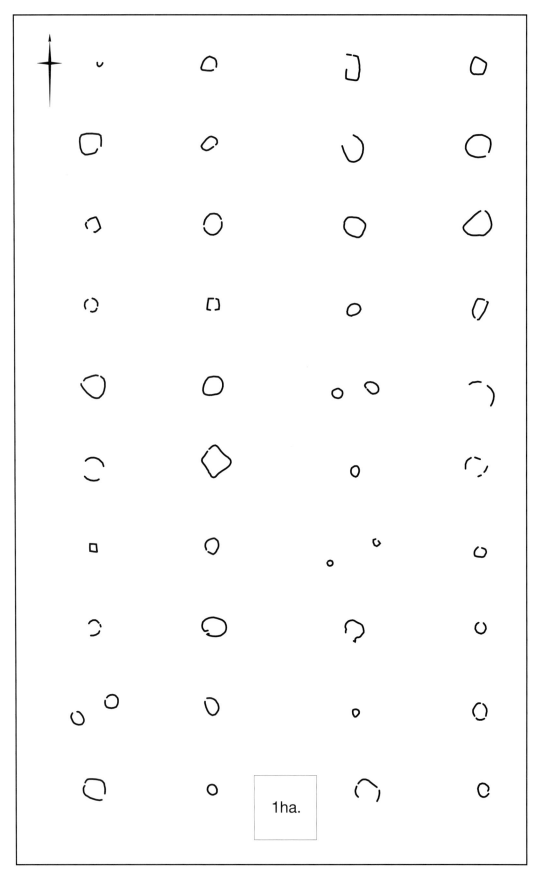

Figure 3.16 (facing page)
Hillslope enclosures: earth-
work surveys showing the
varying shapes and forms
of these sites. Timberscombe
(a) is rectangular and
partly ditched. The small
circular enclosure on
Rodhuish Common (b) is a
platform terraced into the
hillside. At Myrtleberry
South (c) a large rectan-
gular enclosure is also
formed by terracing the
steep slope. The enclosures
at Ley Hill (d) and
Monkslade Common (e)
are both sub-rectangular.

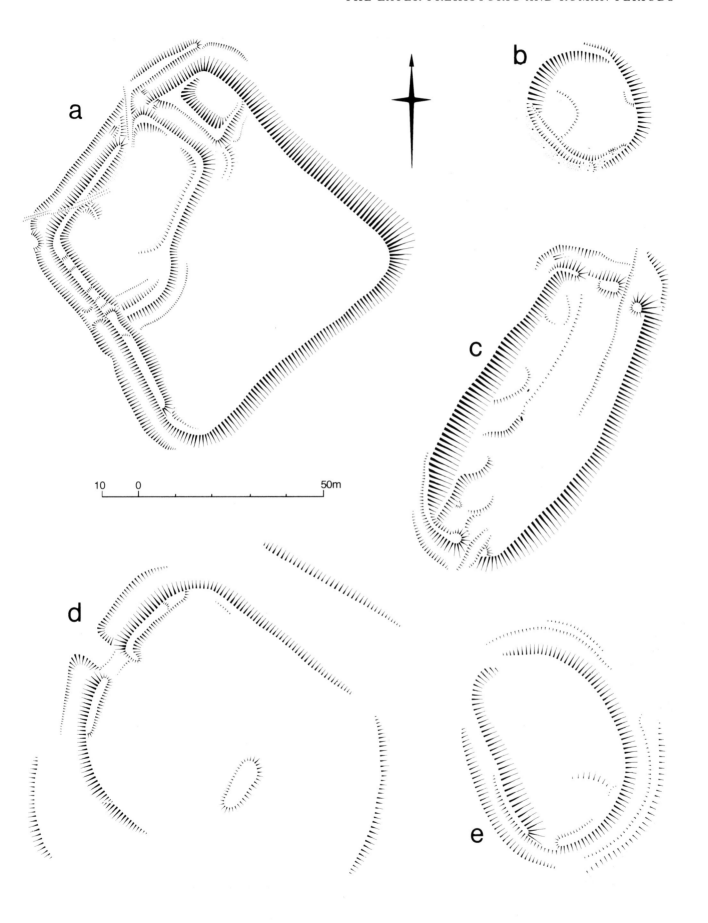

10   0   50m

Figure 3.17
Roborough Castle, a
typical hill-slope enclosure.
The site lies in pasture
fields and has been reduced
by ploughing, but the
remains of a hut circle can
be seen inside the enclosure.
(NMR 15606/14)
(© Crown copyright.NMR)

Figure 3.18
Hill-slope enclosures with
outworks. Myrtleberry
North (a); Berry Castle,
Porlock (b); Voley Castle (c);
Staddon Hill Camp (d) and
Bury Castle, Selworthy (e).

a

b

c

d

e

1ha.

KEY

bank

top of ditch

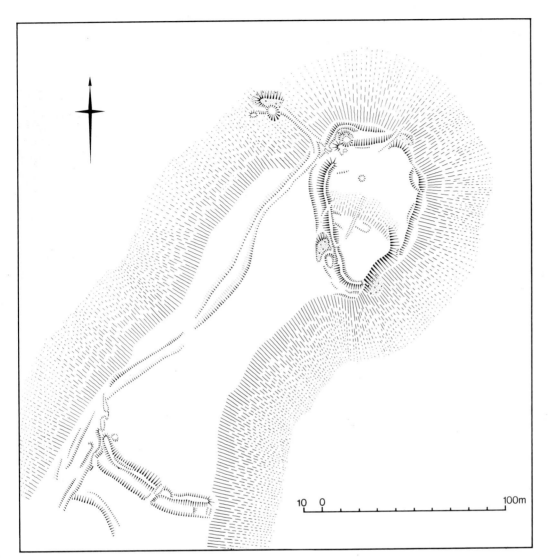

Figure 3.19
Myrtleberry North: this irregularly shaped enclosure occupies the end of a spur in the Lyn Gorge. The outwork, to the south, is overlooked and is unlikely to be defensive. A sunken way runs from the outwork entrance to the main enclosure entrance.

10 0   100m

Beyond Exmoor some enclosures are more complex, such as Clovelly Dykes or Milber Down, where the central enclosure is comparable to the Exmoor examples, but has been embellished either contemporaneously or later with the addition of a whole series of outer enclosures, causing them to be termed multiple-ditched enclosures.

Distribution and siting

The hill-slope enclosures are widely distributed across Exmoor, although they are not found on the highest parts (Fig 3.1). Because of their often substantial form the enclosures prove intractable to ploughing and often occur as smoothed earthworks, or survive by being incorporated into later field systems. The enclosure at Trottsway Cross is a good example of an enclosure much reduced by ploughing: it is barely discernible as an earthwork. Some survive because they are on land that was never subsequently intensively worked. A salutary lesson, however, is that such enclosures have been revealed by air photography where no earthworks survive. This almost certainly means that on Exmoor the distribution of surviving enclosures is not the complete picture. Equally, late prehistoric settlements that were unenclosed might not survive as well if at all, so that the picture is biased in favour of enclosed settlements.

*Figure 3.20
Staddon Hill Camp:
a hill-slope enclosure with
two outworks.*

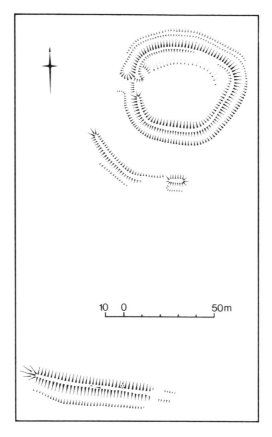

10   0   50m

Some hill-slope enclosures occupy what might be termed defensible locations such as spur ends, while others occur on open hillsides (above). Such a marked variety in their siting might imply different dates or different functions. Only excavation could resolve such issues.

There are marked concentrations on the north-western corner of Exmoor National Park, on the eastern side of the moor and in the hinterland of Porlock Vale. This distribution no doubt reflects the climatic imperative to move away from the high moor, but such a shift meant that these sites were ideally placed to exploit the moor grasslands for pasture, while utilising the more fertile grounds near at hand for more intensive agriculture. As yet, though, only a handful of enclosures have been recognised with directly associated field systems, and in most of these cases, for example the Valley of Rocks and Withycombe Hill, the enclosures are small.

The context of later prehistoric settlement on Exmoor

The evidence for comparable sites in Devon and Somerset is restricted. Small enclosures are found as earthworks across most of Devon, but more evidence is being revealed through air photography (Griffith 1994, 85–100). Many of these enclosures are rectilinear or square in shape, which is strikingly different from the varied though predominantly ovoid examples from Exmoor, although many are similar in terms of the area that they enclose. The dating of these sites is also uncertain at the present time.

In Cornwall, similar non-defensive enclosures or rounds, might be a similar phenomenon to Exmoor's hill-slope enclosures. They date from the 4th century BC, with some continuing in use until the 6th and 7th centuries AD. The Cornish rounds are, however, almost always circular, in marked contrast to the Exmoor sites (Johnson and Rose 1982). Closer to Exmoor, a recently excavated hill-slope enclosure at Rudge, Morchard Bishop, provided dating evidence for occupation during the period of c AD 55–80 (Todd 1998).

Hill-slope enclosures form the bulk of settlement evidence for the Iron Age on Exmoor, and yet at present we understand very little about them. We can see them as originating in the gradual shift from unenclosed to enclosed settlements at the end of the Bronze Age, but there is hardly any correlation between hill-slope enclosures and later settlements, and this suggests a lack of continuity. This is entirely explicable in the more marginal landscapes, but farther away from the moor the pattern is complicated. Existing settlements in these more favourable locations might be on the sites of earlier enclosures, the latter concealed or obliterated by the more recent farms and fields.

As yet the dating of these sites is problematic. They might mark an enduring tradition of enclosed settlement into the Roman period, or they might be part of a much greater settlement pattern the main component of which is unenclosed settlement. They might be in a sense untypical, the indications of status of minor fiefdoms. What is certain is that they are the single most important area for further research on Exmoor. For without greater insights into their chronology and function, we are unable to answer many of the fundamental questions about Exmoor in the 1st millennium BC, and perhaps the 1st millennium AD as well.

Landscape Study 8 Higher Holworthy and South Common: later prehistoric settlement on the moorland margin

The north-western edge of Exmoor National Park is strikingly different from the higher ground of the former Royal Forest to the south-east. Here is an area of gently undulating rich farmland between the moor and the coastal heaths and commons. The river Heddon and its tributaries break up the landscape. The edge of cultivation has been a shifting line on the edge of the moor. This is truly marginal, with the losers littered across the landscape in the form of abandoned settlements and field systems of all periods.

At South Common are two oval enclosures, below the bleak ridge now occupied by the Chapman Barrows (Fig 3.21). They now lie in a landscape of agricultural improvement close to the head of one of the tributaries of the West Lyn River. Nearby is Parracombe Common with its straight enclosure road and neat square fields laid out in the 19th century. Close at hand are the straight beech hedges of Woolhanger Farm. The enclosures lie on north facing slopes on former moorland, that is, land that was previously grass or heather moor and that is now improved pasture. It has been periodically cultivated since the 19th century, but this has

not had a very detrimental effect on the archaeological remains, which appear largely to have been ploughed around because of their high stone content.

Two oval enclosures are visible defined by low, broad stony banks. Within each enclosure are traces of a single building, the most westerly enclosure has only a building platform at its upper edge, the other has a very well defined round stone building, surviving as a stony bank. Close to the enclosures there are two more hut circles – freestanding, as it were, on the open hillside (Fig 3.21).

The remains at South Common illustrate the problems encountered when trying to date such sites by the surface evidence alone. The freestanding huts and the hut circles within the enclosures might be thought of as Bronze Age – enclosed settlements of this period are known from elsewhere in south-west England. What is unusual is the presence of substantial enclosures with well-built single huts within. This is indeed more typical of late prehistoric enclosures, and enables us to interpret them as such. At South Common, with its freestanding huts and enclosures, are we seeing the evolution from unenclosed to enclosed settlements?

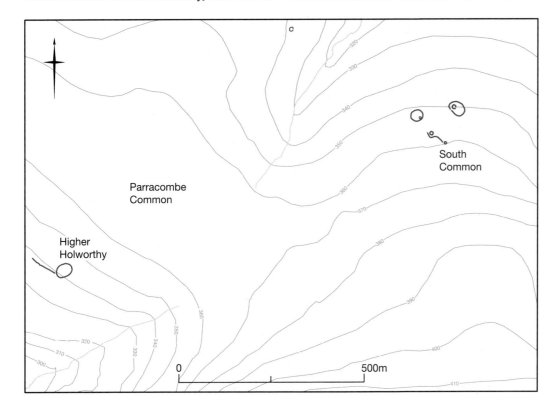

Figure 3.21
Hill-slope enclosures at Higher Holworthy and South Common: both lie close to the sources of tributary streams, and close to the margins of medieval agriculture, ensuring their survival. (Based on an Ordnance Survey map, with permission. © Crown copyright. All rights reserved)

Figure 3.22
Higher Holworthy: this
oval hill-slope enclosure
was discovered through air
photography. It lies close to
the source of a tributary of
the River Heddon.
(NMR 1459/470)
(© Crown copyright.NMR)

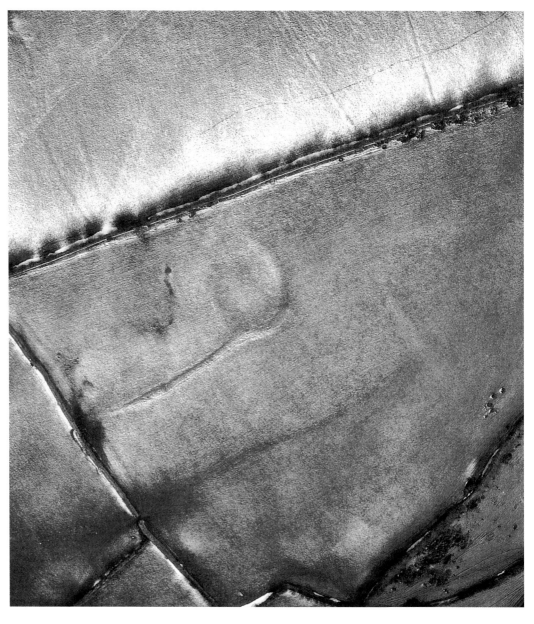

Figure 3.23
Higher Holworthy: the
earthwork survey of the
enclosure reveals an
entrance and traces of a
building platform within.
A lynchet joins the enclo-
sure on its south side,
and this might be the last
trace of an associated field
system. Beyond the hedge
bank to the east of the
enclosure was Parracombe
Common, enclosed during
the 19th century.

Separated from South Common only by the watershed of Parracombe Common is another enclosure, at Higher Holworthy (Fig 3.22). It lies on steep south facing slopes overlooking the tributary of the River Heddon. This is a classic hill-slope enclosure, defined by a spread earthwork bank. Within the enclosure are slight remains of a circular platform. Near the enclosure a substantial lynchet might be the last relic of an associated field system (Fig 3.23).

The positions of this site and the South Common examples are very similar. They both occupy hill-slopes above tributary streams and morphologically they are practically identical. Taken together they illustrate the problems both in dating individual sites, and also in explaining the origins of this type of settlement.

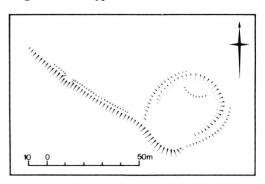

Landscape Study 9 Sweetworthy and Bagley: Iron Age enclosures and the later landscape

The archaeological remains at Sweetworthy and Bagley on the edge of Dunkery are untypically rich and concentrated. Although untypical they do hint at the role that enclosures might have played in determining how the landscape developed. They might be indicative of some of the processes involved. At Sweetworthy and Bagley there is evidence of chronology: both in the adaptation of sites, itself implying prolonged use, and more fundamentally in continuous habitation in one place through three millennia. This is the only site on Exmoor where such strong continuity can be demonstrated. It is not a template for what happened elsewhere, but shows how such sites can play a fundamental role in the development of the landscape.

The northern slopes of Dunkery Beacon are Exmoor at its most sublime, a landscape of restrained grandeur. But what makes it so interesting is people's achievement and failure played out on this grand backdrop. This is a landscape littered with archaeological monuments. There are four enclosures, a deserted medieval hamlet and a farm abandoned in the 19th century. Together they bear witness to a continual struggle to inhabit and farm a very marginal landscape. The name Sweetworthy, formerly 'Sweet Tree', is now attached to one of Exmoor's most impressive hill-slope enclosures (Fig 3.24). It lies just inside enclosed fields where they abut the open moor, and survives as a prominent bank and ditch enclosing an area of 0.28ha. Within it are the traces of a second, earlier enclosure. Close by, on the open moor, are two further enclosures about 40m in diameter, each with a single hut circle inside, and each enclosing about 0.12ha. At Bagley less than 1km to the west is a fourth enclosure, very similar in size to Sweetworthy (Fig 3.25). Such a concentration of late prehistoric activity is of great interest in itself, but at both sets of enclosures is ample evidence to demonstrate that people continued to live in the immediate vicinity until comparatively recently.

Figure 3.24
Sweetworthy complex: the Sweetworthy enclosure is top left, two other enclosures lie on moorland (top). The earthworks of a deserted medieval settlement lie at the bottom centre of the photograph. (NMR 15856/5) (© Crown copyright.NMR)

Figure 3.25
Bagley: the slight earth-
works of the circular
enclosure are revealed by
low sunlight. To the right
of the enclosure are the
remains of a farm aban-
doned in the 19th century.
Close by is the open moor
of Dunkery Hill and the
ancient woods at Clout-
sham. The beech hedges
are a characteristic feature
of post-medieval enclosures
on Exmoor.
(NMR 15856/13)
(© Crown copyright.NMR)

At Bagley, the enclosure sits immediately adjacent to the ruins of a farmstead. This was in use at the beginning of the 19th century but had been abandoned by its end. Bagley was a manor at the time of Domesday, and regularly referred to in subsequent historical sources.

The enclosures at Sweetworthy lie to the east of a deserted settlement comprising the traces of 12 buildings (Fig 3.26). Most are visible as slight rectangular scoops on the hillside, but one seems more complex. Traces of field boundaries and a small stock corral lie within the settlement, while on the hillside above is a substantial embankment, possibly indicating contemporary attempts to enclose more of Dunkery or a substantial stock pound. The settlement does not occur in historical sources, but in 1791 a reference to Bagley might refer to buildings here, so we can suggest that at least some of the

buildings survived until the end of the 18th century, the rest having been already abandoned.

It is tempting to see such continuity of settlement through so long a period as a gritty determination to soldier on. This is clearly wrong, because such strong continuity is so rarely seen on Exmoor. Rather it shows a strong sense of economy: sites that were well placed continued to be used. The landholding pattern here might well show a greater rigidity, for Bagley was a Domesday manor, and it is likely that the field systems in which these sites lie are indeed very ancient. As important was the exploitation of open moorland for fuel and grazing. It is no coincidence that all of these abandoned settlements, whether late prehistoric, medieval or 19th century, lie virtually on the boundary between enclosed land and the open moor.

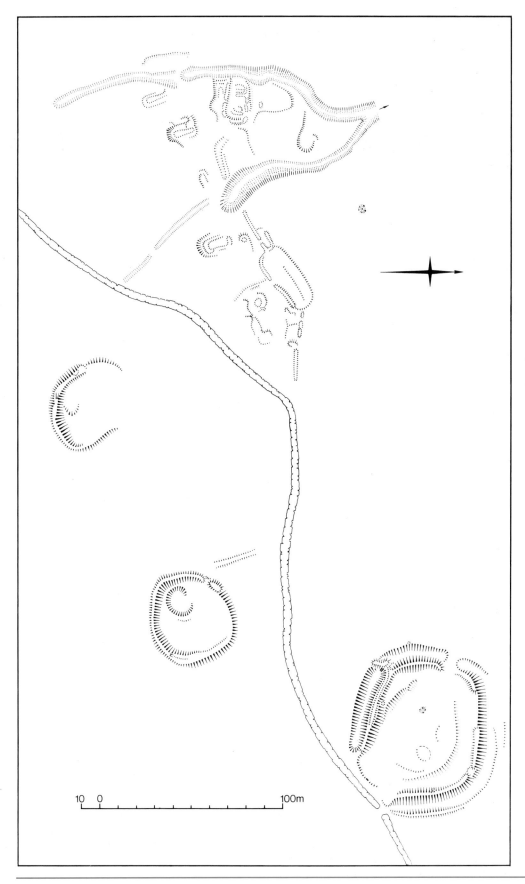

Figure 3.26
An earthwork survey of the remarkable Sweetworthy complex, showing the two enclosures on moorland to the south, the Sweetworthy enclosure to the north-east, and the remains of the deserted medieval settlement to the west.

10   0   100m

Figure 3.27
Martinhoe Roman fortlet
occupies a dramatic cliff
edge position overlooking
the Bristol Channel.
(NMR 15604/32)
(© Crown copyright.NMR)

Figure 3.28 (facing, top)
Old Burrow Roman
fortlet, here under light
snow, lies on an isolated and
exposed spur above Glen-
thorne. (NMR 18242/08)
(© Crown copyright.NMR)

Figure 3.29 (facing, bottom)
Old Burrow Roman fortlet:
the earthwork survey reveals
the outer sub-circular
enclosure and the inner
square one with its entrance
on the north side.

Roman military sites

The Roman conquest of the south-west is not mentioned in literary sources at the time. The chronology and nature of the conquest remain very obscure, and there are great difficulties in placing the archaeological evidence into such a framework. Nevertheless, sites that are distinctive of the Roman military have been found on and around Exmoor; namely, forts and fortlets (Fig 3.1).

Exmoor's best known archaeological monuments, and certainly the most thoroughly examined, are the two fortlets at Old Burrow and Martinhoe. Outside Exmoor National Park are a number of Roman forts and other sites on the edges of the moor. Very recently a probable addition to this group was discovered on air photographs at Rainsbury in the south-eastern corner of the National Park.

The nature of the Roman military involvement in this part of the south-west is at present far from certain. As yet no roads, which are the hallmark of any Roman infrastructure, have been identified although a road through mid Devon to Barnstaple is postulated. Recent work suggests that some of the iron mining and smelting on the moor might have had military associations, if it was not under direct military control, and while this still remains unproven, it is an exciting avenue for further research.

The Roman fortlets: Old Burrow and Martinhoe

The fortlets at Old Burrow and Martinhoe, both overlooking the Bristol Channel, were built in the 1st century AD. They were lookout posts from which the channel could be observed, perhaps linked to the security of shipping in that stretch of water, or built in response to the threat of an invasion by the Silures, the native tribe in southern Wales. Today they are very evocative sites, occupying dramatic and spectacular cliff top positions (Fig 3.27). Both have been extensively excavated, Old Burrow by St George Gray in 1911, Old Burrow and Martinhoe by Lady (Aileen) Fox and Professor Ravenhill between 1960 and 1963 (Gray and Tapp 1912; Fox and Ravenhill 1966).

The surviving earthworks at each site represent the remains of a small square fortlet surrounded at a distance by an oval enclosure that presumably acted as an additional defence, or as suggested by the excavators, an initial temporary defence. Of the two, Old Burrow is almost perfectly preserved, while Martinhoe has been degraded by subsequent land use and the frenetic activity of rabbits. A description of Old Burrow in 1908 conveys the magical atmosphere of this site: '....a very toy wall, nestling close to the foot of the inmost rampart, suggests in its glow of purple heather some exquisite effect of the gardener's art – it is positively a thing of beauty in its very design....' (Allcroft 1908, 117–18) (Figs 3.28 and 3.29).

The excavations have suggested, on quite slender evidence, that the fortlets were sequential: Old Burrow was built in the 50s AD and was shortlived. It was replaced by Martinhoe, which was occupied between AD 55 and AD 75. No buildings were discovered at Old Burrow and it was concluded that the soldiers lived in tents. An elaborate field oven was built against the rampart for all of the soldiers' cooking requirements.

The entrance to the inner fortlet faced the sea. Here an elaborate timber gatehouse was built spanning the gateway. The uprights for this structure were so massive that the excavators suggested that the gatehouse also served as a platform for a signal beacon. This would have made it possible to communicate along the coast as well as to any naval detachments in the channel.

Old Burrow was abandoned, the excavators suggest, because it is so exposed. The garrison of 65–80 men were transferred to Martinhoe. Here the practically identical fortlet was perched on the cliff edge and the soldiers accommodated in timber buildings around a small courtyard, but even these would have been used only in the summer months. Other structures included field ovens and a small forge.

The material found at these sites comprises a small number of coins (on which the dating evidence is largely based), a selection of Roman and native pottery and other miscellaneous items. The native pottery suggests that the soldiers were trading with the native population. Indeed, it is hard to imagine that such a small and defenceless garrison could exist in any other way than on friendly terms with the local people.

Martinhoe was abandoned in the 70s AD at a time when the threat from the Silures was diminishing, although the excavations revealed patches of burning and broken native pottery suggesting that squatters had camped there after the garrison had left.

Rainsbury

During the course of air photographic transcription work on the Brendon Hills, a rectangular enclosure was identified at Rainsbury. The site was investigated on the ground and proved to be a substantial earthwork of 'playing card' shape. Such a precise shape is usually indicative of a medieval or later site, for example a manorial complex, but can also be indicative of a Roman military site. Documentary research failed to identify a medieval or later context. It therefore seems very likely that the enclosure is a Roman fort, although this cannot be conclusively proved without datable finds from the site.

The fort lies on the end of a spur overlooking the valley of the River Haddeo, at the extreme south-east corner of the National Park. It is now incomplete, nevertheless enough survives to gain a good

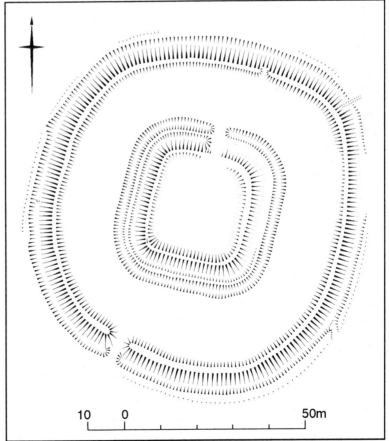

10   0   50m

impression of its defensive capability (Figs 3.30 and 3.31). The almost level interior was defended by an outward facing rampart 1.5m high, with an external ditch, which has silted up, but which shows on air photographs. It also appears to have had a second line of defence, but this is now barely discernible. No traces of buildings were found inside the fort.

The distribution of Roman military sites on and around Exmoor

The wider distribution of Roman military sites shows how few were built on Exmoor itself (Fig 3.32). The hinterland was much more important with a number of forts in valleys around the moor. This shows that the moor was not of strategic importance – it was bypassed – but that its margins and hinterland needed some form of control.

As yet no sites of Roman date have been found at or near Barnstaple, although it has been suggested that a fort must have existed there (Todd 1987, 199). It is inconceivable that it was not used as a port and that the rich hinterland was not exploited. As yet the only certain military site in the area is the marching camp at Alverdiscott. Perhaps the presence of rich iron ore deposits around Exmoor influenced the siting of these forts, and made the area worthy of military attention. Such a connection between the military presence and a local industry is hard to prove, but it would explain the presence of these sites in an otherwise unimportant part of the south-west, and would also help in understanding concentrations of military activity (Griffith 1997, 365).

The evidence for Roman occupation on Exmoor is still very sparse. Nevertheless, the concentration of military sites to the south of the moor and the small sample of iron-working sites now dated to this period, suggest that Exmoor was the subject of military interest in this period.

The complete absence of villas or other high status building complexes around Exmoor is not surprising when viewed against the wider backdrop of Devon. The thin presence of high status Roman objects, such as brooches (information from the Barnstaple and North Devon Museum), however, hints at the existence of such sites. Todd (1987, 234) has pointed out the strange absence of Roman pottery kilns in an area where there is so much suitable estuarine clay. These dilemmas and inconsistencies show how much work remains to be done in uncovering Roman Exmoor and its hinterland.

Romano-British iron working

The Devonian rocks of Exmoor, in particular those making up the Brendon Hills on the eastern edge of the moor, contain important iron ore deposits. The ore was exploited during the 19th and early 20th centuries (Chapter 5), but documentary references to ancient workings, together with surface features such as extraction pits that obviously pre-date the 19th- and 20th-century mining, suggest that Exmoor's iron ore deposits have been exploited for a significant length of time.

Documentary references

Some of the most compelling evidence for Roman iron-working on Exmoor is to be found in Bristol Museum. At some time before 1906 two lumps of iron slag

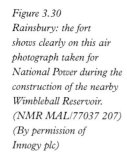

*Figure 3.30
Rainsbury: the fort shows clearly on this air photograph taken for National Power during the construction of the nearby Wimbleball Reservoir. (NMR MAL/77037 207) (By permission of Innogy plc)*

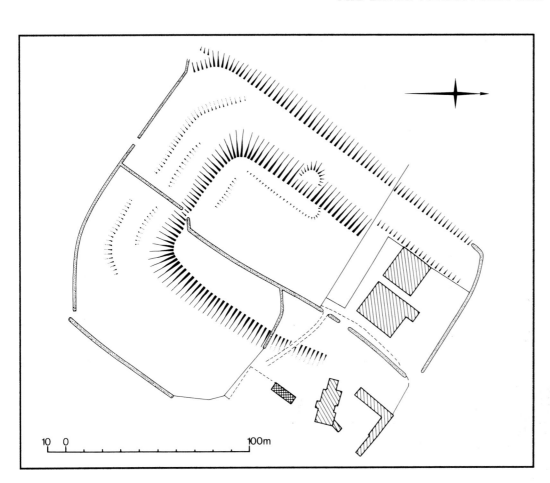

Figure 3.31
Rainsbury: the incomplete
'playing-card' shape is
marked on the ground by
ramparts 1.5m high. The
north-east end has gradually
been effaced by the buildings
of Rainsbury Farm.

10 0   100m

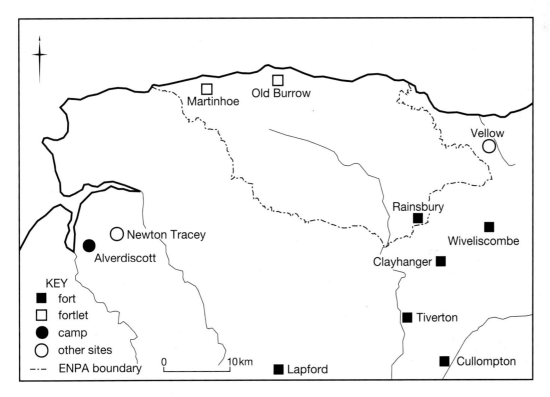

Martinhoe
Old Burrow
Vellow
Rainsbury
Newton Tracey
Wiveliscombe
Alverdiscott
Clayhanger
KEY
■ fort
□ fortlet
● camp
○ other sites
--- ENPA boundary
0   10km
Tiverton
Lapford
Cullompton

Figure 3.32
Roman military sites in the
Exmoor area. (After Griffith
1997, with additions)

containing fragments of oyster shell and four Roman coins were found near Dulverton. Only two of the coins were available for examination in 1958, when they were identified as from the reign of Constantine (AD 308–337) (Grinsell 1958). The 19th-century miners found a coin of the reign of Domitian (AD 81–96) in old workings on Kennisham Hill, and Roman coins are alleged to have come from iron mines in the parish of Luxborough. The name Roman has been applied rather indiscriminately to traces of pre-19th-century mining. Hence Colton Pits was called Roman Mine and a large openwork at Burcombe was given the name Roman Lode (Sellick 1970, 11–12).

Figure 3.33
Air photograph showing location of late Iron Age/Romano-British iron-smelting site at Sherracombe Ford. The large working platforms can be seen on the hillside above the stream; the slag heaps lie below. (NMR 18335/12)

Iron mining and iron smelting

There are two broad types of field remains resulting from early iron working on Exmoor: the evidence from mining the iron ore and the evidence from processing it. The extraction pits and openworks have yet to be securely dated. One problem in identifying early extraction sites is that later mining of the same ore body often destroys such evidence. The early mining sites on Exmoor, such as Colton Pits and the Roman Lode, are generally thought to result from medieval or later mining (Chapter 4).

Slag heaps are the unglamorous result of processing iron ore. Recent work is now beginning to establish a chronology for these sites on and around Exmoor. Iron slag can be roughly divided into that resulting from smelting the ore, and that which occurs from smithing. On Exmoor, the known smelting

sites are located close to fuel – charcoal – and to water. Hence there is a cluster of earlier medieval smelting sites in the Barle Valley between Dulverton and Mounsey Castle (Juleff 1997). The earliest dated smelting site on Exmoor lies at Sherracombe Ford, deep in the upper Bray Valley (Fig 3.33). The remains of two large slag heaps and a range of platforms terraced into the hillside survive as earthworks on a steep slope in a pasture field (Fig 3.34). The three large double platforms are probably smelting platforms, with furnaces and bellows, perhaps within shelters. The smaller platforms on the periphery of the site might be charcoal burning platforms. This site was thought to represent the remains of medieval or post-medieval iron smelting on Exmoor, but radiocarbon dates have now placed the two large slag heaps in the late Iron Age – Romano-British period (Juleff 2000) (Appendix 2). Another potentially very early site is a surface find of some smithing slag from the Iron Age enclosure at Timberscombe (Juleff 1997, 18). The proximity of several of Exmoor's hillforts to significant iron ore deposits should be noted, although there remains much work to be done on the chronology of both the hillforts and the iron-working sites.

Chronology

So far, we have hints of a very early beginning to the exploitation of Exmoor's mineral reserves. The Roman coins from Dulverton and the radiocarbon dates from Sherracombe suggest that the Romans took an active interest in getting what they could from Exmoor. The association of smithing slag and a later prehistoric enclosure point to local use of the metal. The openworks and extraction pits, however, remain to be securely dated. The earliest historic reference to iron working on Exmoor comes from the Domesday Survey (1086). Recent excavations on the fringes of Exmoor have produced evidence of iron working of Iron Age and Roman date. At Sindercombe, south of Twitchen, a slag heap was dated to the Iron Age by radiocarbon determination on associated charcoal (*Devon Arch Soc Newsletter* **70**, 11). Roman pottery was found in close association with iron slag at Syndercombe on the western side of Clatworthy reservoir (NMR no ST 03 SW 9).

Farther afield, iron-working sites in the Blackdown Hills, south-east of Exmoor, have produced Roman dates, with the suggestion of a military context for the

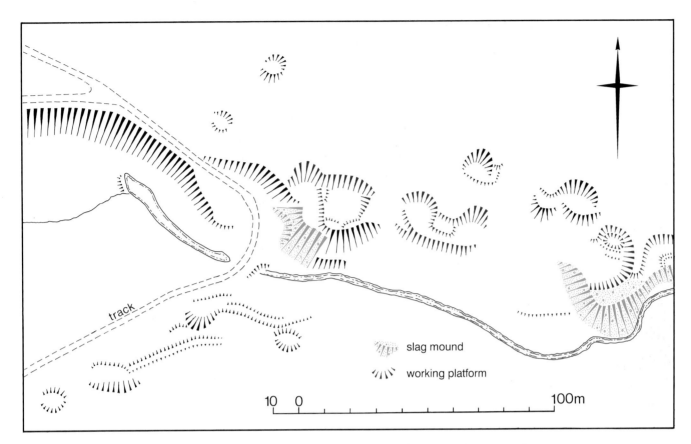

track

slag mound

working platform

10   0   100m

industry in the 1st century AD in this area (Griffith and Weddell 1996, Todd 1984). These early dates for iron working in the environs of Exmoor suggest that the 'Roman Lode' could have had its origins in the Roman period. It might have been the source of iron ore for the smelting site at Sherracombe, although we have no firm evidence, as yet, to link the two sites.

The later prehistoric and Roman landscape

The hillforts and hill-slope enclosures form only part of the later prehistoric landscape of Exmoor. Aerial photography and excavation elsewhere in England show that many of the lowland river valleys were densely settled during the Iron Age and Romano-British periods. In Cornwall the characteristic rounds of the Iron Age and beyond are thickly spread across areas such as West Penwith. On Dartmoor, settlement and agriculture retreated down to the moorland fringe, as climatic deterioration occurred. Aerial reconnaissance of Dartmoor's fringes is continuing to expand the range of settlement types known to have occurred in the 1st millennium BC (Griffith 1994). For the

less extreme parts of Exmoor, however, the worsening climate might not have resulted in the abandonment of fields established in the Bronze Age. The enclosures at Valley of Rocks and Codsend Moors show a continuing use of earlier field systems (Chapter 2). The enclosures on Porlock Allotment and Pinford suggest that these upland areas were suitable for settlement in the 1st millennium BC, presumably based on stock rearing rather than arable farming. Exmoor's diverse and dissected landscape favours dispersed settlement, as the settlement pattern of today shows. For the later prehistoric period, we might be seeing only part of the settlement pattern, as farmsteads built mostly of timber are difficult to detect in Exmoor's pasture fields. Their stone-built counterparts survive in more marginal areas, such as Rodhuish Common and Withycombe Hill. The arrival of the Romans is not well told by Exmoor's landscape. The enclosures of the Iron Age might well have been occupied into the Roman period and beyond. The impact of iron-working on Iron Age and Roman Exmoor is only now coming into focus.

During the Neolithic and Bronze Age, the landscape was dominated by the burial and ritual monuments of the people who

Figure 3.34
Earthwork survey and interpretation of the late Iron Age/Romano-British iron-smelting site at Sherracombe Ford.

lived on Exmoor. In the later prehistoric period the landscape was dominated by their settlements. Their spiritual needs might have been served in hillforts – Danebury and South Cadbury contained shrines – or in places that, until recently, have left little trace in the landscape apart from place-names. The 'Nympton' and 'Nymet' names south-west of Exmoor derive from a Celtic word meaning sacred place (Todd 1987, 204). The recent discovery of an early prehistoric ritual complex south of Nymet Rowland raises questions about the longevity of such sites (Griffith 1985). A few miles away, on the edge of Exmoor, the beautifully decorated bronze bowl from Rose Ash, interpreted as a votive deposit from a lake, suggests that the landscape itself played an important role.

Landscape Study 10 Later prehistoric sites in the Dunster area

Figure 3.35
Later prehistoric sites in the Avill Valley. (Based on an Ordnance Survey map, with permission. © Crown copyright. All rights reserved)

There is a remarkable concentration of later prehistoric field monuments in the north-eastern corner of Exmoor, south of the village of Dunster. Eight hill-slope enclosures and hillforts, together with an extensive field system, lie in hills to the south of the River Avill (Fig 3.35). The enclosures at Timberscombe, Longwood, Rodhuish Common and Monkslade Common were discovered only recently. Timberscombe and Longwood have survived despite their location in 20th-century forestry plantations. As their

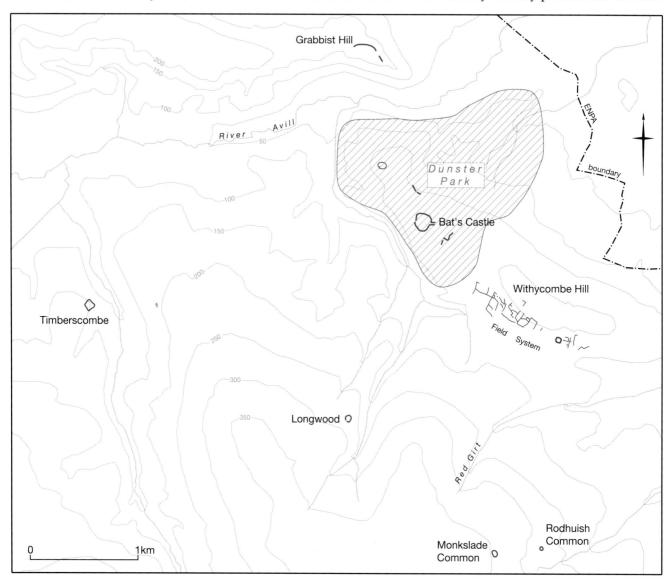

Figure 3.36
Air photograph showing
part of the later prehistoric
field system on Withycombe
Hill. A rare survival on
Exmoor, it is preserved on
rough pasture fields and
unenclosed common land.
(NMR 15864/35)
(© Crown copyright. NMR)

names suggest, the enclosures on the Commons of Rodhuish and Monkslade are on land that has remained unenclosed until very recently. An extensive later prehistoric field system lies on the southern slopes of Withycombe Hill. Unusually, this was recognised as early as 1830 in Savage's *History of the Hundred of Carhampton*:

> Most of the estates in this parish have rights of common on this hill, and as formerly the occupiers of estates having rights of common used in many instances to cultivate certain parts of the same, there can be little doubt but such was the case here, which accounts for the ridges and decayed mounds that might have been boundaries, which are still to be seen.
>
> (Savage 1830, 274)

Part of Withycombe Hill remains as common land, on the northern edge forestry plantation encroaches, the rest is now enclosed. The prehistoric field system survives on this common land, and in some rough pasture fields below (Fig 3.36). A small enclosure lies within the fields, also recognised by Savage as a 'druidical remain' (1830, 274). The heart-shaped deer park, enclosed in the 18th century for the Luttrells at Dunster Castle, contains the hillfort of Bat's Castle and the enclosure on Gallox Hill (named thus because here the gallows were set up). Just across the Avill Valley is another hillfort on Grabbist Hill, again only discovered recently, on the margins of common and woodland.

Here we can get an impression of the density of later prehistoric settlement on the more favourable parts of Exmoor, with the proviso that the exact chronology of when each of these sites was in use remains to be established. The large hill-slope enclosures at Timberscombe, Longwood and Monkslade Common overlook the major tributaries of the River Avill. Ordinary farmsteads are represented by the small enclosures at Withycombe Hill and Rodhuish Common. A mixed economy was practised. The field system on Withycombe Hill covers about 24 hectares, and about 20 small, rectangular fields can be seen. These were for arable agriculture: ploughing has caused lynchets to form on the downslope sides of the fields. Field clearance is also evident, and there are some very faint lines on the surface of one of the fields, which also show that ploughing was taking place.

Access to the Avill Valley was considered so important that the valley was overlooked by two sites: the hillfort on Grabbist Hill and the large enclosure on Gallox Hill (Fig 3.37). The elaborate hillfort of Bat's Castle represents the seat of the elite of society. The two outworks are designed to impress and dominate the landscape, perhaps they also acted as barriers to exclude some groups of people from parts of the landscape. Bat's Castle might have been a focal point in that landscape, an awe-inspiring and sacred place, designed to be viewed from a distance. As well as fulfilling ritual

Figure 3.37
The Iron Age enclosure on Gallox Hill (bottom right) and the hillfort of Bat's Castle dominate the north-eastern edge of Exmoor. The impressive outworks can be seen on the edge of the woods below and to the left of Bat's Castle. On the commons of Withycombe Hill (top left) lies a small later prehistoric enclosure and field system.
(NMR 1459/177)
(© Crown copyright. NMR)

and religious needs, parts of Bat's Castle might have functioned as a communal place, such as a market or medieval fair. As at Danebury, there might have been storage areas for the grain produced down at Withycombe Hill and for the leather and wool from the cattle and sheep that grazed the higher ground. Crafts including metal-working might have been carried out. There is evidence that smithing was carried out inside the Timberscombe enclosure. Deposits of ironstone lie close by: there are easily worked surface deposits on the Brendon Hills to the south, with more local sources at Red Girt.

The position of these sites is crucial, because access to the sea was important. They are close to the coast, in fact in the 1st millennium BC much of the low-lying land north and east of Dunster was at least seasonally flooded. At this time the south-west peninsula had links with groups of people in Iberia and Brittany, as trading networks for tin were developing. Exmoor, and particularly its eastern fringe, was an area with influences from both the south-west, and from the tribes of the Dobunni and Durotriges, whose western limits might have been around the Parrett Valley in central Somerset.

4
Medieval Exmoor

Introduction and chronology

The early medieval period
(AD 410–1066)

Contemporary archaeological evidence for life on post-Roman Exmoor is practically non-existent. The only monuments of the time are three inscribed stones. They are a very restricted and personalised body of evidence in an otherwise truly Dark Age landscape. To colour this picture we could add, in passing, the scant evidence of historical sources; place-names can also be used to provide a very generalised impression of the pattern of settlement in the centuries after the Roman period.

It is generally assumed that the Roman retreat from Britain would have gone unnoticed by the ordinary people in the South West (Todd 1987, 236). Life on Exmoor and its hinterland, organised within petty territories, would have carried on. A striking aspect of the time, however, and one that might well have effected parts of the region quite significantly were the emigrations from Devon and Cornwall to Armorica (Brittany). These were so intense that the name 'Brittany', reflecting the British origin of so many of the inhabitants, originated then. The reasons for the movement of people are unclear. The most compelling historical event was the advance of the Anglo-Saxons into southern Britain. But this alone is too convenient to explain such a large movement of people out of Devon and Cornwall. It is more likely that several reasons caused the emigration, one of which might have been the extensive trading contacts already established between the regions. That is not to say that parts of Devon and Cornwall were deserted. We should imagine, rather, a drift of people away from the south-west causing a dip in the population level.

We know little of the organisation of the Kingdom of Dumnonia at this time. The difficult and fragmentary evidence suggests a society where ties of blood and honour were most important among the aristocratic elite (Pearce 1981, 175). The names of a few of its shadowy kings have come down to us, such as Constantine, Cadwy and Geraint (Pearce 1978, 139–44). It was rightly called, from afar, the 'Land of the western Welsh'.

What we know of the period on Exmoor after AD 410 is derived largely from historical material from elsewhere in south-west England. There is a huge lack of archaeological material. Despite this absence of evidence it would be wrong to assume that the population levels declined due to the emigrations from the south-west to Brittany. Neither was there a great influx of Saxons in the 7th and 8th centuries. Rather the pattern that emerges is perhaps one of continuity of socio-political systems, which might well have originated in the pre-Roman era, and were exploited by the conquering Saxons.

What we are missing is the story of the inhabitants of Exmoor at this time. For example, very little is known of the settlement pattern. Understanding the mechanisms that caused the settlements of the Iron Age to evolve into or be replaced by the pattern of farms, hamlets and organised field systems of the medieval period is a big historical challenge.

Early church dedications

A few of Exmoor's churches are dedicated to early Christian saints. This is a trend in the south-west, Wales and Brittany and commemorates the crossing of Irish, Welsh and Breton missionaries to and from the south-west peninsula in the 5th and 6th centuries (Grinsell 1970a, 103). Most of these dedications originate some 500 years later in the 11th century, the culmination of a hagiographical tradition and association between the great abbey of Glastonbury and south Wales (Pearce 1978, 136–8).

On Exmoor such dedications occur at Culbone (to St Bueno); Brendon (to the 6th-century Irish saint, St Brendan);

Porlock (to St Dubricius; the Welsh saint who died *c* 550 and was active in the spread of Christianity in South Wales and the west); and Timberscombe (to St Petrock) (Farmer 1978; Pearce 1978, 136).

While the evidence for most of these being 11th century in origin is compelling, they do express yet another link between Exmoor and the rest of the south-west and Wales. In addition, it is intriguing that some of them have coastal and remote locations away from centres of settlement. Do some of them indeed perpetuate earlier foundations?

The Anglo-Saxon conquest and the use of place-names

The chronology of the Anglo-Saxon conquest of south-west England is uncertain. It appears to have been a haphazard affair with battles leading to advances and setbacks on both sides. This probably continued for more than 100 years, but by the beginning of the 9th century AD the kingdom of Dumnonia had fallen under Anglo-Saxon control, after which it seems to have existed as a subject kingdom.

Place-name evidence can be a valuable indicator in charting the progress of Anglo-Saxon influence in southern Britain. On Exmoor and in the rest of Devon hardly any British names can be found, and it would be easy to overestimate the impact of the Anglo-Saxon conquest. The great mass of Saxon place-names does not mean that the British population was overwhelmed, instead it shows us a gradual process of renaming, perhaps throughout 300 years when British elements gradually gave way to the new language. No doubt this process was largely due to a new landowning elite (Todd 1987, 273–4; Gover *et al* 1969, xix–xxi). Many place-names have an element implying woodland or clearance of woodland, suggesting perhaps a period of colonisation and agricultural improvement under this new regime, or did these names refer to ancient farmsteads and holdings of the native British population?

Some place-names give insights into how the landscape was organised at this period. For example the *hiwisc* element refers to the one hide unit. This manifests itself today as *huish* in modern place-names. The distribution is restricted to south-west England and presumably represented the holding of a free peasant. Rodhuish is an example, the size of the unit calculated as 586 hectares, reflecting the

poor quality of the ground on the north escarpment of the Brendons.

Cott and *wyrth* names also originate at this period, and are generally assumed to represent small, low status settlements. Woodland names also abound, such as *wudu, bearu, graf, hyrst* and *holt*. Other names suggest the clearance of woodland, such as the element *leah*, commonly found as the suffix, -*ley*.

Place-names with Celtic connections on Exmoor are rare. Of the few, Countisbury (with the later *bury* suffix) is an example. Wallover near Challacombe is interpreted as 'farm of the Britons' (Gover *et al* 1969, 60; 62; Cameron 1979, 17).

Elsewhere in England Anglo-Saxon church architecture and crosses form an important part of the cultural material from this period. These remains are very rare in south-west England, however, and Exmoor is no exception with only fragments of an Anglo-Saxon cross-shaft built into St Dubricius' church, Porlock (Pevsner 1989, 275).

The Viking Raids

In AD 851 the Anglo-Saxon Chronicle records that Ceorl and his kinsmen of Devon defeated the Danes somewhere near Tor Bay. Thus began a series of Viking raids on the south-west. In AD 878 an unnamed brother of Ivar the Boneless and Halfdan crossed the Bristol Channel and attacked the north Devon coast at a place called Arx Cynuit. The battle was decisive with more than 800 Vikings being killed. The location of this battle has been suggested as Countisbury where the substantial prehistoric earthwork on Wind Hill no doubt could have been reoccupied and would have proved an ideal defence. (Todd 1987, 275–6; Gover *et al* 1969, 62). There are problems with associating the place-name Arx Cynuit with Countisbury, and other contenders have been put forward (Grinsell 1970a, 114–15). Specific archaeological evidence is needed to prove a 9th-century reuse of this site. Porlock was raided by the Vikings on two occasions, on the second of which it was extensively burnt.

Inscribed stones

Within Exmoor National Park are three inscribed stones dating from the early medieval period (Fig 4.1). Two memorial stones, the Caractacus stone on Winsford Hill and the Cavudus stone near Lynton,

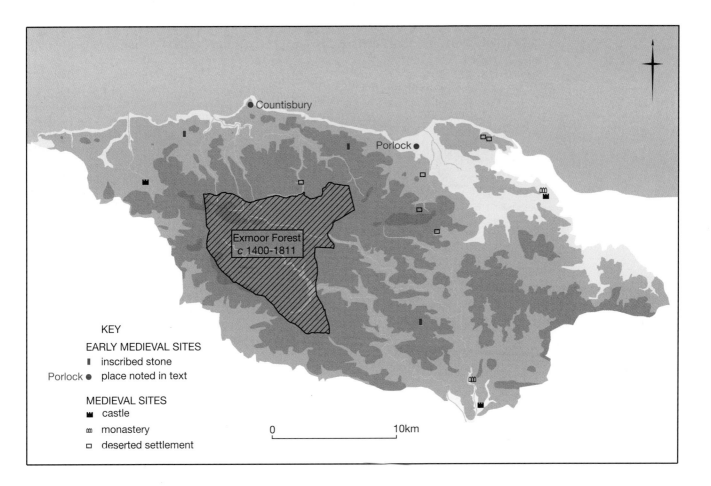

KEY

EARLY MEDIEVAL SITES

❚ inscribed stone

Porlock ● place noted in text

MEDIEVAL SITES

🏰 castle

♨ monastery

▫ deserted settlement

0   10km

Figure 4.1

Exmoor: selected medieval sites and the Royal Forest of Exmoor (c 1400–1811). (Based on an Ordnance Survey map, with permission. © Crown copyright. All rights reserved)

bear inscriptions – such stones usually indicate the site of a grave. The third is the Culbone stone, inscribed with an early Christian symbol. They are part of a culture concentrated farther west in Cornwall, in south Wales and in Brittany. As with so much of Exmoor's heritage, these examples lie on the extreme edge of the tradition. Hardly any of these stones are found across the rest of southern Britain. Such marginality makes them difficult to assess, but they are generally seen as indicative of a wealthy aristocratic class in the process of conversion to Christianity.

The Caractacus stone bears the inscription CARAACI NEPUS – kinsman of Caractacus – and is assumed to represent the proud claim that the deceased was a descendant of Caractacus, the defiant British rebel of the 1st century AD (Grinsell 1970a, 104). The stone lies on medieval common land, close to a former track running northwards out of the Exe valley. Much has been made of its position close to a former ridgeway, presumably at a place where it would have been clearly visible to passers by. The Cavudus stone is not in its original location, but stands in a private garden. Its inscription, CAVVDI FILIUS CIVILI means (the tomb of) Cavudus, son of Civilis. Both stones date from the 5th century AD an attribution made because of the style of the lettering. The Cavudus stone has recumbent final Is, a reversed D, and the Is in FILIUS have been joined to the F and L. All of these are features typical of lettering of the period (Pearce 1978, 24; Grinsell 1970a, 108).

Landscape Study 11 Culbone, St Bueno and the impact of early Christianity on the landscape

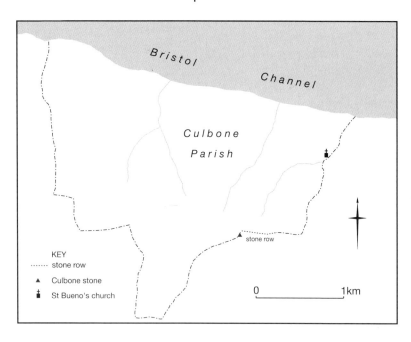

Figure 4.2
The parish of Culbone:
St Bueno's church, the
Culbone stone and the
prehistoric stone row. The
south-eastern corner of the
parish boundary follows the
line of the stone row.
(Based on an Ordnance
Survey map, with permis-
sion. © Crown copyright.
All rights reserved)

The remote parish of Culbone stretches from the Bristol Channel southwards onto the northern ridge, and encloses an area of steep, thickly wooded cliffs, above which is the productive coastal strip segmented by deep combes. Above this again is an area, formerly moorland, of late enclosure and plantations.

The earliest feature of the landscape is a stone row on the southern edge of the parish (Fig 4.2). The stone row was discovered during the 1970s. The coastal strip is occupied by several hill farms, two of which, Broomstreet Farm and Silcombe Farm, have been associated with the 'land for 2 ploughs' mentioned in Domesday (Thorn and Thorn 1980, 5, 5).

Culbone church stands beside a stream at the bottom of a steep combe, so close to the sea that the waves can be heard crashing on the rocky shore below. Estate cottages

Figure 4.3
The Romanesque window
on the north side of
Culbone church has an
animal's head carved
between the two window
lights. (© Copyright
Elaine Jamieson)

were built near it in the early 20th century, but before this it must have stood virtually on its own in a most unusual and remote situation. The church, claimed to be the smallest medieval parish church in England, has traces of Norman building within it and a delightfully primitive window (Fig 4.3) on the north side that is likely to date from the 100 years after the Norman conquest. Also on the north side are traces of an Anchorite cell.

The parish was originally called Chetenore or Kitnor, but in the 17th century its present form – Culbone – emerged, duplicating the dedication of the parish church. The church's dedication to St Culbone is seen as a corruption of Kil Bueno, meaning 'the church of Bueno', and the dedication has therefore now reverted to St Bueno. St Bueno was a Welsh saint of the 6th and 7th centuries. It is likely that the dedication of the church dates from the 11th century (as does the earliest fabric), at a time when hagiographical tradition resulted in a large number of dedications to Celtic saints.

Definitive evidence of early Christianity in the area is provided by the Culbone stone (Fig 4.4). This standing stone was discovered in 1940 and re-erected close to the spot where it was found. The stone, an unworked slab, is inscribed with a simple wheel cross; that is a circle with a diagonal cross within it. One of the arms of the cross has been projected beyond the circle. The stone might date from the 6th century, although dates in the 7th–9th centuries have also been suggested.

The stone lies close to the end of a prehistoric stone row, and it has been suggested that it might originally have been one of the terminal stones of the row.

Figure 4.4
The Culbone stone.
(AA00/0386)

Recently a second cross was found faintly inscribed on one of the stones of the row itself. The Christianisation of prehistoric monuments is well attested, but here it is noticeable that the parish boundary follows the prehistoric stone row almost exactly. It seems probable that the Christianisation of the row happened at a time when it was adopted as part of the boundary of the parish.

At Culbone we see the conscious adoption of a prehistoric monument as part of a medieval boundary system. It seems likely that it was necessary to imprint the sign of the new religion on this pagan structure – an event that must have occurred sometime between the 600s and 900s AD because of the style of the inscribed stone.

The later medieval period (1066–1600)

The later medieval period spans the time from the Norman Conquest to the end of the 16th century. Its archaeology is characterised by the familiar pattern of farms, hamlets, villages and towns, with their organised fields. Churches, castles and monasteries feature in the landscape. Settlement spread to take in more marginal land, but some farms and villages failed and fell into ruins during the latter part of the period.

During this period, the disciplines of archaeology and history begin to work together, to provide a more complete understanding of past communities and how they worked. Devon and Somerset existed as shires as early as the 8th and 9th centuries AD (Hoskins 1992, 10; Dunning 1987, 5). The process of parochial organisation, which began in the late Saxon period, was formalised in the 11th and 12th centuries.

At the beginning of this period the Domesday Survey (1086) provides a picture of the whole of England, county by county.

England was settled and farmed, having more than 100 towns and thousands of rural settlements (Rowley 1997). The entries for the Brendon Hills suggest a landscape of hamlets and numerous farms, each appearing as separate entries: on the northern slopes of the Brendons the farms of Huish, Leigh Barton, Woodadvent and the villages of Rodhuish and Treborough are all described in Domesday. It also hints at the composition of Exmoor's landscape at this time, which was one of woodland, pasture and areas for arable cultivation. A typical entry is that for Stoke Pero, which had land for two ploughs, 50 acres of pasture, 60 acres of woodland, 5 cattle, 7 pigs, 20 sheep and 20 goats (Thorn and Thorn 1980, 21, 60). In the Domesday Survey we first see the names of the people who lived and worked on Exmoor. For Devon, Domesday gives a vivid picture of farming the margins of Exmoor: at Radworthy, below the Chapman Barrows, Alric farmed (at *c* 400m) and at 'Lacoma' (Hoccombe Water, Lanacombe) Edwin ploughed a solitary furrow (at *c* 350m) (Thorn and Thorn 1985, 21, 1; 34, 14).

A remarkable survival of a Somerset Coroner's Roll gives us a picture of daily life (and death) on Exmoor in the beginning of the 14th century. A typical entry tells the story of one Thomas de Pyrkeslade, who, on October 3rd 1320, was working on his forge at Prickslade. 'As he wanted to go out of the door a beam of the forge fell on his head, whereby he died; but before that he had the last rites of the church and he lived until 6 Oct' (translation in Stevens 1985, 459). The verdict was misadventure and the beam that killed the unfortunate Thomas was valued at 1d. The reason for this diligent recording is that any article or animal said to have caused a death was forfeit to the king: hence the valuation of the beam.

Archaeology and, increasingly, the built environment, contrive to add the background to the glimpses of everyday life contained within such documents, which are generally concerned with money and the administration of justice and property rights. The archaeology of medieval settlement is illuminated by the fact that most farms, hamlets, villages and towns documented from this time exist today. Some of Exmoor's churches contain fabric from this period, and several medieval churchyard crosses survive. Only the marginal or unsustainable fell into disuse, and so were preserved as earthwork sites. The study of

this period, however, has benefited from recent excavations and recording work. Ley Hill, a deserted settlement on the edge of Horner Wood, has dating evidence placing its occupation in the 13th and 14th centuries. Buildings with medieval fabric have been recorded on the Holnicote Estate. Timber in a cottage in East Lynch, across the valley from Ley Hill, has been dated to the beginning of the 14th century by dendrochronology (Richardson 1999, and personal communication). Radiocarbon dating has placed an iron-smelting site in the Barle Valley in the 13th and 14th centuries (Juleff 2000).

The Royal Forest of Exmoor

A royal forest was an area where deer and other wild animals were reserved for the king, and protected by forest law. Such reserves existed before the Norman Conquest, but the Norman kings introduced the forest laws and greatly extended the areas of royal forest. These areas were not necessarily heavily wooded, but were outside the common law and subject to special forest law. South-western England was favoured by royalty for hunting. Royal forests were created at Selwood, in the Parrett Valley, at North Petherton, on the Mendip Hills, and at Neroche, on the Blackdown Hills, together with those that encompassed the central wastes of Dartmoor and Exmoor.

The existence of such an area on Exmoor during pre-Conquest times is indicated from the Domesday Survey, which mentions that three foresters held half a hide of land in Withypool (Thorn and Thorn 1985, 46, 3). Much of the history of the Royal Forest of Exmoor is contained in documents concerning the administration of forest law. These documents have been studied in great detail and the results published as *A History of the Forest of Exmoor* (MacDermot 1973). The royal forests were a preserve for the king's game – red deer on Exmoor. There are no records of royalty actually hunting on Exmoor, but in 1315 the Sheriff of Devon was ordered to take 20 stags from 'Exmore Forest' as part of a large requisition for salted venison for King Edward II (MacDermot 1973, 29).

At the beginning of the 13th century, the Royal Forest appears to have encompassed a large part of Exmoor. During the reign of King John it contained the parishes of Hawkridge, Withypool, Exmoor Forest, Oare, Culbone, Porlock, Luccombe, Stoke

Pero, Cutcombe, Exford, Winsford and Dulverton, together with parts of Selworthy, Wootton Courtenay and Exton (MacDermot 1973, 114). The afforested area was reduced following Magna Carta in 1215, when most of the eastern parishes were disafforested and by *c* 1400 the area under forest law was the equivalent of the present day parish of Exmoor (Fig 4.1). By this time, the Royal Forest was a central portion of unenclosed land, surrounded by the commons of the parishes that abutted it. A map drawn in 1675 – 'The Map of Exmore' – illustrates this graphically (Fig 4.5). The Royal Forest was uninhabited from the time it was formalised until James Boevey moved into Simonsbath in the 17th century (Chapter 5).

Forest law was administered at the Swainmote Courts, held yearly at Landacre Bridge – where the fields were named Court Hams on the Withypool tithe map of 1839 – then a fortnight later at Hawkridge churchyard.

Figure 4.5
The Royal Forest of Exmoor, 1675. Original in the Public Record Office, Kew.
(PRO E112/389 f.269)

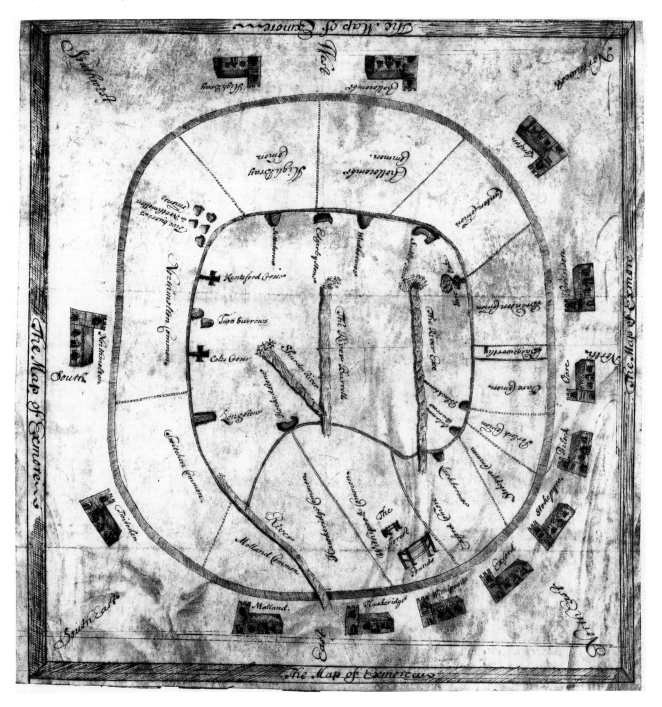

Both the Free Suitors (from Hawkridge and Withypool parishes) and the Suitors at Large (from the parishes bordering the Royal Forest) had to attend the courts. The Free Suitors had certain duties to perform, such as perambulating the Forest boundaries and organising the drifts of stock off the Forest, in return they had rights of common pasture, turbary and fish. The Suitors at Large had a right of common in the Forest. Stock from farther afield, mainly from north Devon, was also pastured on the forest, and profits from this practice went to the king's officers. An estimate of the numbers of animals taken to Exmoor for summer grazing towards the end of the 16th century was 40,000 sheep, 1,000 rother (horned) cattle and 400 'horse beasts' (ponies). The custom of Crying the Moor grew from this practice, when the forester sent men to neighbouring market towns to proclaim the prices for taking in the different animals. The sheep were put out on the moor in the spring, then brought down again for shearing. A teller counted and recorded the numbers of sheep leaving the moor. Any unshorn sheep were impounded in the Forest pound, south of the river at Withypool. Cattle drifts occurred two or three times a year, those for the 'widge beasts' – another name for ponies – happened five times annually. A new Forest pound was built at Simonsbath in the middle of the 17th century, but the ancient pound at Withypool continued to be used. The ways of the Royal Forest continued down through the centuries, until 1819, when the area was enclosed and sold to John Knight of Worcestershire (Chapter 5).

The actual traces of the former Royal Forest of Exmoor in the landscape are hard to detect. The most obvious is that of the Forest edge, now the boundary of Exmoor parish. By its nature, it was a wild place, a waste, and only the pasturing of stock was allowed. There is anecdotal evidence for telling houses at Yarde Down (Poltimore) and at Moles Chamber but no definite remains of these survive. Likewise, there are no traces of the two forest pounds, although that at Withypool is shown on the map of 1675 (Fig 4.5). The only monuments dating from the early days of the Forest are the boundary markers, often parts of the landscape itself or deliberately placed boundary stones. Bronze Age ridge top barrows and isolated large cairns were pressed into service as markers of the limits of the king's lands (Fig 4.6).

Rural settlement

The evidence for medieval settlements on Exmoor comes mainly from those settlements that failed – deserted settlements. Information can also be gleaned from the surviving medieval buildings on the moor, from documentary evidence and from existing settlements that reflect medieval patterns.

The existing pattern

Without doubt the most common settlement unit in the modern landscape of Exmoor is the single farm. A typical parish has a settlement that might include a small village or hamlet with a parish church, while the remaining population is scattered across the parish in small hamlets or isolated farms. Commonly on Exmoor the barton farm and parish church stand together; examples of this are Upton near Brompton Regis and Barton Town, Challacombe. Larger, nucleated villages, also occur, but are less common. To what extent these modern settlements are derived from medieval precursors is the subject of this section.

Research by Aston (1983) showed that personal names mentioned in the Lay Subsidy tax return of 1327 were commonly the same as existing farms or of those that survived until the 19th century before being abandoned. An example is Littlecombe in Luccombe parish: Alice de Litlecombe is mentioned in 1327 and a small farm of 37 acres, called Littlecombe, survived into the

Figure 4.6
Setta Barrow: this Bronze Age ridge top barrow was used as part of the boundary of the Royal Forest of Exmoor. (AA97/1352)
(© Crown copyright. NMR)

early 20th century; the site has now been demolished (Aston 1983, 94). Aston's work showed that this continuity of settlement from the 14th century was not rare. Undoubtedly the situation is generally much more complex and subtle than that, because what the Lay Subsidy is not able to tell us is the nature of the places mentioned in 1327. Neither does it rank between the settlements nor does it prove that place-names have not shifted in the landscape.

Documentary research and excavation in the south-west shows us that many modern farms are the product of a whole series of amalgamations or engrossments through time, and that many single farms began life as hamlets of several holdings. This has been demonstrated repeatedly, for example at Hartland and Roadford in north Devon and on Exmoor itself (Fox 1983, 40–42; Henderson and Weddell 1994, 131; I Richardson, personal communication). Wilmersham Farm, now a single holding, has architectural and documentary evidence to suggest that it was once a hamlet. It is recorded in the early 19th century as being four separate farms and the remnants of two houses still survive. This story might be much more common than we are yet able to prove, and the archaeological evidence for medieval settlements backs up the model of the hamlet as by far the most common settlement grouping on Exmoor in the medieval period (see below). King's Brompton Farm, near Brompton Regis was called Ratshanger in 1629 when it contained three tenements. The 1st edition 25in Ordnance Survey map of 1889 (Fig 4.7) shows an awkward arrangement where the single remaining farm lies on the south-eastern edge of an open space. With the aid of this valuable 17th-century reference, we can perhaps see the three tenements lying to the south-east, south-west and north-east of a communal area, which also contained a pond. So, at King's Brompton the awkward layout of the existing farm echoes the arrangement of the former medieval hamlet.

Evidence for medieval settlement is also contained in the few surviving medieval buildings on Exmoor. This is a valuable level of information for it provides the physical evidence of construction techniques and the materials used. While it will only ever be able to tell us about a few individual buildings, it does enable us to make the important link between archaeological and architectural evidence. Nowhere is this

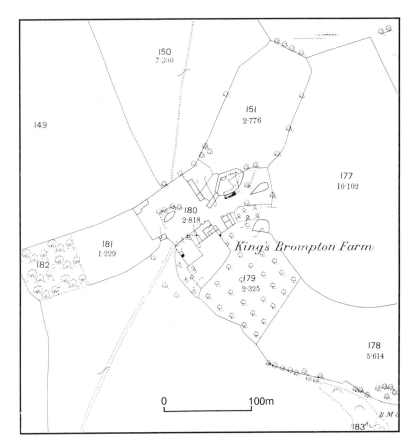

more powerfully demonstrated than at East Lynch, owned by the National Trust, where roof timbers in the building, were dated by dendrochronology, and gave a felling date of 1316. The building is therefore precisely contemporary with the nearby deserted settlement on Ley Hill currently being excavated (I Richardson, personal communication).

Some settlements, in part, no doubt perpetuate the arrangements of their medieval antecedents. This is particularly true, and more importantly provable, among the planned villages and towns of the area, but is less demonstrable among the dispersed rural communities.

Figure 4.7
King's Brompton Farm was called Ratshanger in 1629 when it comprised three tenements. The awkward arrangement of the farm and the open space to the north-west might echo its medieval origins. (Reproduced from the 1889 Ordnance Survey map, Somerset LVIII.5)

Deserted settlements

Most medieval settlements were successful and continue in use to the present. As such they evolved and changed through time, their very success often obliterating their origins. In order to discover the form and nature of medieval settlements and to see how the people who occupied them lived, it is necessary to turn to those that failed – the archaeological evidence. Deserted settlements are a rarity, yet they contain an enormous amount of information about the life of those who lived on Exmoor in the medieval period about the years 1200 to 1500. They are caught in time, with none of the trappings of later developments and change. There are five major deserted settlements on Exmoor, at: Badgworthy, Mansley Combe, Ley Hill, Grexy Combe and Sweetworthy (Fig 4.8). They are recognisable from the field evidence because of the large number of simple rectangular buildings clustered together – they are hamlets of varying sizes. This distinguishes them from later deserted farmsteads, which although possibly having as many buildings, are generally more substantially constructed and are focused around a single yard. A number of sites exist that might be found to have been deserted in the late medieval period, however, and that are indistinguishable from 18th- and some 19th-century desertions.

Documentary sources

Of the five deserted settlements only Badgworthy is definitely named in contemporary sources, and that is mainly because it was the subject of a grant of land. The settlement at Sweetworthy seems to be mentioned (although not by name) in the 18th century, perhaps a reference to its final phase of use (Riley 1996, 8). The medieval settlement on Ley Hill is not referred to in any medieval documents and yet the modern Ordnance Survey map marks the place-name 'Higher Wells' nearby at an otherwise featureless spot. Is it possible that this name somehow perpetuates that of the settlement some 500 years after it was abandoned?

Reasons for and date of abandonment

It is unlikely that these settlements were abandoned for one reason only. It is more

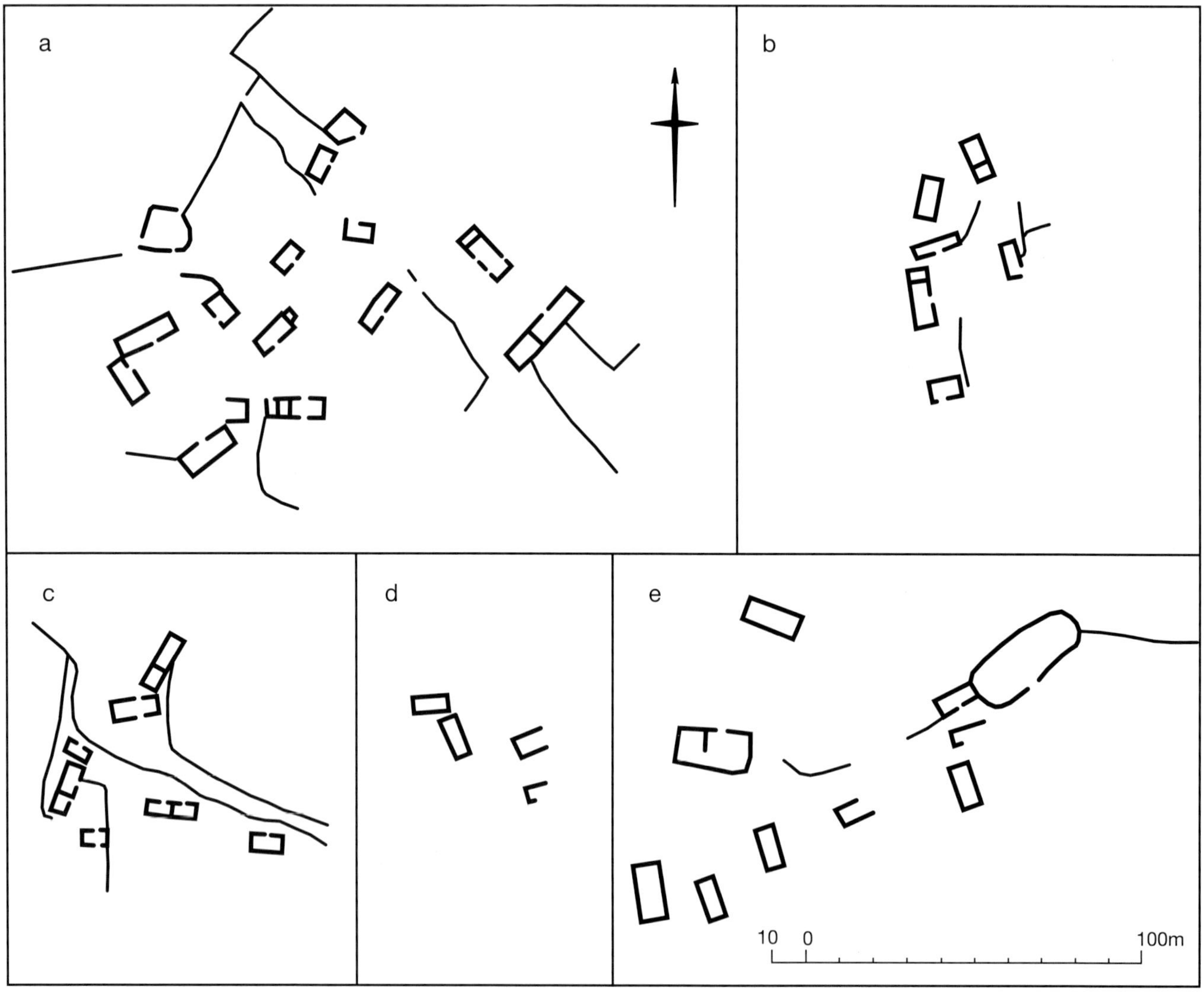

Figure 4.8
Deserted medieval settlements on Exmoor: Badgworthy (a), Mansley Combe (b), Ley Hill (c), Grexy Combe (d) and Sweetworthy (e).

plausible that several factors combined through time to make them unviable. Without doubt the most significant of these was climate. At a time when this country was becoming colder and wetter, such marginal communities might well have been pushed over the edge. Combine this with other factors such as plague epidemics and changes in land ownership, and life on the edge might well have become intolerable.

Documentary sources suggest that Badgworthy was abandoned by the beginning of the 15th century (Wilson-North 1996, 3) and at Ley Hill pottery recovered during excavations by National Trust staff in 1998 and 1999 was mainly 13th- and 14th-century in date, but a few 15th- and 16th-century glazed sherds have been found (Richardson 1999 and personal communication). The similarity between these and the other deserted settlements means that it would not be unreasonable to suggest that they were abandoned during the same period. Badgworthy and the settlement at Sweetworthy each have one holding that looks to be later in date, suggesting that a single farm continued in use.

Physical characteristics

The form of dispersed settlements such as these varies greatly throughout England, but the classic nucleated medieval settlement has a well marked sunken street with rows of former buildings sometimes with yards (tofts) fronting onto it. Each of these has a separate parcel of land (crofts). The settlement can appear very ordered (Astill 1992, 50–51, 59). The evidence of the buildings is usually less apparent than that of the street pattern and property boundaries, and this gives the settlement a coherence and assists in its interpretation. Deserted settlements on Exmoor could not be more different from this. They are characterised by a haphazard collection of buildings, a few of which have yards or closes attached to them, but the majority do not. There is usually no clear road pattern, which is a considerable obstacle to understanding how the settlement worked. It is often difficult to identify which buildings formed part of a single holding.

Exmoor's deserted medieval settlements are strikingly similar to some of its surviving hamlets, and to others in north Devon. Earthwork evidence for similar settlement forms has been reported from elsewhere in England, such as on and around Dartmoor and in Shropshire. This all serves to emphasise the robustness of the hamlet as a settlement form (Aston *et al* (eds) 1989).

Buildings and building construction

The main evidence within these abandoned settlements is that of the buildings themselves (Fig 4.9). All that remains are the footings of stone walls, now visible as low stony banks. Sometimes doorways are visible as gaps in these banks and often, internal partitions can be seen. The buildings vary between 9 to 26m long and 4 to 6.5m wide. In places walls poke through the turf and it can be seen that they are constructed of unmortared, roughly coursed stone. The walls are stone-faced, both externally and internally, with a rubble core. Some buildings appear to have been constructed of cob (an earth and straw mix). Excavations at Ley Hill failed to encounter evidence of roofing material, and it therefore seems likely that the roofs were constructed of timber with a covering of thatch.

The variation in size hints at the different functions performed by the buildings, and it is possible to identify four distinct categories: longhouses, houses, shippons (cattle sheds) and barns (grain stores). The field evidence is such that some buildings could be placed in several of these categories. For example it is very difficult to distinguish, on the field evidence alone, between longhouses where animals were housed under the same roof as people, and houses where people lived at one end of a building the other end of which was used for storage (Astill 1992, 55). Equally it is not always possible to distinguish between houses and shippons. It should also be borne in mind that excavation has repeatedly shown that elsewhere buildings changed their use and were adapted for other purposes (Astill 1992, 54, 58–9). A possible example of this on Exmoor is at Ley Hill, on the building partly excavated by National Trust staff in 1999. It appeared to be of cob construction; later internal timber partitions suggest that it was subsequently used for cattle. From this same part of the building were recovered more than 100 sherds of mainly 13th- and 14th-century pottery, implying a change from domestic to agricultural use (I Richardson, personal communication).

The houses display a varied form, but are usually two- or three-roomed and sometimes have small annexes attached to them.

The internal partitions are sometimes evident as stone footings or more commonly level changes within the building. It is not always possible, however, to identify internal partitions; and this is so in the settlement at Sweetworthy where their almost complete absence on the surface suggests that partitions were constructed of timber. The general lack of stone on the building remains also suggests that cob might have been used extensively here. Shippons or byres have been found standing alone or in association

Figure 4.9
Ley Hill: the remains of a medieval building.
(AA00/0382)

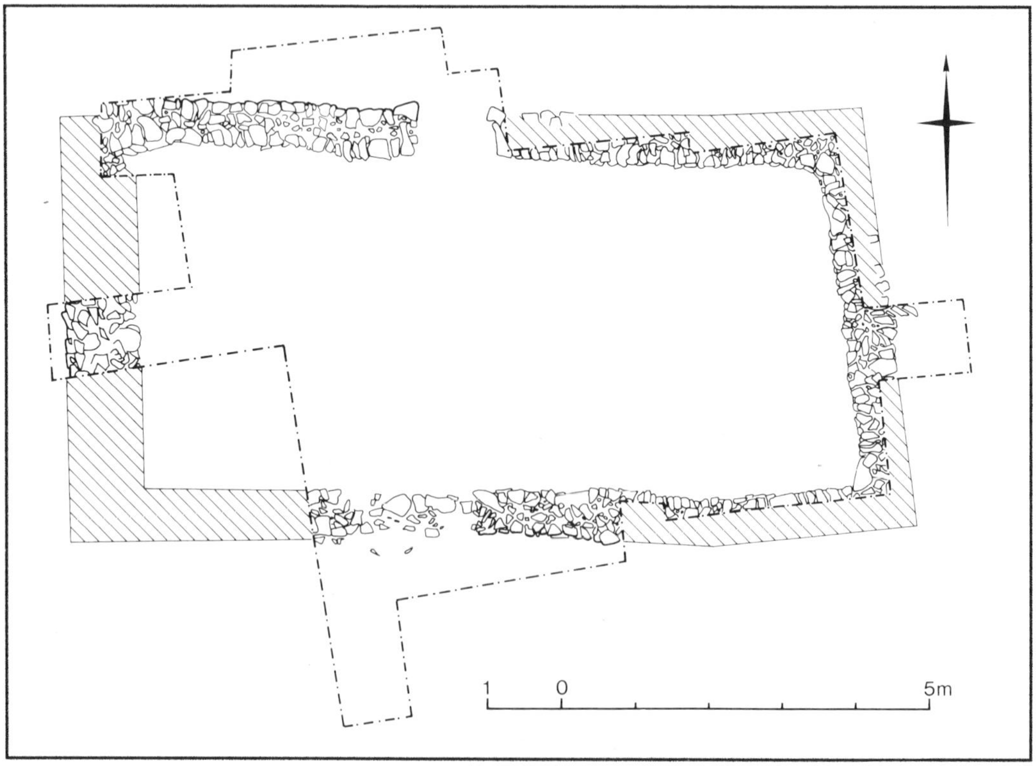

Figure 4.10
Ley Hill: plan of a medieval barn excavated in 1998 by the National Trust. A few sherds of 13th- and 14th-century pottery were found on the floor of the building (hatched walls are conjectural, pecked line shows edge of excavation).
(© Copyright National Trust)

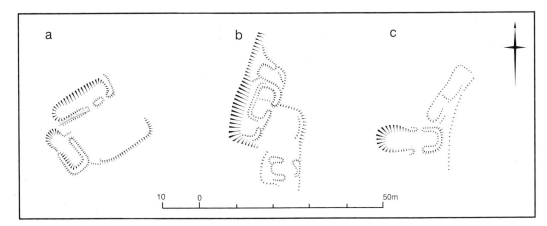

Figure 4.11
At several deserted
medieval settlements, some
buildings are paired
forming small farmsteads,
as at Badgworthy (a) and
Ley Hill (b, c).

with houses (below). In general when standing alone it is often impossible to distinguish them from houses.

Barns for the storage of grain and for other purposes have been identified at Badgworthy, where they are distinguished from other buildings by being short and noticeably wider, and they usually have a single entrance. At Ley Hill excavations in 1998 revealed a building that had a beaten earth floor and practically no artefacts. It was interpreted as being a barn and is likely to have been used for grain storage (Richardson 1999) (Fig 4.10). It is noticeable that these buildings occur at sites where there is evidence for arable cultivation in the form of strip lynchets. At Hound Tor on Dartmoor similar structures have been examined and yielded internal corn drying ovens and kilns where oats were dried, although so far no such features have been found on Exmoor. The decline of cereal pollen in the environmental record at Hound Tor in the 14th century might echo the problems encountered on Exmoor (Henderson and Weddell 1994, 123–4), which no doubt contributed to the ultimate demise of the settlement. At Badgworthy the small barns seem to be placed at the northern end of the settlement. Does this indicate a communal purpose among the inhabitants or is it simply more convenient for buildings to be arranged in this way?

There are three examples of what we might describe as farmyards. These occur at Badgworthy and Ley Hill. At the former, two similar buildings have been placed to form an L-shape along two sides of a yard, the remaining sides formed by a bank (Fig 4.11). The similarity between the buildings suggests that one was a house, the other a shippon. Organisation of the settlement might also take the form of the grouping of buildings of certain function together.

It is by no means clear that the presence of a separate shippon in a holding marks either a development from the longhouse or an indication of higher social status or wealth. It might, however, represent the origins of the courtyard or nucleated farmstead so familiar to us today.

Field systems

The evidence for medieval agricultural practice on Exmoor comes largely from two sources: firstly, medieval field boundaries fossilised as the boundaries of existing field systems, and secondly, relict field systems surviving as earthworks or visible on air photographs. The former can be studied from map evidence, such as 19th-century and modern Ordnance Survey maps, the latter chiefly through air photographs and fieldwork.

Extant field systems

The identification of medieval fields fossilised within later systems is an imprecise and imperfect science. It relies on identifying certain characteristics of such systems, recognising at the same time that some of these characteristics might well also originate in the post-medieval period. It is impossible therefore to create a map of the medieval agricultural landscape of Exmoor. Rather we should attempt to identify windows of surviving medieval landscape, and seek to understand them better, and hence understand the systems that operated across the landscape as a whole.

A common feature of Exmoor's landscape is a curving continuous boundary enclosing a farm holding. Such features seem to represent the planned intake of land from the waste or woodland. These features are most apparent around the

Figure 4.12
South Radworthy: the
Ordnance Survey map of
1890 shows fossilised
medieval strip fields in a
combe to the west of the
hamlet. (Reproduced from
the 1890 Ordnance Survey
map, Devon XV NW)

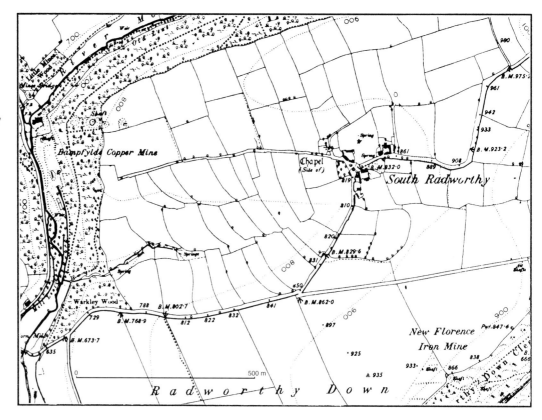

margins of the moor. Sometimes the boundaries are irregular and curving, marking periodic intakes of woodland or waste. This is more difficult to date and might take the form of very gradual encroachments during long periods of time, equally this method of enclosing land would have operated as well in the medieval period as in the 18th century. More useful is the identification of features that can be seen as diagnostic of medieval agricultural practice.

The characteristics of the medieval agricultural system in the south-west is that it originated as a mixed system, but a deteriorating climate meant that more and more emphasis was placed on pastoralism. There is some evidence that parts of the south-west adopted a communal or open field system, characterised by cultivation of strips of land by individuals as part of a system of rotation. This phenomenon manifests itself in the landscape by strikingly uniform narrow fields often defined by curving, parallel hedgelines. These perpetuate individual strips or bundles of strips. A striking example of this occurs at South Radworthy. Here the isolated hamlet of two farms, some cottages and a former chapel had its own strip field system, which is recognisable from a glance at the 1st edition Ordnance Survey map of 1890 (Fig 4.12).

Relict field systems

Relict field systems that can be confidently ascribed a medieval date are best preserved on moorland where they survive in association with deserted settlements. Elsewhere they are found within enclosed land and their survival is, therefore, partial.

The moorland examples generally show that, where it is an adjunct to a discrete settlement, there are two distinct parts to the field system: these are conventionally termed infield and outfield. The infield was intensively cultivated strip fields in the case of a hamlet or village, or intensively worked fields near the farm in the case of a single farmstead. The outfield was an area of poorer grassland (or moorland) that was ploughed up from time to time, but was primarily used for grazing. This two part system is clearly demonstrated at both Badgworthy and the settlement at Ley Hill where there are well preserved and developed systems of strip lynchets (see Fig 4.14). These are communal strip fields, and in both cases have developed on steep south or south-east facing slopes near to the settlements. On Ley Hill they are organised into two distinct bundles or fields. The second part of the field system – the outfield – survives on Ley Hill and at

Badgworthy as large enclosures of moorland varying in size between two and five hectares. These appear to have been subdivided and might well have been partly ploughed up from time to time in the medieval period. At Grexy Combe the field system comprises a regular pattern of large fields and is of very different character from those at Badgworthy and Ley Hill. This might indicate that it continued in use until a later date.

The evidence of medieval field systems within later fields generally takes the form of ridge and furrow or strip lynchets. Both are assumed to be evidence for open fields, although on Exmoor there is some evidence that ridge and furrow of a medieval or late medieval date was constructed as part of the process of land improvement prior to enclosure into conventional fields (Chapter 5). On Exmoor the

occurrence of strip fields – ridge and furrow or strip lynchets – is not as common as elsewhere in southern England, but it does exist in striking concentrations around the western edge of the moor, noticeably around Parracombe and Challacombe. It is certain that more examples will be discovered. Like the strip fields at South Radworthy, the Challacombe examples appear to concentrate around hamlets within the parish: there are areas of lynchets around Barton Town and around North and South Swincombe. This might well be confirmation that such hamlets operated their own communal field system. (Fig 4.13). The striking factor at these sites is the way in which the later field system does not reflect the earlier pattern. This implies that the strip system was largely disregarded; or maybe some other factor drove such radical change.

Figure 4.13
Air photographic transcription of strip lynchets around hamlets and farms in the Challacombe area. (Based on an Ordnance Survey map, with permission. © Crown copyright. All rights reserved)

Landscape Study 12 Badgworthy: a deserted medieval landscape

*Figure 4.14 (below)
Badgworthy: the medieval
settlement and its
adjoining field system.
(Based on an Ordnance
Survey map, with permis-
sion. © Crown copyright.
All rights reserved)*

*Figure 4.15 (facing page)
Badgworthy: reconstruc-
tion of the village and fields
in the 13th century.
(© Copyright Jane Brayne)*

When R D Blackmore, the author of *Lorna Doone*, walked up Badgworthy Water in the years before 1869 and came across the ruins of some buildings clustered along the banks of a moorland stream, they inspired him to dream up the lonely Doone village: 'But further down, on either bank, were covered houses, built of stone, square and roughly cornered, set as if the brook were meant to be the street between them. Only one room high they were, and not placed opposite each other, but in and out as skittles are.' (Blackmore 1994, 35). What Blackmore so eloquently described were the remains of a medieval settlement largely abandoned some 200 years before the legendary Doones were meant to have existed. That an archaeological site should inspire him is hardly surprising, for the place is timeless. The large numbers of visitors to the site go there, however, not because it is a deserted medieval settlement, instead they come to

drink in the atmosphere of the fabled Doones. This is a pity because Badgworthy is one of the finest pieces of undisturbed medieval landscape in south-west England (Fig 4.14). The site has a completeness that enables us to begin to see the workings of an isolated medieval community in the 13th and 14th centuries.

The place-name means Baga's Farm and certainly pre-dates the Domesday Book although nothing is recorded there in 1066. The concentration of Bronze Age monuments nearby implies that the area has always favoured human occupation. The first mention of the place in contemporary documents is in 1170 when the land was given to the Knights Hospitallers and was described as the land of the hermits of Baga Wordia. Who these hermits were and how they lived is a mystery. By the 13th century there was a priest named Elias and a chapel at the vill of Badgworthy and

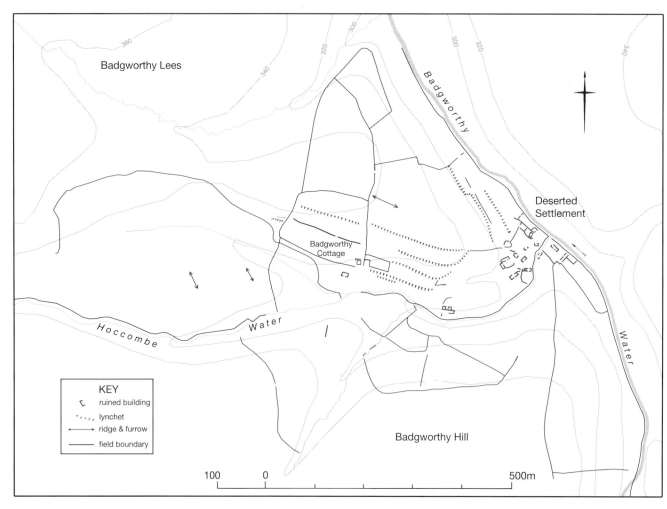

KEY
ᔑ   ruined building
'··,,   lynchet
←——→   ridge & furrow
———   field boundary

Badgworthy Lees

Badgworthy

Deserted
Settlement

Badgworthy
Cottage

Hoccombe   Water

Water

Badgworthy Hill

100   0   500m

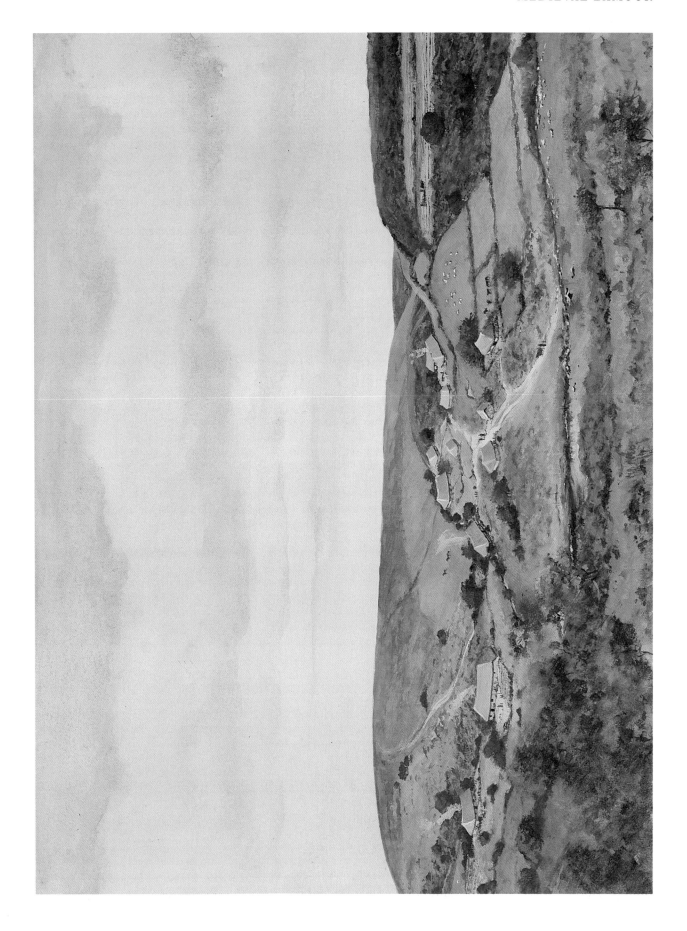

several tenements are mentioned there. By 1423 the settlement was largely unoccupied.

In the early 19th century only an old man named Tucker and his granddaughter lived there, and they died in a terrible snow-storm in the winter of 1814–1815, on their way home from Challacombe. A shepherd's house was built in the 1860s, but that was blown up by American artillery fire during World War II.

Fifteen structures make up the settle-ment (Fig 4.15). Thirteen are grouped together at the confluence of Badgworthy Water and an un-named tributary stream, two more lie to the south-west at some distance from the main settlement. The buildings are arranged in a haphazard way, their siting dictated by the dramatic topog-raphy and nearby river rather than by any overall plan. From their appearance they are all, except one, of similar construction suggesting that they are broadly contempo-rary. The settlement comprises houses, shippons and grain barns or stores. Some of the buildings have small paddocks or closes attached to them, and a few of the smallest structures might be better interpreted as animal pens for sheep or pigs.

The buildings seem to have had walls of roughly coursed stone, and were presum-ably roofed with thatch or reed. It might be that some of the structures were long-houses, with people and animals under the same roof, although only excavation could prove this arrangement. Elsewhere the presence of houses and shippons together suggests that the accommodation was sepa-rated. Three or four grain barns have been identified, and these seem to cluster at the northern end of the settlement, and provide compelling evidence, supported in the adjacent field system, of the cultivation of arable crops at more than 300m above sea level.

On the slopes and spurs around the deserted settlement are traces of its fields. They make up a classic medieval arrange-ment of infield and outfield. Long, terraced strip fields or lynchets stretch along the free-draining, south-facing slopes to the west of the main settlement and along the east-facing slopes to the north. These would have been intensively worked and provided the main source of vegetable and cereal food for the inhabitants. Farther away from the hamlet were large fields or enclosures carved out of the moorland. Traces of broad ridge and furrow show that these were ploughed up and cultivated from time to time, but their main purpose was to provide a managed system of grazing for livestock. Here the cattle and sheep would have been pastured when not oversummering on the commons or Royal Forest.

During the late 1400s and early 1500s the hamlet declined: tenants could not be found for the land and tenements. But was the hamlet totally abandoned? The archaeo-logical evidence suggests that at least one holding was able to carry on. Sheltered from the weather by a mass of rock on the valley floor are the substantial remains of a small farmstead that is strikingly different from all the other medieval buildings at Badgworthy. Its complexity suggests that it is later in date. It was a well-constructed house with a number of rooms and annexes probably used as stores. Facing the house across a narrow courtyard was a barn. Was this the house that Tucker and his grand-daughter never returned to on that fateful night in the winter of 1814?

Castles

The stone keeps and grassy castle mounds in the centres of many English towns are familiar aspects of the historic landscape. Castles, however, were direct imports from France, an important feature of the Norman Conquest of England. Only three castles occur within the bounds of the Exmoor National Park, and all are on the fringes of Exmoor (Fig 4.1). The three are all very different in date and form. At Parra-combe, the castle has influenced the pattern of subsequent settlement. At Dunster the medieval castle site was used in the later landscaping of the grounds for a grand stately home, which replaced the outmoded motte and bailey castle. Bury Castle, on a lonely spur above the Exe valley, was only occupied for a few decades in the 12th century, but it also figured in a grand land-scaping plan in the 18th century.

Chronology, function and form

There is a growing body of evidence, both from excavation and documentary work, enabling some generalisations to be made about the chronology, form and function of the castle. The commonest type of early castle in England and Wales was the motte and bailey castle. There are examples of motte and bailey castles in northern France that date from the earlier part of the 11th century. The first castles in England date to the period of the Norman Conquest. William I marked his military progress through the land by building royal castles in England's county towns – hence those built at Exeter, Okehampton and Totnes. Many smaller castles, built by the new Norman land-owners and often called baronial castles, also date from this time. The process of the re-organisation of the English landscape, so prosaically described in the Domesday Survey, inevitably led to a prolonged period of instability. A peak was reached in the mid-12th century with the Anarchy of King Stephen's reign. A significant number of the smaller castles seem to date from this unsettled period.

The castle had two main functions. One was military – it was both defensive and offensive. The castle was not just a place of safety and security, but was also a base for conquering the surrounding countryside and imposing the rule of the new Norman lord. The second role was that of a residence for the lord and his household – in effect a stately home. Alongside his castle, a Norman lord aspired to a deer park, rabbit warren, fish ponds, vineyards and gardens – all the trappings of high society. The combination of the domestic and military requirements of the day influenced the development of castles.

The bailey, enclosed by a bank and ditch, contained all the buildings required by the feudal household, including the hall, chambers, stables and kitchens. To one side of the bailey, and rising high above it, was the motte. It was the most important part of the castle, both practically as the final refuge, but also symbolically as an expression of power and domination. For this reason, the siting and appearance of castles in the landscape was important (*see* Figs 4.31 and 4.33). The motte, circled by its own ditch, was connected to the bailey by a timber bridge. Although natural landscape features were used, the motte was usually an artificial earthern mound. On its summit was a timber tower – the keep – surrounded by a timber palisade. As it usually contained the lord's apartments, the keep could be an elaborate building.

Castles changed and developed through time, as their owners reacted to circumstances and fashions. Stone keeps and curtain walls generally replaced the timber buildings and palisades, although on some sites the earliest buildings were of stone. By the later medieval period, the military role of the castle was dying out, and its residential role became more important (Platt 1982; Brown 1989).

Castles in the Exmoor landscape Holwell Castle

On the western edge of Exmoor, close to the village of Parracombe, lies Holwell Castle, a perfectly preserved motte and bailey castle (*see* Fig 4.31). It occupies a spur in the valley of the River Heddon and is overlooked on all sides bar the north-west. The castle is sited to control the valley, a steep, wooded combe, running from the fringes of Exmoor to the sea at Heddon's Mouth. Important factors in its siting were the strategic and economic benefits of controlling the bridging point of the river at Parracombe. Although the castle appears to have been in use during a relatively short period of time, its location has influenced the growth of the settlements centred at Parracombe.

Little is known about the history of Holwell Castle, which is not documented. At the Norman Conquest, the Manor of Parracombe passed from Beorhtwald to William of Falaise. His lands were part of the baronies of Blagdon and Stogursey. In 1284–1246, William Fitzmartin of Blagdon held the Manor of Parracombe. It seems likely that Holwell Castle was built soon after the Conquest, probably in the late 11th century, and that its use was short-lived. No formal excavation has taken place on the castle although Prebendary Chanter, a local antiquarian, cleaned out the motte ditches in 1905 and a roofing slate was found on the motte recently (*VCH Devon* I; Higham 1979).

The motte is a circular, largely artificial mound, surrounded by a deep rock-cut ditch. Preservation on the site is so good that traces of the motte tower or keep are visible on the summit. The bailey, defined by a strong rampart and ditch, is kidney-shaped, with the entrance to the north. Again, the outstanding preservation at Holwell Castle means that the sites of two towers where the bailey rampart meets the motte ditch are visible as earthworks.

*Figures 4.16 and 4.17
Holwell Castle: earthwork
survey and interpretation
plan showing the main
features of a motte and
bailey castle.*

On the western side, a wing wall, surviving as a broad bank, runs up the side of the motte. It connected the tower on the bailey rampart with the keep on the motte summit. Several platforms can be seen within the bailey, arranged around its perimeter. These are the remains of several buildings, perhaps as many as six. The largest is probably the site of the castle hall. The absence of surface stone on and around the castle suggests that the buildings were mainly of timber and cob (Figs 4.16 and 4.17).

Bury Castle

Bury Castle lies on the southern fringes of Exmoor, on a narrow spur between the valleys of the rivers Exe and Haddeo and so dominates these valleys, and also controls the bridging point of the Exe at Hele Bridge (Fig 4.18). The castle is close to the town of Dulverton, a small town in the medieval period, but not sited so as to influence any of the nearby settlements. Bury Castle, like Holwell, appears to be undocumented. The king owned the estates that contained the castle at the time of the Domesday Survey. By the late 12th century they were owned by the de Say family. William de Say might have been the builder of Bury Castle – sometime before 1144 (the year of his death). Bampton Castle, another motte and bailey castle, lies a few miles to the south. That castle might have been built *c* 1136 during Robert of Bampton's rebellion against King Stephen – this local disturbance could also have led to the construction of Bury Castle (Dunning 1995; Higham and Hamlin 1990).

The earthworks of Bury Castle are very different from those at Holwell. Their form suggests that this castle was short-lived, intended only for temporary occupation. Whoever the castle builders were, they had an eye for a good location: the castle re-uses a cleverly sited Iron Age enclosure (Chapter 3). A small, circular motte was placed on the edge of the Iron Age ramparts. The Iron Age ditch was re-used and deepened for the motte defences. The castle builders also strengthened the counterscarp bank. The rest of the Iron Age enclosure was used as the bailey, where a couple of platforms mark the sites of buildings. There is no obvious entrance – perhaps a timber bridge or ramp gave access to the interior (Fig 4.19).

By the late 18th century, Bury Castle formed part of the Pixton Park Estate (Chapter 5). The castle earthworks might have formed part of the elaborate improvements to the Pixton Park Estate undertaken by the second Earl of Carnarvon. They are visible from various drives laid out at this time, and the main approach to the estate passed below the castle earthworks.

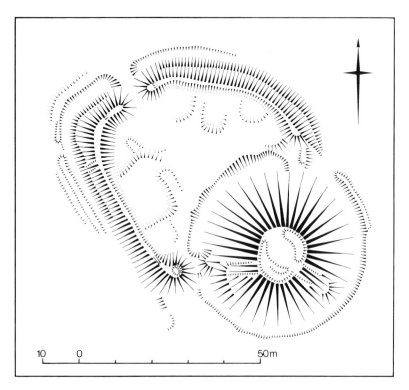

10 0   50m

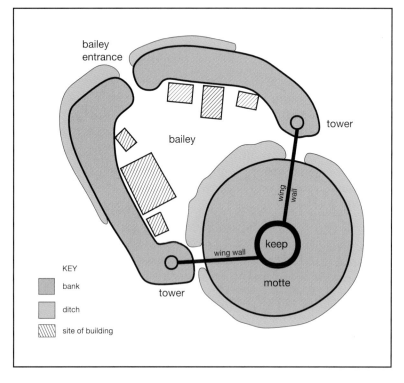

bailey
entrance

bailey

tower

wing
wall

keep

wing wall

tower

motte

KEY

bank

ditch

site of building

Figure 4.19
Bury Castle: the earthwork
survey clearly shows how
the motte has been built on
the corner of an Iron Age
enclosure.

Dunster Castle

Both Holwell and Bury Castle appear to have been used for relatively short periods of time. At Dunster, however, those two great Somerset land-owning families – the de Mohuns and the Luttrells – built and beautified the castle and its surroundings during a period of 900 years. The medieval castle at Dunster, on the north-eastern edge of Exmoor, is well documented. William de Mohun built it before 1086: the Domesday Survey records that 'he holds Dunster himself; his castle is there' (Thorn and Thorn 1980, 25, 2). William de Mohun was one of William the Conqueror's chief supporters. He was granted 69 manors in the south-west in 1066, and chose Dunster to be the seat of his administration. The de Mohuns held the Honour of Dunster (their manors and estates in Somerset and Dorset) until 1404, when it was sold to the Luttrells, who maintained the Dunster Estate for more than 500 years. Its history has been documented in some detail (Lyte 1909).

The site of the medieval castle is on the summit of a steep conical hill, which rises high above the floodplain of the River Avill. It controls access up the Avill valley as well as a bridging point of that river. The site of

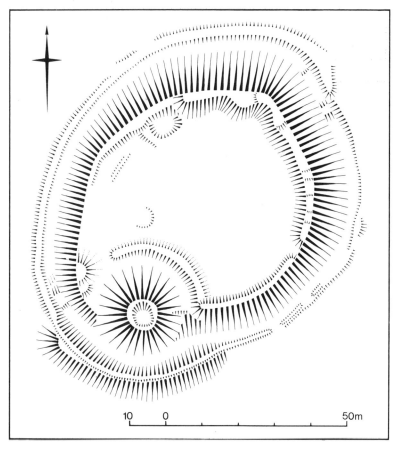

10   0   50m

105

Figure 4.20
Dunster Castle: this tower
(now restored) formed part
of the medieval defences.
(A99/06307)

the original motte and bailey is now obscured by landscaping and planting schemes throughout the centuries, but the motte, later used as a bowling green, then a garden, can be seen on air photographs (*see* Fig 4.33). Major phases of construction were carried out in the 13th and 14th centuries, but only fragments of the medieval fabric survive: the gateway, a tower and part of the curtain wall (Fig 4.20). The construction of a fortified house and the landscaping of the hill have destroyed much of the original medieval fabric.

Monasteries

The monastic tradition in Britain was established well before the Norman Conquest. Monasteries probably developed in Britain by *c* AD 500, spreading from Gaul to Cornwall and Wales. Monasticism began in the early centuries of the 1st millennium AD, with the emphasis on a solitary, contemplative life. The early Holy Fathers sought a life of spiritual devotion in the deserts of North Africa, far away from temptation and worldly pleasures. As the tradition spread, the importance of a 'desert' aspect to the landscape surrounding a monastery continued. The early monasteries in Britain were perched on rocky islands, or, like the important early centre of Glastonbury, in a lonely marshland.

The Viking raids of the 8th and 9th centuries AD contributed to the gradual collapse of organised monastic life in Britain by *c* AD 900. About the middle of the 10th-century, the re-establishment of monasticism began. By the time of the Norman Conquest, there were about 60 of these 10th and 11th-century foundations and re-foundations in Britain; many seem to have acquired significant amounts of property and land. They were re-built by the Normans in their style, and there were a few very early Norman foundations – famously at Battle by William the Conqueror himself. By the time of Henry II – less than 100 years later – there were about 500 monasteries in Britain. The cornerstone of medieval monastic life was the Benedictine Rule – a fierce blend of obedience, poverty and chastity, although several other orders founded important monastic centres in this country (Aston 1993).

The layout of a monastery
There is a growing body of excavated evidence to illustrate the main features of monastic life in medieval England. This is complemented by copious amounts of documentary evidence, often relating to estate administration. A monastery had to fulfil two functions: the spiritual and the domestic. The largest and most impressive

building on the site was the church. The lay brothers and parishioners had access only to the nave. They were often physically separated from the monks by an elaborate screen. To the south of the church, where possible, was the cloister with its garden and range of buildings, which included the Chapter House, monk's accommodation and refectory. The infirmary, guest rooms and service buildings lay outside the cloister, and farther afield were fishponds, watermills, garden plots and orchards, all contained within a precinct. A good water supply was essential to the life of the monastic community. Monasteries were usually sited with access to a spring or well for drinking water and a stream or river for drainage. Elaborate systems of conduits, pipes and drains were laid on. The monastery was often the centre of a large estate, with outlying farms – granges – and access to grazing land. Most members of the community outside the monastery precincts had contact with the monastic way of life. Perhaps they were tenants or worked on the fields and farms, or worshipped in that part of the monks' church reserved for them (Greene 1992).

The Dissolution of the monasteries

Although the beginnings of organised monastic life in Britain are uncertain, we do know exactly when it ended. Between 1530 and 1540 all of the monasteries were surrendered to the king's commissioners. The process of the Dissolution of the monasteries is well documented. The gentry were keen to acquire these sites, which occupied prime positions and held large estates. The ruined or partially demolished monastery buildings provided building materials and there are many examples of 16th-century and later houses and gardens occupying monastic sites. The monastic churches were sometimes completely demolished, or they continued in use for the parish (Bettey 1989).

Monasteries on Exmoor

The remote combes of Exmoor, somewhat surprisingly, did not attract many religious houses. The central part of the moor was a Royal Forest for much of the medieval period and only two foundations were made on Exmoor during this time. At Dunster, the lord of the manor founded a small monastery close to his castle. The Exe valley provided a remote location for a small community of Augustinian canons at Barlynch, near Dulverton.

Dunster Priory

Dunster Priory was a Benedictine foundation, a daughter house of Bath Abbey. In 1090 William de Mohun, lord of the Honour of Dunster and builder of its castle, gave the church of St George, land at Alcombe, the tithes of various manors and two fisheries to the Benedictines at Bath. It was not until 1332 that Dunster received a prior of its own, Robert de Sutton, who moved from Bath accompanied by four monks. There are some tantalising references to the monastic buildings in the 14th century, when the 'sumptuous buildings' and the 'lower chamber next the great gate' are mentioned (quoted in *VCH Somerset* II, 81–2). Some of the monastic church survives as part of the west and north walls of the parish church of St George (Fig 4.21). Apart from the church itself, little is known about the layout of the monastic buildings and the precinct area (Fig 4.22). The cottages known as the Old Priory, at first glance in an odd position, close to the eastern end of the church, are part of the monastic buildings. Although they mainly date from the 16th century they embody the remains of the refectory and the priory offices. The refectory contains a stone traceried window dating from the late

Figure 4.21
Dunster: the parish church was originally part of the monastery, founded in 1090. The great barn, also part of the monastery, lies just beyond the church. (AA99/06304)

14th century and a 15th-century stone fire-place (Hancock 1905, 43). The cloister was to the north of the church, a layout dictated by the restricted space to the south, probably already occupied by shops and houses, squashed hard against the foot of Castle Hill. The dovecote and tithe barn, still standing to the north of the church, belonged to the priory. The monastic precinct appears to be perpetuated by

Figure 4.22
Dunster: the probable areas of the medieval town, castle and monastery. (Reproduced from the 1889 Ordnance Survey maps, Somerset XXV.10 and XXV.14)

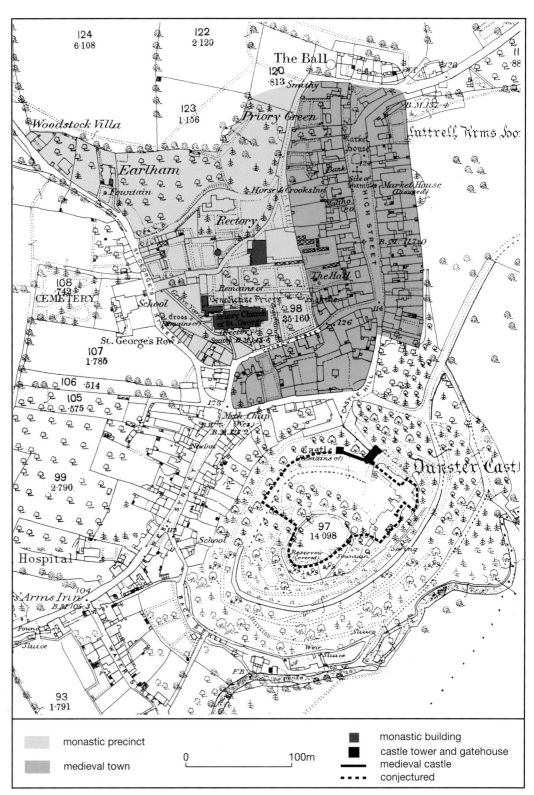

	monastic precinct		monastic building
	medieval town		castle tower and gatehouse
			medieval castle
			conjectured

0   100m

St George's Street and Church Street on its west and south sides; the east side is marked by the end of the tenements of the High Street. The northern boundary, however, remains conjectural, but probably included the areas known as Priory Young Orchard and Priory Green in the 18th century (SCRO *c* 1750).

Dunster Priory shared its church with the townspeople, and this caused some friction, as the parishioners were isolated from the celebration of mass by the monks. The problem was eventually solved in 1498 by the division of the church into two sections – one for the monks the other for the parishioners and their vicar – by a glorious rood screen, which can still be seen in the church. In 1539 the priory was dissolved. The church was given over to the parish of Dunster. Leland wrote in 1540: 'The hole chirche of the late priory servith now for the paroche chirch. Aforetymes the monkes had the est parte closid up to their use.' (Leland *c* 1540, quoted in Eeles 1945, 7). Before its restoration in the 19th century, the eastern part, or old church, had fallen into disrepair: 'shut up, stripped of all its furniture, and totally neglected.' (Savage 1830, 400–401). The rest of the priory estate was leased from the Crown to the Luttrells. The refectory and offices were converted to a farm – Priory Farm – but the other buildings were dismantled (Hancock 1905, 61). Priory Farm sprawled over the old monastic precinct in the 18th and 19th centuries, but later in the 19th century the Luttrells remodelled the area. A splendid new rectory was built on Priory Green and the area between the church and the tithe barn was used by the Luttrells for the glasshouses and kitchen garden – in effect a convenient place for the walled gardens that the steep grounds of the Castle area made impossible.

Barlynch Priory

In contrast to the well-documented history and standing buildings that tell the story of Dunster Priory, the foundation of Barlynch Priory has been paid little attention until very recently. Barlynch Priory lies on the banks of River Exe, not far from the town of Dulverton, and close to, but not within sight of, Bury Castle. The site is typical of a new foundation – isolated on the narrow floodplain, at the foot of the the steep wooded Exe Valley. Barlynch Farm and Barlynch Cottage now occupy the site. Scattered in and around these buildings are fragments of the monastic buildings, including part of the church, together with traces of earthworks associated with the monastery (Fig 4.23).

No excavations have been documented at Barlynch, although recent watching briefs have found encaustic tiles and other medieval material (V Heal, personal communication). Chance finds include a 'paving tile, decorated with a two headed eagle displayed, 14th or 15th century. Found built into a wall of a cottage half a mile from Barlynch Priory' (Additions to the Museum in *Somerset Archaeol Natur Hist* 98 (1953): 8). Much discussion has taken place about the dispersal of monastic fabric after the Dissolution. Legend states that material was removed from Barlynch to local churches, such as the church door at Winsford, the screen at Brushford and a bell at Dulverton. These are now discredited or

*Figure 4.23
Barlynch Priory: air photograph of the priory site on the floodplain of the River Exe.
(NMR 18260/05)
(© Crown copyright. NMR)*

considered unprovable. The east window and colonnade at Huish Champflower church, however, seem likely to have come from Barlynch: it is ill-fitting and not designed for that building. Parish accounts record that a window – with its stonework and glass – was removed from Barlynch and set up in Morebath church in 1537, sadly it is no longer there (Eeles 1928, 30–31). While the merits of such traditions are often hard to establish, they seem to reflect an awareness of the wholesale robbing of architectural fragments from the site. This accords well with the lack of such material around or built into Barlynch Farm and Cottage. Only one piece of decorated tracery can be seen at Barlynch: a small piece of quatrefoil tracery is built into the gable end of a late 19th-century barn. The identification of fragments of monastic buildings derives from early visits to the site by the Somerset Archaeological Society. In 1900 Colonel Bramble described a lofty wall with window openings – part of the church – and an extensive block of buildings to the south of the site of the cloister (Excursion to Barlynch Priory in *Somerset Archaeol Natur Hist* 46 (1900), 34).

The Priory of St Nicholas, Barlynch was founded at the time of Henry II (1154–1189) by William de Say. This was the son of the William de Say who built nearby Bury Castle. The first prior is recorded as Walter in the time of Bishop Reginald (1174–1191). It was a house of Augustinian canons. Barlynch was not a wealthy foundation. There were never more than nine canons – sometimes only three canons elected a new prior. In 1535 the Valor Ecclesiasticus valued the priory at £98 14s 8d. Tregonwell, writing to Cromwell, described the house as in some ruin and decay, with only six canons and the prior. The house was dissolved in February 1536 (*VCH Somerset* II; Orme 1984). The Augustininan canons were priests, unlike many monks. Their tradition of working in the community was borne out at Barlynch, where all we know about the life in the monastery comes from a school boy's notes. The notebook was written sometime between 1480 and 1520 by a pupil studying Latin grammar at Barlynch. It contains references to swimming (in the River Exe?), being woken at dawn by the chamberlain, and to the noise of poultry, dogs and the wind rattling the windows (Orme 1984, 1990).

After the Dissolution, the King granted Sir John Wallop the site in 1538. Wallop rose steadily in favour with Henry VIII. He was a naval man and led campaigns to the Low Countries and France: these were of such ferocity that his name is said to have been the origin of the verb 'to wallop'. He was knighted in 1513 and elected Knight of the Garter in 1543 (Weaver 1908; Watney 1928). Despite Sir John's standing, he appears to have done little with the Barlynch holdings. The site seems not to have had the injection of capital and status that so many former religious houses had after the Dissolution, and was never more than a farm in the succeeding centuries. In the 19th century Barlynch was part of the Baronsdown Estate, and the farm buildings reflect the estate architecture of the time.

A detailed survey of the site and its surroundings has led to an interpretation of the remaining medieval fabric and the monastic earthworks (Fig 4.24). The remains of three monastic buildings survive: a fragment of the church, part of the eastern claustral range, and the south wall of another building. In addition, a massive quarry scarp, marking the edge of the platform for the monastery, lies to the east. Near this is a circular, flat topped stony mound – all that remains of the dovecote that supplied fat squabs during the autumn. The channels and stone sluices that supplied the water for the monastery still run across the fields, and a shallow fishpond, another source of food, still holds water during the wet winter months.

Metal working

The evidence for metal working on Exmoor during the medieval period comes from documentary sources and from a handful of dated sites. Crown mining records tell that the silver/lead deposits around Combe Martin were being worked in the 14th and 15th centuries (Claughton 1997a). The mine workings around Heasley Mill, near North Molton, are some of the oldest documented on Exmoor. The Domesday Survey records four smiths at North Molton (Thorn and Thorn 1985, 1, 27). In 1346 Nicholas de Welliford attended the royal court to be granted the keeping of the king's copper mine at North Molton. He incurred heavy losses, however, and gave up the commission. This mine, probably at Heasley Mill, was mentioned again in the early 16th century (Dixon 1997, 42–3). Another 16th-century document records that, in December 1550, Michael Wynston 'found divers mines of iron and steel within the King's Forests of Exmore and Dartemore . . .' (MacDermot 1973, 223).

On Exmoor, early iron working has left the most traces in the landscape, although some potentially early silver/lead workings have been identified at West Challacombe near Combe Martin (Claughton 1997a). There are two broad types of field remains resulting from early iron working: the evidence from mining the iron ore and the evidence from processing it.

Iron ore mining: extraction pits and openworks

The economics of 19th- and early 20th-century iron production meant that large quantities of good quality iron ore were required. On Exmoor, this meant underground working of the iron ore. Earlier communities needed iron for local consumption, for the small-scale manufacture of tools and weapons. The weathered surface deposits of iron ore were more accessible and also easier to smelt than the underground iron ore. Thus it is possible to separate the 19th- and 20th-century mining remains from earlier extraction efforts.

The early miners dug pits and trenches into the ground surface to obtain the iron ore, the 19th- and 20th-century miners dug deep shaft mines to exploit the iron ore bodies. The later miners were drawn to areas of previous iron ore extraction, so that many of the 19th- and 20th-century mines in the Brendon Hills have evidence for much earlier iron extraction. Such features take the form of extraction pits, where iron ore was dug out from a discrete pit or shaft until it became too deep to work easily. The spoil dump usually remains, close to the pit. Another pit was then opened a short distance away. An irregular trench or openwork develops where such pits are dug close together. Small shallow pits – prospection pits – mark the limit of successful surface working of the iron ore body, as at the head of Roman Lode (Fig 4.25). As mining is a destructive activity, areas that have been mined during a considerable length of time might only show evidence for the latest phases of extraction.

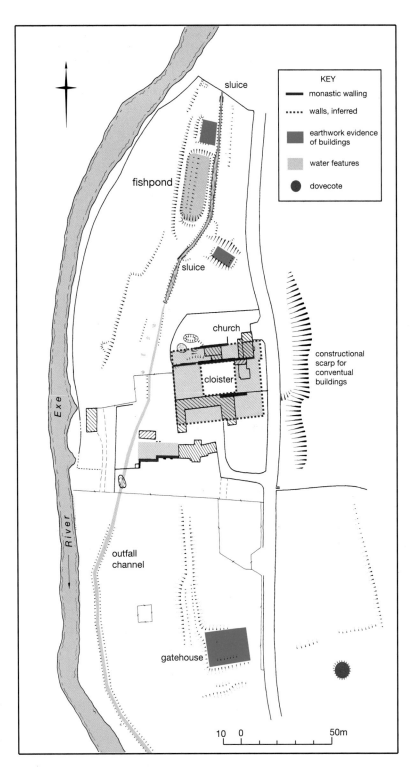

Roman Lode
The name 'Roman Lode' applies to a massive openwork cut into the hillside at Burcombe, above Cornham Ford. It has been suggested that the originators of these early workings were Michael Wynston in the mid-16th century or James Boevey in the 17th century (MacDermot 1973).

Figure 4.24
Barlynch Priory: interpretation plan showing probable layout of the monastic site, based on a detailed earthwork survey.

Recent radiocarbon dates from the nearby iron-smelting site at Sherracombe Ford show that iron working began as early as the Roman period on Exmoor. There is, however, no evidence to link the two sites (Chapter 3). Its form suggests a medieval or early post-medieval date. The size and complexity of the working suggests that extraction was carried out for a considerable period of time (Fig 4.25). The site was also worked in the 19th and 20th centuries (Chapter 5), and the shafts and spoil heaps resulting from this activity have added to its complexity. The openwork extends for nearly 700m east–west right across the valley, cutting into both the east and west-facing hillsides, following the surface outcrop of an extensive iron ore lode.

On the east-facing slope several prospection pits mark the western limit of the early working. The most impressive part of the openwork runs deep into the west-facing hillside, where several of the later shafts cut through it. Possible ore processing areas have been identified on the northern side of the openwork, an indication of an early date for the site (G Juleff, personal communication).

Colton Pits

The late 19th- and early 20th-century iron mining at Colton Pits is well documented (Chapter 5), but scattered across the hillside is a dense concentration of more than 130 iron extraction pits, covering about 15ha. The hillside was planted with coniferous woodland sometime after 1964, and the pits are now covered with closely spaced, tall conifers. Air photographs taken before the area was planted have made it possible for a detailed plan of the pits to be made (Figs 4.26 and 4.27). Some pits cut into the spoil heaps of others, suggesting that the site was used through a period of time. Most of the pits are single, but where small trenches occur they cut through the spoil heaps of the round pits. The date of the extraction pits is uncertain. Reports of old underground workings at depth (Sellick 1970, 13) suggest early post-medieval mining at the site; the pits themselves might well date from the medieval period or even earlier (Chapter 3). On the Blackdown Hills, south of Exmoor, extensive areas of iron extraction pits have been recorded. Excavation of one of these pits gave radiocarbon dates indicating that nodular iron deposits were being worked in the Roman and/or early post-Roman periods (Griffith and Weddell 1996; *Devon Arch Soc Newsletter* 69 (1998), 12).

Iron ore processing: smithing and smelting

The extraction pits and openworks of the early miners are difficult to date, but work centred on identifying the sites of early iron working – smelting and smithing – has begun to establish a chronology for these sites. A large slag heap in the woods at Blacklake, in the Barle Valley near Dulverton, has radiocarbon dates that place it in the 5th to 6th centuries AD (Juleff 1997; 2000). An important site at Eastbury Farm near Carhampton, on the north-eastern edge of Exmoor, has produced evidence for metal working – furnace bases

Figure 4.25
Roman Lode, Burcombe: this impressive openwork might have its origins in the early medieval or Roman period. (Hazel Riley, English Heritage)

Figure 4.26
Colton Pits: this extensive
area of iron ore extraction
pits (probably of medieval
origin) is now densely
planted with conifers.
(RAF: 543/2821 297)
(© Crown copyright
1964/MOD. Reproduced
with the permission of the
Controller of Her Majesty's
Stationery Office)

and slag – associated with imported pottery generally dated to the 5th and 6th centuries AD (interim report in *Somerset Natur Hist Archaeol* 138 (1994), 177). Also in the Barle Valley, upstream from Blacklake, are two recently discovered iron-smelting sites. One of these even contains the remains of buildings among the slag heaps (Fig 4.28), the other has a radiocarbon date that places it in the 13th to 14th centuries (Juleff 2000) (Appendix 2).

In Horner Wood, on the valley floor beside Horner Water, are the remains of a substantial stone building, together with the stub of an earth and stone dam and various watercourses. A large charcoal-rich dump of smithing slag lies in front of the building, and some smelting slag has also been identified (Fig 4.29). The site has been identified as a water-powered smithy, suggesting a date in the late medieval period, as water power was not used in iron working prior to this (Juleff 1997, 24). This has been confirmed by radiocarbon dates that place the site in the 15th–17th centuries (Juleff 2000) (Appendix 2). Documentary references

suggest that the smithy in Horner Wood was in operation in the late 16th century by George Heasley of Selworthy (Chadwyck Healey 1901, 102).

All of these sites are on valley floors, close to the raw materials needed for iron smelting – wood for charcoal and water. The early dates for these iron-working sites – Roman (Chapter 3) and early medieval – are important. Locally, they add to our knowledge of the Roman and early medieval periods on Exmoor. More widely, they contribute to our understanding of the development of iron-working technology.

The medieval landscape

The modern settlement pattern across Exmoor is based on the medieval one, with the main exception of the former area of the late medieval Royal Forest. It is one of farms, hamlets, villages and a few towns. Without doubt the farm is now the essential unit of settlement in the landscape, and the most common grouping is the simple hamlet: a collection of several farms with

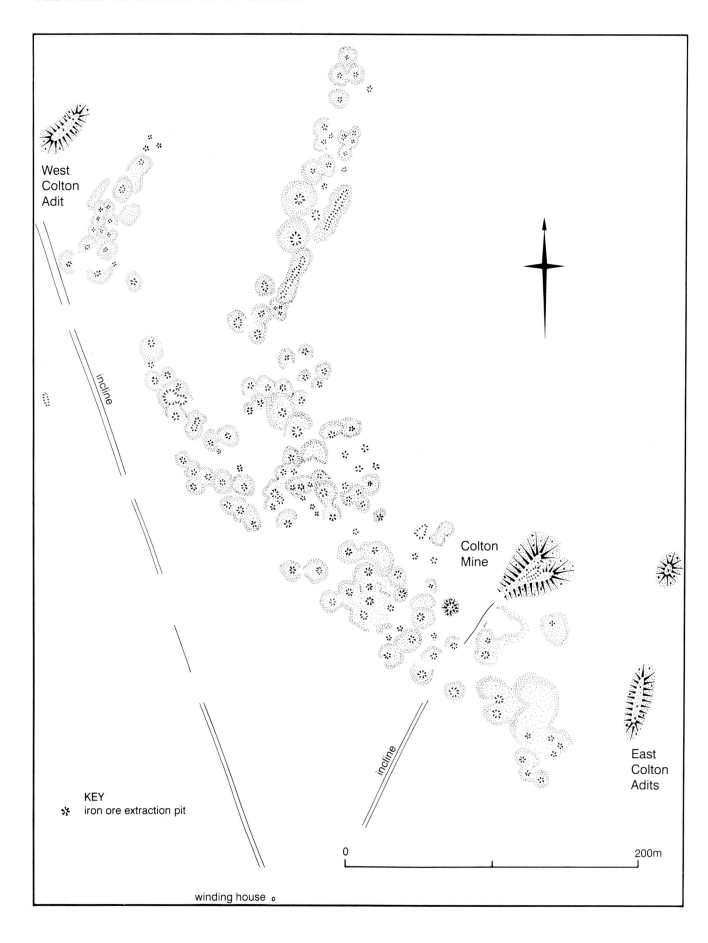

West
Colton
Adit

incline

Colton
Mine

incline

East
Colton
Adits

KEY
❋ iron ore extraction pit

0   200m

winding house ○

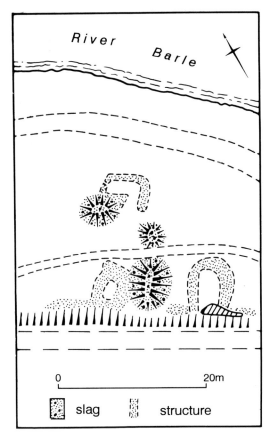

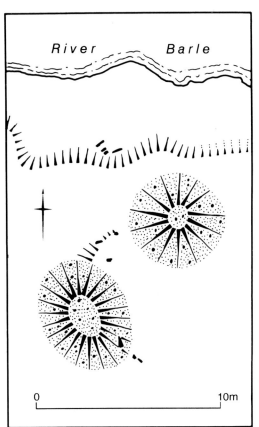

Figure 4.27 (facing page) Colton Pits: survey showing the extent of the iron ore extraction pits (probably of medieval origin) and the 19th- and 20th-century mining features. Based on air photographic transcription.

Figure 4.28 Medieval iron-smelting sites in the Barle Valley: Shircombe Slade (left) and New Invention (right). These sites are defined by small, conical slag heaps.

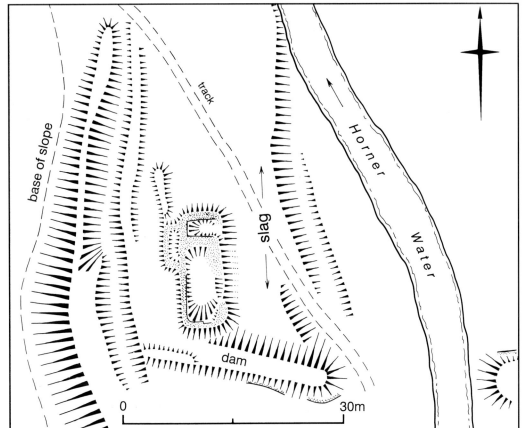

Figure 4.29 Horner Wood: this late medieval iron-smelting/smithing site lies deep in Horner Wood, close to sources of fuel and power.

perhaps some cottages. In the medieval period we should perhaps see the hamlet as the essential unit, with collections of farms being more common than isolated ones. What survives now is the product of the farms in some hamlets amalgamating to eventually form one holding.

Some parishes had what we would recognise as villages, while in others the settlement pattern was made up only of isolated hamlets, one of which would have had a church. The outlying hamlets were therefore more important than they are now. They would generally have supported more people and would have functioned as mini-communities within the parish. Some would have had their own chapel.

The origin of villages in the area is problematic, but Parracombe provides a good example of the processes involved. In rare instances towns developed, usually through economic prosperity and/or planned creation. Dulverton and Dunster are examples. These larger settlements are studied by looking at their plan form in map evidence and in other documentary sources. Analysis of the settlement plan can show how the settlements develop and what the underlying mechanisms are.

Given the essentially rural economy of most of Exmoor, it is impossible to divorce its settlements from their hinterland – it was from here that food, fuel and other essential resources came. We can imagine that the area of regularly cultivated land was much smaller then and was concentrated around the settlements themselves. In between were areas of moorland, woodland and rough grassland. These pastures were periodically ploughed up, and were grazed by everyone with rights to do so. In 1550 a mention is made of 'licence to sow corn upon the lord's common at North Hill and Duncrey this year' (Aston 1988, 87), and this phenomenon appears to have been extensive throughout many of the commons in the late medieval and early post-medieval periods (Chapter 5). The tithe map series of c 1840 shows the pattern of isolated farms or hamlets and commons very vividly. It is sufficiently early to capture the medieval pattern before it was overwhelmed by the immense agricultural changes of the 19th century, which led to the enclosure of so many of the commons and the creation of hedged fields in the large outfield enclosures.

Landscape Study 13 Parracombe: the medieval origins of the settlement

The village of Parracombe lies near the head of the Heddon valley on the fertile strip between the coast and the upland mass of the central ridge to the south. The busy A39 linking Barnstaple with the Exmoor coast crosses the area from south-west to north-east. Much of this modern landscape has been shaped by changes that have occurred within the last 150 years. Stripping these away and seeing what is left, and then adding the evidence of archaeology and documentary sources, starts to reveal the medieval landscape of Parracombe – one that is very different from that seen today.

At the centre of the parish is the settlement of Parracombe, which appears at first sight to be a nucleated village. The real story is more complex than that, however: there are a number of separate foci that make up the settlement, Churchtown, Prisonford, Bodley and Parracombe itself (Fig 4.30). Each hamlet has sprung up at different times in the past for distinct reasons. Churchtown is an integral part of the early settlement and might well be the original core. There are

several reasons for suggesting this. Firstly, the medieval parish church is sited here. Secondly, and most fundamentally, the settlement near the church is arranged around an open space or 'green'. Thirdly, a number of named or 'holy' wells are clustered around the settlement. Prisonford owes its name to the prison – presumably near here – controlled by the powerful St Aubin family in the medieval period. The major focus of settlement, however, is around the crossing over the River Heddon. This settlement has an organised core, suggesting that it was planned; it has also spread out along the lanes that converge on the crossing. The origin of this part of the settlement is uncertain, but its prevalence might well be connected with the construction of the motte and bailey castle at Holwell in the 11th century, which although sited a little upstream, is close at hand (Fig 4.31).

So Parracombe can be seen as a number of separate foci, probably developing fairly independently through time. The ecclesiastical focus at Churchtown might be the earliest,

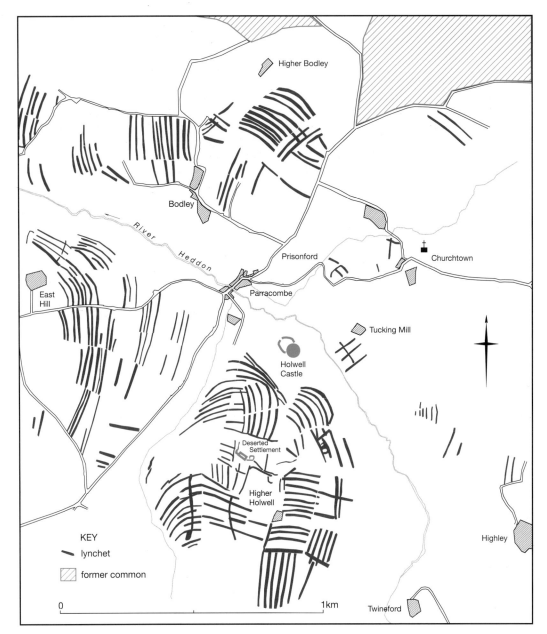

Figure 4.30
Parracombe: the topography
of the settlement, showing
its several foci, the castle
and strip field systems
(recorded from air
photographic transcription.
(Based on an Ordnance
Survey map, with permis-
sion. © Crown copyright.
All rights reserved)

while the emphasis at the river crossing might not have become established until after the Norman Conquest. Into this must be added the other elements of the settlement pattern, which includes the nearby hamlet of Bodley – first mentioned in 1332 when William de Bodeleigh lived there – and which is still a separate entity.

Around Parracombe is an extensive system of strip lynchets now overlain by the present arrangement of hedged fields. These are the former common fields. Beyond them to the west is Parracombe Common, which remained common land until it was enclosed by Act of Parliament in the mid 19th century.

Elsewhere in the area individual hamlets – probably separate townships – developed their own communal system of strip fields, which are likely to be of medieval origin. These are especially striking to the north around Kemacott and Heale, where the strip fields are fossilised within the existing field system. At Kemacott (Fig 4.32) they form a regular and planned system of strips laid out in conventional reversed S-shape, with long boundaries (headlands) or lanes between the bundles of strips. Such planned systems might suggest the original importance and independence of such communities. Kemacott also lies close to Martinhoe Common, which it must have exploited for fuel and grazing.

Figure 4.31
Holwell Castle lies to the south of the crossing point over the River Heddon, where the concentration of settlement might owe its origin to the creation of the castle in the 11th century. At the top of the photograph are the remnants of strip lynchets marking the settlement's former open fields.
(NMR 15604/14)
(© Crown copyright. NMR)

Figure 4.32
Kemacott: the Ordnance Survey map of 1890 shows the hamlet and fossilised system of strip fields, originally organised into furlongs. (Reproduced from the 1890 Ordnance Survey map, Devon VI.3)

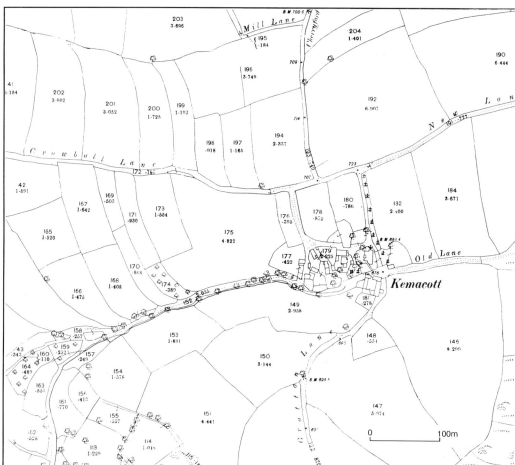

The name means Cyma's cot and is first mentioned in 1330.

At Parracombe, as at so many other places on Exmoor, much of the settlement pattern was in place by the early 14th century, and might have been so for several hundred years. At Winsford, for example, Mick Aston has shown that the pattern was almost identical in 1840 to that in 1327. Such apparent conti-nuity should not obscure the failures and creations that occurred through time. Further, a place could be mentioned in 1327 and again in 1840, but such implied continuity might obscure the fact that it was a hamlet of seven farms, which had amalgamated to just one by the 19th century. Such complex mechanisms need to be grasped when investigating medieval settlement on Exmoor.

Landscape Study 14 Dunster: a medieval town

William de Mohun's choice of Dunster as the site for his castle influenced the subsequent development of Dunster as a town in the medieval period. Described as a borough in 1197, by the middle of the 13th century Dunster had a market and the right to hold

Figure 4.33

Dunster: the site of the medieval motte and bailey castle is marked by the oval lawn at the very top of Castle Hill. Salvin's fairy-tale castle lies to the right. The area of the monastic precinct, behind the priory church of St George, is marked by the garden walls of the Castle's kitchen gardens. The medieval core of Dunster is defined by the long, narrow plots with street frontages. (NMR 18252/09)

fairs in North Street. The area of the medieval town can still be seen in the present-day layout of Dunster (Fig 4.33). The burgage plots – long, narrow strips of land laid out at right angles to the street – and the rectangular market area at the top of North Street are characteristic of a planned, medieval town, as are the dog-leg roads at the bottom and top of High Street. The growth of the town was restricted to the east by the oldest of Dunster Castle's three deer parks. Dunster Priory was the other factor in the development of the town: the precinct (and later, Priory Farm) effectively stopped the town developing between St George's Street and the High Street until well into the 19th century. Dunster's fields lay to the west of the priory, towards Alcombe and Ellicombe. The monks' dovecote and great barn still stand to the north of the church in the old priory precinct.

Medieval Dunster must have had a harbour – in 1375 the French captured the St Marie Cog of Dunster. The course of the River Avill has changed through the years and the exact area of the harbour is not known. It might have been around the foot of the castle mount, or farther downstream towards the mouth of the river.

One of Dunster's main activities in the medieval period was the manufacture of woollen cloth. Adam the dyer, William the fuller and Alice the webber all lived in Dunster in 1266. Dunster's fast flowing streams provided the water power for four fulling mills in 1430. Various types of woollen cloth were manufactured, including dunster – a coarse cloth named after the town. Documents record disputes about the pollution of streams, and about the blocking or diversion of water courses. In 1547 George Luttrell built the famous Yarn Market, but the history of the woollen industry in the town is one of decline after this. By the end of the 18th-century Dunster's woollen industry had virtually disappeared.

During the 18th century Henry Fownes Luttrell began a programme of landscaping the old castle and its grounds. A new deer park was created, which took in a large area of land to the south of the town, including the impressive Iron Age earthworks of Bat's Castle and Gallox Hill. Conygar Hill, the site of the medieval rabbit warren, was adorned with a ruined tower and archway. The fairy-tale appearance of Dunster Castle today results from the embellishments and additions of Salvin in the 19th century.

5
The post-medieval period

Introduction and chronology

The post-medieval period encompasses the years 1600 to 1900. The transition from medieval to post-medieval is not easy to identify in Exmoor's historic landscape. It was a time of gradual change and evolution, but by the end of the 19th century its quickening pace had profoundly shaped what we see today.

The end of the medieval period was a time of slow recovery from the epidemics and setbacks of the previous centuries (Crossley 1990, 3). This process continued in the early post-medieval period, which was a time of relative economic stability coupled with huge social change. This was caused by many factors, not least the Dissolution of the Monasteries, which caused a quarter of England's land to change hands. A century later the English Civil War had little direct effect on Exmoor, but the Royal Forest passed briefly into private hands; other estates around the moor were consolidating by this time, and were increasingly to shape the post-medieval landscape. The rising population levels during the post-medieval period fuelled agricultural improvements, which in turn caused fundamental changes to the landscape. The commons on Exmoor seem to have been increasingly exploited and farmsteads continued to amalgamate – a gradual process that we understand only imprecisely.

The Industrial Revolution influenced the development of Exmoor, with the mining of its iron deposits. The appearance of the rural landscape was also changed by rural industries such as charcoal burning and tanning, which led to the increased importance of coppiced woodland. Estate owners saw this as a lucrative alternative to farmland and one that suited Exmoor's dissected and wooded landscape. Other industrial processes that came to dominate landscapes elsewhere in England – such as the woollen industry – were carried out on Exmoor extensively, but were 'woven into the fabric of a rural, largely agricultural society' (Atkinson 1997, 10) and did not have an industrial appearance.

The post-medieval period can be seen as one of emergence and change. The rural landscape provided the backdrop for a variety of processes, agricultural and industrial, which became inextricably linked. By the 19th century many of these activities, which together make up the distinctive rural landscape of Exmoor, cannot be separated from each other. In these and other developments, such as tourism and hunting, estates played an increasingly pivotal role. The key to them all was a transport infrastructure to overcome the remoteness of Exmoor. Whether by sea, road or rail the development of good links with the outside world was critical to the success of all these ventures. Despite several attempts to open up the moor in this way, in the end its remoteness, the poverty of its soils and its scarcely viable mineral reserves combined to make this, physically and economically, a truly marginal landscape. By the end of the 19th century iron mining had mostly ceased and Page, writing about the Brendon Hills in 1893, described 'the gaunt chimneys, the ugly pumping houses' and 'rows of ruinous cottages bordering the roadside' (Page 1893, 215).

The food shortages caused by the European wars at the beginning of the 19th century had driven forward agricultural improvement and the enclosure movement: the changes that resulted had profoundly transformed and shaped the rural landscape. The essential building blocks of settlement in the modern landscape, the farmsteads, were by 1899 very distant descendants of their medieval forbears.

Farms and farming

Most evidence for farms on Exmoor dates from the post-medieval period. This reflects the insubstantial nature of earlier agricultural buildings and the fact that fewer buildings were needed then. But it does not follow that the post-medieval period on Exmoor was one of continual expansion; on the contrary a large number of farmsteads have been abandoned in the last 150 years.

The 16th and 17th centuries are shadowy: the evidence for farms and farming is scant (but *see* landscape study 15), and this is made worse by the fact that the transition from medieval to post-medieval cannot be precisely identified for farming processes in the archaeological evidence. Firmer ground is reached in the 18th century when more documentary evidence survives. If this is combined with the increasingly reliable maps from the beginning of the 19th century – particularly the tithe map series – a fuller picture of the earlier post-medieval period can be gained by extrapolating back. By the 19th century, map evidence and the census returns make it possible to compile a detailed picture of the agricultural landscape. Many buildings also date from this time, adding yet another layer of evidence to the historical map.

Fields provide direct archaeological evidence for the development of the landscape in the medieval and post-medieval periods. We have seen that many fields were laid out in the medieval period and remain in use to this day. It is usually impossible to date them precisely, but they sometimes provide a key to the way in which the landscape was enclosed. In this way archaeologists can build up a broad chronological framework.

Despite the increasing importance and reliability of historical documents, archaeology and the evidence of the landscape as a whole continues to play an essential role in uncovering what actually happened, as opposed to the historical version of what occurred. It is only when these varied forms of evidence – the pieces of the jigsaw – are put together that we can begin to see the origins of today's farming units.

The origins of the farm

The essential agricultural unit that we see on Exmoor today is the courtyard farm: a farmhouse and a collection of specialised buildings arranged (sometimes very loosely) around a yard. Some originated as hamlets of several holdings, which have gradually amalgamated into one. Others were impoverished hill farms; these subsisted on small areas of infield, and exploited the moor, commons or Royal Forest for extra grazing and sometimes for temporary cultivation. Others again were model farms or were part of massive agricultural expansion during the 19th century. Most reflect medieval or earlier settlements, but by the 1800s had changed beyond all recognition.

Many of the early farms are sited in or close to major valleys, on spring-lines in minor combes or folds in the valley sides.

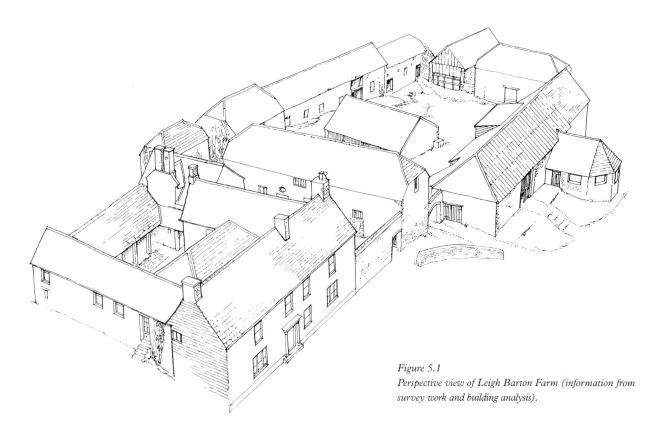

Figure 5.1
Perspective view of Leigh Barton Farm (information from survey work and building analysis).

KEY to FARM DEVELOPMENT

- 17th cent
- 17th or early 18th cent
- early-mid 18th cent
- late 18th or early 19th cent
- mid 19th cent
- late 19th cent

0   100m

Figure 5.2
Leigh Barton: the development of the farm. 1. house; 2. cider press and wool store; 3. bank barn (incorporating former domestic building); 4. bank barn; 5. wagon shed and sheaf store; 6. threshing barn and granary; 7. threshing barn, granary and horse-engine house; 8. shelter shed; 9. stable, oxen house and granary; 10. shelter sheds and calf house; 11. mangold shed; 12. field shelter; 13. sheep linhay (collapsed). (Based on an Ordnance Survey map, with permission.

They were placed to have easy access to water, comparative shelter, convenient for the better pastures on the valley sides, and yet not too far from the extensive grazing on the moorlands and commons above. In many cases, the heavily wooded valley bottoms provided a ready source of fuel.

The range of farmsteads on Exmoor reflects a number of factors such as the gradual development and evolution of some, such as Kersham and Barton Town, or the impact of estate ownership in the form of 19th-century building campaigns, such as at Cloggs. At Leigh Barton, exceptional in many ways, the wealth of the Poyntz family in the 17th century caused the creation of high quality buildings that substantially influenced what followed (Figs 5.1 and 5.2). In other cases farms were created in the 19th century on new sites, such as Horsen (*see* below). They are model farms of the time, and yet often have characteristics that have become distinctive of the Exmoor landscape.

As we have seen, the evidence from deserted medieval settlements shows that they were mainly hamlets of several holdings sited close together (Chapter 4). In some rare cases, the evidence of standing buildings confirms that these hamlets might have continued to survive into the post-medieval period. For example at Kersham Farm – now a single holding – there are the remains of four domestic buildings of the 17th century (Fig 5.3). Two of these seem to have been courtyard farms, one was a cottage and the fourth survives now as fragmentary evidence within a later stable building so that its original status is unclear. The picture that emerges at Kersham is one of evolution in which the various components of the settlement amalgamate. By the 19th century a single farm predominates. Here, the fragile survival of architectural evidence points to the evolution of this place from hamlet to simple farm.

On some farms the rebuilding campaigns of the 19th century, often carried out by estates, removed the evidence for the earlier farm buildings. This is true at Cloggs (*see* landscape study 15), but at Barton Town the earlier phase of the farmstead is partly preserved (Fig 5.4). The southern end of the existing yard is a former house that is now used as a farm building. It appears to date from the late 17th or 18th centuries and is contemporary with, or slightly earlier than, a neighbouring barn.

Figure 5.3
Kersham is now a single farm. In the 17th and 18th centuries there were at least four domestic buildings here – probably two courtyard farms and two cottages. 1. storage barn incorporating former house; 2. animal shed; 3. threshing barn; 4. farmhouse; 5. stable incorporating remains of former house; 6. cart shed; 7. animal shed; 8. cottage. (Based on an Ordnance Survey map, with permission.
© Crown copyright. All rights reserved)

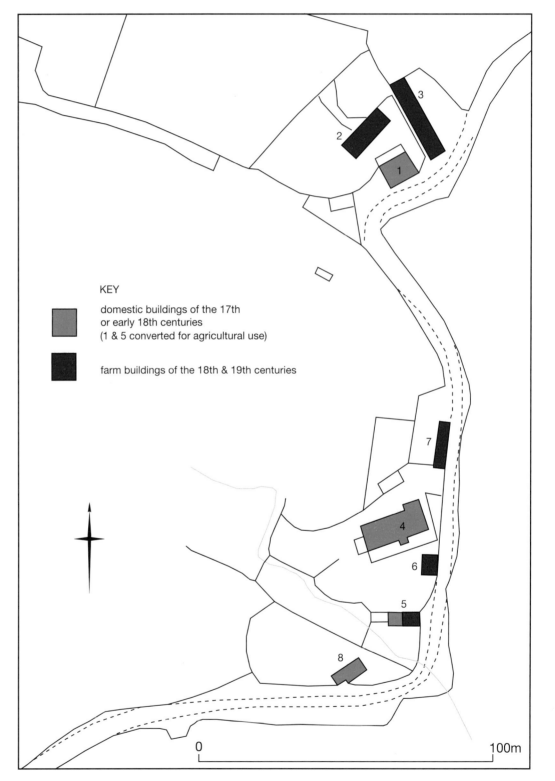

KEY

domestic buildings of the 17th or early 18th centuries (1 & 5 converted for agricultural use)

farm buildings of the 18th & 19th centuries

0   100m

Figure 5.4
Barton Town: the 17th or 18th century farmhouse, now an agricultural building, stands at the lower end of a farmyard of 19th century buildings. These accompanied a larger farmhouse to the north. (AA00/0942)

These two buildings give an insight into the farm that existed during the 17th and 18th centuries. Earthworks in the field to the north represent another abandoned farm. In the 19th century a massive reorganisation took place, which involved the farmhouse being taken out of the yard. The new house was built to the north-east while a complete yard of 19th-century farm buildings was constructed.

The principal building, a bank barn, is industrial in scale and reflects the way in which agriculture was seen by that time.

Amalgamation and failure

A common feature of Exmoor's landscape are deserted farmsteads; they are a constant occurrence in the marginal landscapes around the moor. They often manifest themselves as an area of scrub and some tumbledown walls, scarcely recognisable today as the remains of a once active farm. Some are better preserved, such as the remains of the small farmstead at Darlick in North Molton parish (Fig 5.5). Some have already disappeared completely and their locations are known only from 19th-century maps and from local knowledge. Many failed in the 1800s, the victims of agricultural improvement. This led to more land being enclosed and improved, so that farms were often cut off from the moorlands on which they depended for seasonal grazing and outfield pastures. Some failed as part of a long process of amalgamation, which we have already encountered in an earlier chapter. The agricultural economy was changing and these were the casualties of that change.

In Somerset, Aston has shown that many of these recently deserted sites were occupied in the 14th century (Aston 1983). They survived to be included on the tithe map series in the early 19th century, and were abandoned after that. It could be said, therefore, that the most radical changes to the distribution of settlements have occurred in the last 150 years. Many abandoned farms were single holdings before they failed, such as Road in the Exe valley. Others were more complex and included cottages and other buildings. At Clicket, in the valley south of Timberscombe, a small hamlet was abandoned, partly because of its remoteness. Some farms were not completely abandoned, a single building being retained for agricultural use.

The development of field systems

During the medieval and later periods, the Royal Forest and the surrounding commons dominated the agricultural economy of Exmoor.

Figure 5.5
The ruins of Darlick
farmhouse stand among a
clump of grown-out beech
hedging. The house was
probably abandoned at the
end of the 19th century or
might even have limped on
into the early 20th century.
(© Copyright Jane Brayne)

They directly affected the amount of livestock that could be raised in the area. Records for the Royal Forest clearly show this (MacDermot 1973).

While the Royal Forest could only be used for pasturing livestock, the commons were used for the cultivation of crops as well. This practice is sporadically documented in the late medieval and early post-medieval period. The Swainmote Court Rolls for 1548 record that seven acres of Withypool Common were enclosed and 'with Oxe and plough turned and putt to tillage' (MacDermot 1973, 447). Again in 1678 'sixpence an acre rent is paid to the Lord of the Manor for enclosing and ploughing parts of the commons' (MacDermot 1973, 352). The archaeological evidence shows, however, that vast areas of the commons were cultivated in this way, and that the fields were planned and laid out in organised systems. Hundreds of hectares of field systems comprising low field banks and areas of slight ridge and furrow ploughing have been noted on most of the commons. They are particularly visible on Molland Common, Withypool Hill and Common, and on Winsford Hill, where they have been recorded by air photographic transcription (Fig 1.16). In at least one case a drove road has been formalised between the enclosures to make it possible to drive livestock onto the Royal Forest (Fig 5.6), implying that the field system was planned and was of some duration. It is very surprising that such a widespread system should be so poorly reflected in the historical sources and yet so strikingly visible in the landscape today. Much more work needs to be done on these field systems before we can fully understand the agricultural economy of the Exmoor hinterland.

The practice of enclosing land from the waste in the medieval period no doubt continued, and the characteristic curving intake boundary is diagnostic of this process irrespective of when it occurred. It has been noted on the open moor, where attempts to intake land obviously failed, but it is most commonly seen as the ring-fence around some farms, suggesting that they were enclosed in one operation, as at North Lyshwell and Cloggs (*see* Fig 5.12).

Parliamentary and private enclosure

In much of England commons were enclosed by act of Parliament throughout the late 18th and 19th centuries. That process also occurred in the West Country, but enclosure seems to have taken place on parts of Exmoor at a late date, with some of the last instances of the practice.

Parliamentary enclosure entailed the dividing of the commons into hedged fields, characterised by very straight, regular boundaries; the landscape is regimented and planned. Straight roads were laid out to provide access to the fields. Examples on Exmoor are Kentisbury Down and Parracombe Common. At the latter, the rights of the commoners were served by a tiny square of open ground among the sea of hedged fields. This area was called the pleasure ground and was reserved for the recreation of the people of Parracombe. Such results illustrate the background to the undoubted unpopularity of the process. Elsewhere commoners'

rights were more effectively asserted. At Holdstone Down in the 1870s, the common was 'enclosed' by dividing it into a series of strips, the corners of which were marked only by numbered standing stones. Each commoner was entitled to a single strip, thus ensuring that the common could never fall into the hands of one individual. Parliamentary enclosure was here exploited to prevent the very result for which the process was set up.

Many of the private estates and wealthy farms took in areas of waste ground and woodland throughout the 19th century. Farms were created and fields, often very like those of parliamentary enclosure, were laid out. In some instances the areas enclosed were former outfield land or common. The process of enclosure often entailed elaborate drainage schemes. Another feature of the process was the clearance of surplus stone. This was either incorporated into the new field boundaries or was piled into heaps at the margins of the newly made fields. On North Hawkwell

Figure 5.6
To the north of Landacre Bridge are the extensive remains of a field system comprising field banks and ridge and furrow. A former drove road runs through the field system, preserving a route to the Royal Forest.

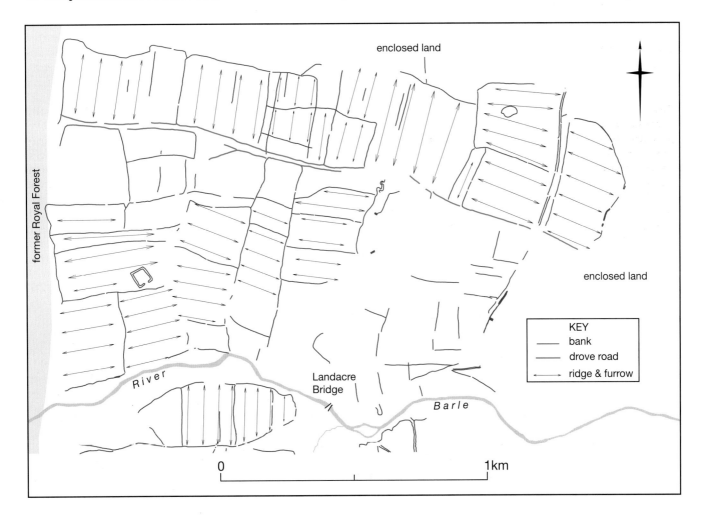

Farm south-east of Dunkery, the stone clearance heaps stand more than 4m high.

Often the enclosure of this land meant that the holding from which it was farmed was too far away from the new land. To save transporting harvested crops and animal feed, barns were built within these new fields. Hill Barn and Moor Barn are still common names on the map. These could be highly specialised buildings. Some were outfarms (*see* Glossary), such as Marshclose Barn north of Hawkridge (Fig 5.7). The animals could freely use the yard and could seek shelter within the ground floor of the barn. Its upper floor was used to store hay and other feed crops, which were thrown down into the mangers below as required.

New Barn at Ashott Farm (west of Exford) was another specialised barn. It, too, lies beyond the area of the farm's main fields in an area of 19th-century enclosure. Here the barn was provided with a water wheel and leated water supply, and so was used to thresh grain and to store fodder as well as for other stock handling purposes.

Field gutter systems

Most of Exmoor's farms had a field gutter system, sometimes called a water meadow or catchwater leat system. These comprised a series of channels cut along the hillside, usually in pasture fields close to the farmstead (Fig 5.8). The traces of these are often visible on hillsides close to the farm today. In the autumn and winter water was fed out onto these pastures via the series of leats. The flux of water across the pasture at this time of year raised the ground temperature and encouraged a flush of grass. Livestock could graze it during the winter months, or new lambs could be turned out onto it in the spring. Field gutters are first mentioned on Exmoor at the end of the 18th century (Francis 1984, 15). By this time the practice was already well established, but it was not until the 19th century that most farms possessed a gutter system, their popularity being fostered by the agricultural improvements promoted by the estates (Francis 1984; Cook 1994, 61–2).

Although gutter systems were primarily designed to irrigate the infield pastures, the water supply was often enriched by the

Figure 5.7
Marshclose Barn: an outfarm used for overwintering cattle away from the farm itself. Livestock were kept in the yard adjacent to the barn and had access to its ground floor for shelter and feed. Hay and fodder were stored in the upper storey and could be thrown down into the mangers below as needed.
(AA00/0924)

Figure 5.8
A working field gutter system in the hillside meadows around East Nurcott Farm.
(AA99/09622)

addition of manure. This was easily achieved by passing the supply leat (or carriage gutter) close to, or often through, the farmyard. Manure was thus conveniently added to the supply and carried onto the fields. Examples of this occur at Cloggs, and deserted sites such as Morehouse (*see* landscape study 15), and Road near Exford.

Despite their popularity, even into the early 20th century, only a few gutter systems are still in use. The system at East Nurcott near Winsford (Fig 5.8) is one of these. The leats are gradually redug through the late autumn and winter months, and sections of them flooded, so that piece by piece the entire field is irrigated by the end of the winter. Cattle are still fed in the sunken yard into which the carriage gutter brings the water supply. It passes across the floor of the yard collecting the animal waste as it passes, and then flows out into the gutter system in the meadow below. The water is diverted from leat to leat by temporary, earthen dams. Similarly a few sods of soil are deposited in the gutter to enable it to overflow and spill water across the desired part of the field.

Landscape Study 15 The development of farming in the Dane's Brook Valley

The Dane's Brook is a tributary stream of the River Barle. Along much of its length it forms the county boundary between Devon and Somerset. It flows south-westwards from a source close to Withypool Common between spurs and ridges of poor grassland and heather moorland. At Cloggs and Lyshwell is more fertile land, with a series of moorland edge farms along the valley sides with areas of former common and patches of woodland. The valley becomes increasingly wooded as it approaches its confluence with the Barle.

In this relatively fertile valley are a series of farms and abandoned farms. They show how settlements formed and changed through time, how enclosure took place, and how agricultural techniques developed. The fascination of this landscape is in the wealth of archaeological information it contains, which helps us to think about how settlement patterns formed in the medieval period. This landscape also emphasises the value of archaeology in the study of settlement patterns, for although we have some invaluable documentary sources, they are not precise or detailed enough to be reconciled with the number of deserted farms littering the landscape. The settlements lie close to Molland Common, a large tract of moorland that has traces of medieval field systems across much of it. These show that the marginal farms in the Dane's Brook valley and elsewhere were exploiting this resource and that it was a key factor in their development.

There are three farms in the modern landscape: Lyshwell, Shircombe and Cloggs, although formerly there were nine. Cloggs occupies a moorland edge location and is sited on the slopes of the Dane's Brook Valley. It overlooks the valley of a tributary stream. The position has a number of advantages: it is relatively sheltered, it is on free-draining ground and yet is close to an abundant water supply. Cloggs is shown on a map of 1688 but its earlier history is less certain. The existing farmhouse dates from the late 17th or 18th centuries. The farm buildings are arranged around a yard and date from the mid to late 19th century and show the influence of the

Figure 5.9
Cloggs: development of the farm. 1 farmhouse 2 shippon 3 bank barn and stable 4 pigsty/calf house 5 linhay 6 sheep shelter/store 7 hay barn 8 oil engine house on site of earlier water-wheel pit. (Based on an Ordnance Survey map, with permission. © Crown copyright. All rights reserved)

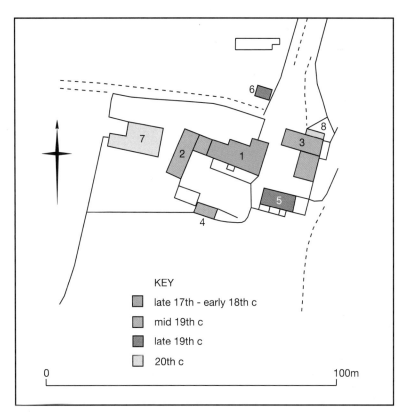

KEY
■ late 17th - early 18th c
■ mid 19th c
■ late 19th c
□ 20th c

0   100m

Figure 5.10
Perspective view of Cloggs
Farm (information from
survey work and building
analysis).

Carnarvon Estate. They comprise a shippon, bank barn with attached stable and loft, a linhay and a pigsty or calfhouse. The original farm buildings that were contemporary with the farmhouse do not survive, but two buildings are shown on the tithe map and it seems that they formed the working farm buildings that predated the more elaborate and extensive group created in the 19th century. (Figs 5.9 and 5.10)

Cloggs typifies the Exmoor farmstead in its use of water for a variety of purposes. A leat runs south towards the farm and brings water from a tributary valley. At the farm the water was used for domestic purposes as well as for the farm dairy. It also supplied a water wheel, on the outside wall of the bank barn, that powered the threshing machine and a grinder. The water was then fed under the yard to re-emerge in a manure clamp on the southern side of the yard. Here it collected slurry before passing out of the yard and onto the field gutter system in the meadows on the valley side to the south. The system at Cloggs shows how individual farms harnessed Exmoor's abundant, if unpredictable, water supply.

The use of water developed into an ambitious and highly focused aspect of the farm.

Five abandoned farmsteads, surviving as earthworks or ruined buildings, can be found in the fields of the modern Lyshwell Farm. Another farmstead, West Shircombe, is documented and was lived in during the 18th century, although its site is lost. Lyshwell is first documented in 1318, and by the 17th century South Lyshwell is named, implying that a North Lyshwell existed. The archaeological evidence confirms that Lyshwell was more than one farm. To the north three deserted farms, surviving as earthworks, lie close together. One is in a field called North Lyshwell, and is documented in the 17th century but was abandoned by the beginning of the 19th century; the other two cannot be identified. At present it is not known whether these farmsteads were contemporary or whether they were occupied in succession.

We cannot be sure when the settlements at Lyshwell came into existence, but we might guess that the peak of settlement was in the late medieval period. The documents do not reflect this, only becoming a usable source for the 17th and 18th centuries. The picture is further complicated by the presence of two other abandoned farms at Lyshwell. On the very edge of enclosed land, close to where it abuts the open heather expanse of Molland Common, are the remains of another farm called, appropriately, Morehouse. This farm was documented in the 17th century but was abandoned by the beginning of the 19th century. It is the final piece of enclosed land before the valley opens onto the moor. The most recent farm to emerge was Landcombe, which was built in the mid-19th century but was abandoned earlier this century (Fig 5.11).

Most of the farms lie within blocks of fields with a continuous outer boundary. Each seems to have been enclosed from the waste or woodlands in one operation. Morehouse, North Lyshwell and Cloggs are particularly good examples of this. All the farms have the Dane's Brook or one of its tributaries as a common boundary. North Lyshwell (Fig 5.11) and West Shircombe, although no longer in existence, can both be recognised in the landscape today because they continue to be farmed as a single field. North Lyshwell was occupied in the 18th century, when it was a ring-fenced farm subdivided into a series of regular fields. Later it was rented out as a single unit

Figure 5.11
The Dane's Brook Valley: the map shows existing and abandoned farms, the regular pattern of ring-fenced farms and other field systems. Molland Common has traces of field systems representing temporary cultivation, probably by the farms within the valley. (Based on an Ordnance Survey map, with permission. © Crown copyright. All rights reserved)

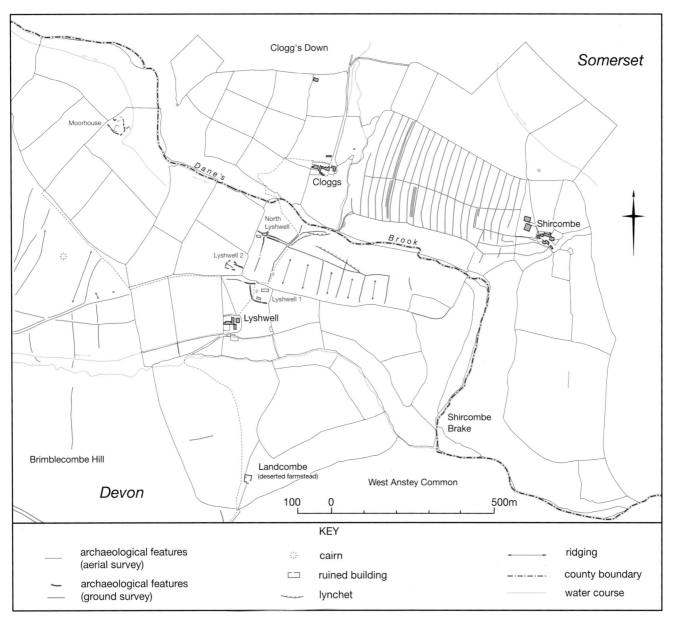

KEY

archaeological features (aerial survey)	cairn	ridging
archaeological features (ground survey)	ruined building	county boundary
	lynchet	water course

Figure 5.12
Cloggs: a ring-fenced farm.
Its regular outline suggests
that it was enclosed in one
operation. Beyond the
enclosed fields lies the
outfield of Clogg's Down,
where later fields have
encroached. (Reproduced
from the 1891 Ordnance
Survey map, Somerset
LVI SE)

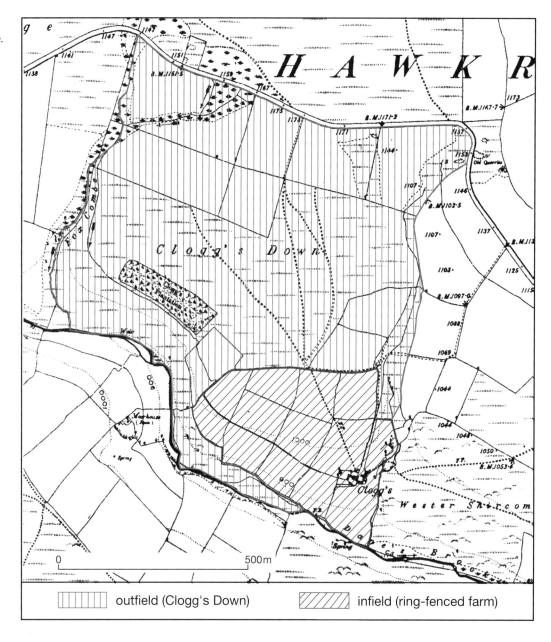

outfield (Clogg's Down)   infield (ring-fenced farm)

of land even after it ceased to be a farm in its own right. This illustrates how persistent such units are in the landscape. Within these holdings the fields are arranged in a systematic if not planned fashion. We can assume that these fields were intensively worked – in effect they were the infield system. Beyond lay the open moor with its intakes of land or the commons. Cloggs Farm has an area known as Clogg's Down, which is now part of the farm, but originally served as additional poor grazing – the outfield. Subsequent improvement and enclosure of land in the

19th century has blurred this pattern, but it can still be traced (Fig 5.12).

The extensive field systems on Molland Common abut the enclosed land, and it is probable that they were farmed from the deserted sites close by. The field system is made up of large regular fields, marked by low earthen banks. Within the fields are large areas of very slight ridge and furrow indicating where the ground has been ploughed. The area of ridge and furrow is so great that it must have had an important bearing on the operation of the farms in the Dane's Brook Valley and beyond.

Exmoor estates: archaeology and impact on the landscape

Estates have played a huge part in the economic and social development of Exmoor. Without doubt their zenith was during the 19th century, although some can be traced back to the beginning of the post-medieval period and earlier. The purpose of this section is not to describe in detail the history of estate ownership on Exmoor. Rather it is to show, by selected examples, the reasons why estates developed here at all, the ways in which they exploited and changed Exmoor's landscape, and to characterise the often disparate archaeological traces they leave.

The character of Exmoor's estates was dictated as much by fashion as by the distinctiveness of its topography. From the Knight family's dream of reclaiming a wasteland and turning it into a sea of corn, to the Halliday's vision of picturesque Glenthorne; from the elegant and gentle parkland at Nettlecombe to the formal Italianate terraces of Ashley Combe. They form a very diverse group – the product of their owners' vision, wealth, aspirations and energy. Together they are an eclectic addition to the rich variety of Exmoor's historic landscape, and often form a defining factor in its development.

Origins, history and archaeology

Exmoor's first estate was the Royal Forest. Its creation was partly due to the native red deer herd – not for the hunting of them, but for the supply of meat. The area was not settled and was of limited agricultural use, except for the summer grazing, which later on was to become one of its most profitable aspects.

By the 17th century the freehold of the Royal Forest had been purchased by James Boevey, who set about creating his own estate. At that time the Royal Forest was uninhabited, and Boevey built himself a house at Simonsbath, traces of which survive. Very little is known about the Royal Forest at that time, but one archaeological site could be directly associated with Boevey. The Warren lies in a wild and remote valley – fewer than 5km from the source of the River Exe. It is a lonely and beautiful place, the steep, sweeping valley sides broken by rugged outcrops of rock. On the slopes around the 19th-century Warren Farm are eight rectangular mounds

with flat tops and flanking ditches. These are pillow-mounds, the artificial homes of rabbits. Their presence is not documented in the 19th century and they are unlikely to be contemporary with the farm that was built in the 1840s. It is probable that they date from the 17th century, and were built by Boevey to provide food (and an income) from his new estate.

Estates on Exmoor often emerged as a collection of separate manors, farms and holdings. Such estates were common throughout the whole of the south-west. Examples on Exmoor are the Holnicote and Pixton Estates owned by the Acland family. At Pixton, latterly the property of the Earl of Carnarvon, the estate was so large that it is impossible to gain a sense of it in the landscape today.

A number of estates and parks flourished in the late medieval period, and many of them continued to prosper in the 16th, 17th and 18th centuries. Nettlecombe and Combe Sydenham are examples of such emerging country houses with settings that reflect the status of their owners. Both had deer parks adjacent to the house, and small walled formal gardens. Nettlecombe was embellished in the 18th century with a landscape park, the creation of which involved the removal of a hamlet. The buildings were swept away and the settlement's field boundaries flattened. Many of the parkland trees stand on the flattened banks of the hamlet's fields and can be shown to be hedgerow trees from the pre-parkland farming landscape (Fig 5.13).

On other estates more practical reminders of early activities are encountered. A near perfect duck decoy, perhaps

Figure 5.13
Late 18th-century parkland at Nettlecombe Court. (Hazel Riley, English Heritage)

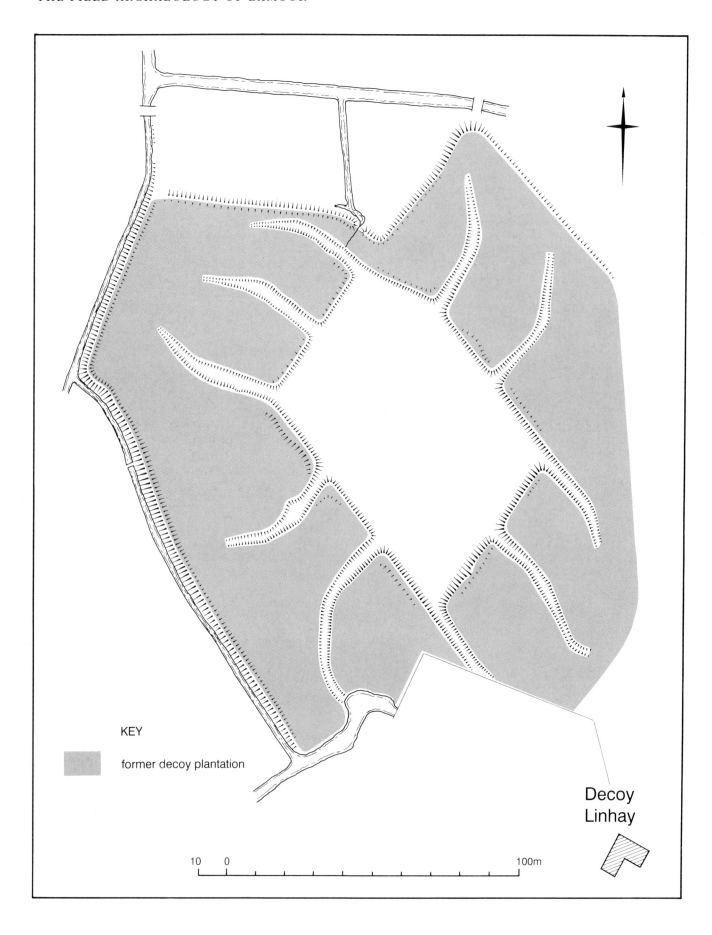

KEY

former decoy plantation

Decoy
Linhay

10   0   100m

constructed in the 18th century, has recently been submerged within a saltwater lagoon following the inundation of Porlock Marsh. It was recorded beforehand; the survey showed that it was a rectangular pond with ten, tapering, water-filled channels. The channels were netted over and the ducks ensnared at the ends (Fig 5.14).

Dunster Castle was embellished in the early 18th century by Henry Fownes Luttrell (Binding nd, 33) who improved its immediate setting by turning the top of the Norman motte into a bowling green, building elegant bridges in the grounds and improving the park (Fig 5.15). Conygar Tower was built at this time both as an eyecatcher to be seen from the castle and as a place to be visited; its approach is dominated by an elaborate ruined gateway. The Luttrell's improvements at Dunster were intended to develop the medieval ambience of the place. Conygar Tower has the feeling of a medieval fortification at the opposite end of the town to the castle, one of the castle's angle towers was restored as a folly and a packhorse bridge was included in the overall design.

Great improvements were carried out at Pixton Park in the late 18th century. Replanting was carried out in the park, a new carriage drive built, ponds were constructed below the house and a menagerie was made at Weir House. Rides were built stretching away through the estate. Lady Harriet's Drive can be followed for several kilometres up the valley of the River Haddeo. On Haddon Hill are well-preserved tree rings, which once supported clumps of trees. They are lone survivors in an otherwise agricultural and heathland landscape, but illustrate well the far-reaching impact of such estates

Farther down the social scale a small estate briefly flourished at Withiel Florey. It was the product of the linking by marriage in 1776 of the Bryants, a wealthy yeoman family, and the Stawell family of Rhyll Manor. The 'very neat house and gardens' described by Collinson (1791, III, 295) are scarcely traceable today, but early maps show a string of two or three small lakes stretching away from the former house towards a castle-like folly or eyecatcher, which was also a pair of estate cottages. The whole, while on a modest scale, clearly had greater pretensions. Today, the ponds are silted up, the house has gone and the eyecatcher is in ruins.

Figure 5.14 (facing page)
The duck decoy on Porlock Marsh.

Figure 5.15
Lawns Bridge, Dunster: the area around Dunster Castle was landscaped in the 18th century. (AA99/06608)

Without doubt the 19th century was the peak of Exmoor's estate tradition, seeing the emergence of its most spectacular examples. Most of these are on the coast and reflect a time when the picturesque was the height of fashion. The turmoil in Europe at the beginning of the 19th century brought an end to the European Grand Tour, and the Exmoor coast became a popular destination because of its dramatic scenery. The Glenthorne Estate was created from scratch with the eventual purchase of the entire parish of Countisbury (Halliday 1995). Glenthorne has all the attributes of an estate at the beginning of the 19th century: a new house, bath house, boat house, ice house, walled kitchen garden and greenhouses, lodges and follies. Most spectacular, though is its setting at the foot of the immense cliffs. Its approach, 'with serpentines as daring as in the Alps' (Cherry and Pevsner 1989, 292), was conceived to emphasise the drama of the landscape. Glenthorne epitomises one of the central ambitions of the picturesque: the house is at one with its natural setting.

At Ashley Combe the house was originally built in the 1830s on steep ground overlooking Porlock Bay, and surrounded by elaborate Italianate terraced gardens, summerhouses, turrets and tunnels (Fig 5.16). Its builder was Lord King, later the first Lord Lovelace who married Lord Byron's daughter, Ada. The house had a variety of uses after World War II, and was demolished in the 1960s. Its levelled site is still surrounded by the magnificent gardens. They are cut out of the steep cliffs and form a series of terraces at different levels connected by stairs concealed within turrets. The sense of mystery and surprise, one of the garden's main features, is heightened by its lost feeling today. A series of distinctive estate buildings were constructed from the 1860s to the 1930s, some the work of Lady Lovelace and the architect Voysey. They stretch along the coast to Culbone where the truncated spire of the tiny church might have been the inspiration for the distinctive tapering chimneys of the estate. Even the extensive planting of contorted Corsican Pines, which are so memorable on this coastline, were planted by the estate to provide cover for deer.

In the 18th century, Holnicote was as much a sporting estate as an agricultural one. The estate farms exploited the fertile Porlock vale, while in the woods and moors

Figure 5.16
The Italianate terraced gardens at Ashley Combe. (Hazel Riley, English Heritage)

the red deer herd was encouraged by extensive plantations, such as those around Webber's Post. In Mansley Combe the circular clumps of Scots Pine still adorn the valley side. One of the estate farms, Cloutsham, perched on the lip of a precipitous, wooded valley, was converted from farmhouse to alpine-style lodge in the late 19th century (Fig 5.17). Nearby, the Mound, an earthen embankment around a former tree clump, has such elaborate bastions that it was wrongly described as a fort of the Civil War. Its true purpose has only recently come to light (Fig 5.18).

Figure 5.17
Cloutsham Farm: the 'Swiss style' gable end of the farmhouse dates from the 19th century, when the Acland family added accommodation for their own use. (BB00/1235)

Figure 5.18
The Mound was a circular tree clump enclosed by a square bank with projecting angle bastions, built by the Acland family in the 18th or 19th centuries. The tree clump has long vanished, and only a few bushes of the beech hedge that enclosed it now survive. (NMR 15865/35)
(© Crown copyright.NMR)

Landscape Study 16   The archaeology of improvement

The Royal Forest was enclosed in 1818. Its purchaser was John Knight of Worcestershire, who bought the Crown Allotment and a number of other allotments on the forest amounting to more than 15,000 acres. The formation of this estate has had the most dramatic and profound effect on Exmoor's landscape (Fig 5.19), giving the moorland margins their distinctive character. The former Royal Forest is characterised by its wild yet gentle moorland alongside the regimented enclosures and farms of the Knight Estate. But the impact of the estate goes deeper than that. When John Knight purchased the Royal Forest there were no roads within it, and the only building was Simonsbath House built by James Boevey in the 17th century. Exmoor Forest was extra-parochial; it had been largely a wilderness since the medieval period. There were no fields and no farms except for a single enclosure at Simonsbath. When the estate was sold in 1898 Exmoor Forest had a network of roads, farms, fields and a village with a church at the centre of the largest parish in Somerset. Much of the

land in the Barle valley had been converted from grass moor into good pasture, other outlying areas of moorland, such as Exe Plain, Trout Hill and Lanacombe, while still moorland, had been extensively drained.

John Knight began the Exmoor enterprise and although he lived until 1850, his son Frederic Winn Knight effectively took over in 1841 (Orwin *et al* 1997, 37). The Knights were a family intimately connected with the development of the iron industry in the west midlands, but as much as this they were concerned with 'artistic life and rural development' (Orwin *et al* 1997, 35). The development of the former Royal Forest after 1818 is primarily about agricultural improvement, but it is also concerned with social history and improvement in its widest sense. The story of the reclamation has been told from the viewpoint of the economic historian by Orwin (Orwin 1929; Orwin and Sellick 1970; Orwin *et al* 1997), and added to in detail from the perspective of the local historian by Roger Burton (1989). The archaeological dimension still has much to tell us.

Figure 5.19
The former Royal Forest after 19th-century improvements by the Knight family. On the left is the open grass moor, to the right the lower slopes of the moor have been enclosed and improved. (NMR 15606/17) (© Crown copyright. NMR)

Figure 5.20
Horsen: one of the new
estate farms built by the
Knight family in the
1840s. The farmyard and
ranges stand behind the
house and beyond the beech
trees of the shelter belt can
be seen. (AA00/0958)

The process of improvement entailed the construction of a stone wall around most of the former Royal Forest. Drains were dug to remove water from areas of the moor and these survive as sharp-sided gulleys even after nearly 150 years. The leat known as the Pinkery Canal – its grandiose name reflecting speculation as to its function – is merely a large drainage channel. Its most impressive aspect is that it shows the scale on which John Knight envisaged his improvements – it is nearly 9km long.

The process of agricultural improvement spawned a large number of buildings, mainly constructed during the 1840s. Eleven of the farms constructed by the Knight family survive on the former Royal Forest. Horsen is a typical example (Fig 5.20). It lies in a remote setting at the end of a long lane, near Wintershead, another Knight farm. Horsen is one of the highest farms on the moor at an elevation of 380m. It is on a south-facing slope below the brow of a hill to afford the best shelter at this altitude. The usual Knight practice was for the house to be built by the estate when the farm boundary was defined. The construction of the other farm buildings and field boundaries was usually left to the incoming tenants, although at Horsen the estate seems to have completed the work by 1848. This means that the farms differ across the Forest, with subtle variations on the same basic layout. The plain and rather solid appearance of these farmsteads is one of the distinctive features of the former Royal Forest (Fig 5.20).

Horsen has a quadrangular layout with the house at the eastern corner (Fig 5.21). The farm buildings were formerly surrounded on all sides except the south by broad shelter belts of beech trees. The north-west range of buildings is single-storeyed and included a cow shed, calf house and root store. The south-west range had a cart shed at its north-west end, a barn in the centre, an additional room, possibly a loose box or implement shed adjoining the barn and a stable. Part of the range was one and a half-storeyed, providing for additional storage space. The simple, restrained treatment of the farm buildings reflects the limited resources of the Knight Estate and the use of local materials from estate lands.

The surrounding fields are disposed so that each one tapers towards the farmyard, and in this way six fields border the farm buildings. This arrangement greatly increased the ease of stock and feed movements between the fields and farm buildings. Such details are characteristic of the extensive planning that accompanies estate agriculture.

Apart from the evidence for improvement contained in the buildings and field systems themselves, there are a number of other sites that form part of this broad picture. An example lies in the valley of Hoaroak Water. A trail of large slate slabs tumbles down the steep hillside. Closer inspection reveals that many of the pieces of slate are rough-out gateposts, drilled for gate hangers but never transported from the site. Below are a working area and crude shelter.

Figure 5.21
Horsen: plan of the farm
showing its layout around
a quadrangular yard.
1. farmhouse; 2. shippon;
3. ?shippon; 4. barn;
5. cart shed; 6. cow shed,
calf house or root store;
7. implement house, loose
box or store; 8. stables and
shippon with hayloft above;
9. later horse engine house.

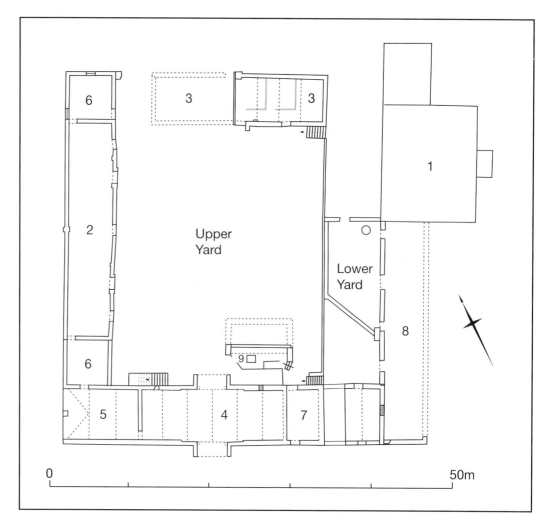

Figure 5.22
Plan of gate post factory on
the slopes of the Hoaroak
valley.

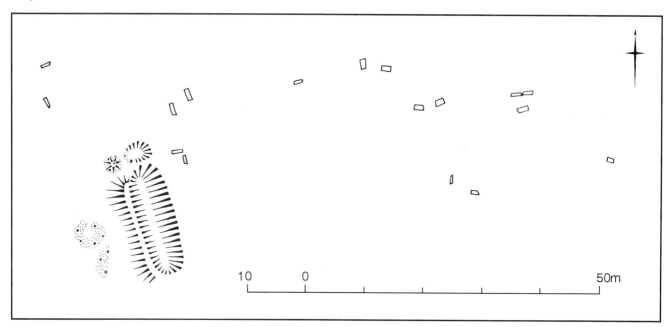

The site is a gatepost factory. Undocumented, it was from here that the Knight estate workers obtained their gateposts. It is one of the few outcrops of suitable stone on Exmoor (Figs 5.22 and 5.23).

Agricultural practice on the former Royal Forest was initially directed at growing cereal crops. When this proved unviable, there was an increasing emphasis placed on sheep ranching. Herdings were created. These usually had a cottage for the shepherd and sheepfolds placed at convenient points on the moor. They were generally placed in valleys, both for shelter and to facilitate stock being driven to them. Examples are at Three Combes Foot, Hoaroak, East Pinford and Lanacombe (Fig 5.24).

Figure 5.23
Recording gate post factory in the Hoaroak valley.
(Hazel Riley, English Heritage)

Figure 5.24
A sheepfold at Lanacombe.
(NMR 15606/25)
(© Crown copyright. NMR)

Simonsbath was the centre of the enterprise, although they never lavished money on it as befitted an undertaking on this scale. A great house was begun, but was never completed; it was pulled down after some sixty years. A deer park was enclosed to the south of Simonsbath and plantations of beech trees were established on Birchcleave. No doubt a grand setting had been planned for the great house.

A stone tower sometimes thought to have been used as a hide for deer shooting, stands just north of Simonsbath beside the Lynton road (Fig 5.25). Its true function is, however, by no means certain. It is as likely to have served as a point from which the Knight family could have viewed the deer park and the improvements they were carrying out in the Barle valley. It has been suggested recently (S Pugsley, personal communication) that it might even have served as part of a formal gateway to the estate.

Farther afield the Knights' aspirations for Exmoor sometimes were not fulfilled. The intended railway from Simonsbath to Porlock – which was to be the artery of the Exmoor estates – was never completed. Its proposed course is traceable along much of its length as an earthwork, and it was clear that it would have entailed some huge engineering challenges if it had been built. From the dock at Porlock Weir, two inclines were to have brought the railway up onto the top of the cliffs. From here the trackbed can be followed across Porlock Common and into the former Royal Forest (Fig 5.26). It is clearly visible as far as Ramscombe; west of this it was apparently never built. Its exact course to Simonsbath would have entailed elaborate engineering works, either to cross the Exe valley or, if it crossed at Exe Head, to descend from Dure Down. Like the mansion, the boldness was in the vision, and we are left wondering at how different Exmoor would be now, if these schemes had been completed.

Figure 5.25 (top)
A tower beside the road north from Simonsbath might have been built as a viewing point from which to view the improvements on the former Royal Forest. (AA96/6232) (© Crown copyright.NMR)

Figure 5.26
The course of the proposed Simonsbath to Porlock Weir railway, looking west towards Larkbarrow Corner. (NMR 15608/14) (© Crown copyright.NMR)

Industry and communications

Exmoor is relatively poor in natural resources. Minerals include iron ore in the central, eastern and southern parts of the moor, copper and gold near North Molton and silver-lead and manganese around Combe Martin. Thin deposits of limestone within the Devonian slates and shales occur in a narrow band from Combe Martin in the west, around Exford and across to Roadwater in the east, providing lime for both the building industry and agricultural improvement. Good quality roofing slate is found on the eastern fringes of the moor, while sandstones and slates have been used locally as building materials right across Exmoor. The high moors contain a certain amount of peat, still dug for fuel in places, while the wooded valleys are a source of fuel from both standard and coppiced trees and a source of raw material for the tanning industry. Exmoor's fast flowing rivers and streams provided a ready source of water for power and for processing material, particularly pertinent for cloth manufacture, once notable at Dulverton and Dunster. Transport of materials within and around the moor has been a constant problem, and remains so. Many of the cliffs are very steep and much of the shore is virtually inaccessible by land, so only Porlock and Lynmouth have grown as coastal settlements. Inland, only Dulverton has become large enough to be called a town.

Mining

Geology and mineralisation

The date and origin of Exmoor's minerals is still a matter for debate. The Devonian slates and sandstones that make up Exmoor contain low temperature hydrothermal mineral deposits. They are of a different nature from those caused by the intrusion of the south-western granite batholith and might well pre-date this event, being the result of earlier metamorphism of the Devonian rocks. Silver-lead ore, in the form of galena, outcrops around Combe Martin. Iron ore is present around North Molton and across the central part of the moor from Simonsbath across to the Brendon Hills. The lodes of ore are at their richest in the Brendon Hills, and are more sporadic

Figure 5.27
Exmoor: major post-medieval mines. For key to numbered mines see Gazetteer. (Based on an Ordnance Survey map, with permission. © Crown copyright. All rights reserved)

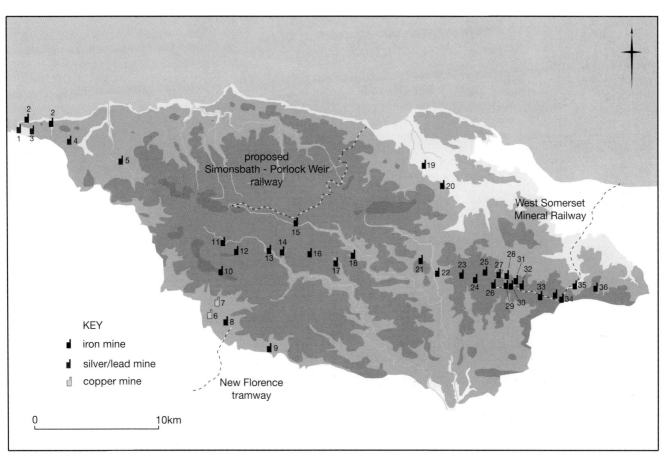

moving westwards across the area of the former Royal Forest. Mineralisation has followed the dominant trend of the country rocks, and so the lodes run WNW to ESE. The iron ore is in the form of siderite at depth, which weathers to haematite near the surface. The iron ores are sometimes found in association with small amounts of copper ore. The ores around North Molton are the only ones with a high enough copper content worth exploiting, where deposits of chalcopyrite occur. Gold has also been recorded from this area, from Britannia and Bampfylde mines (Fig 5.27) (Dines 1956; Beer and Scrivener 1982, 121–6).

The Brendon Hills: 19th-century iron ore mines

The solitary engine house at Burrow farm is a reminder that the Brendon Hills was a flourishing iron ore mining district in the 19th century (Fig 5.28). There is no documented mining activity before the 19th century, but the presence of openworks and trial pits around the later workings suggest earlier working of the deposits (Chapters 3 and 4). The first documented mining of iron in the Brendon Hills was by Sir Thomas Lethbridge, owner of the Chargot Estates near Luxborough. Lethbridge was a principal shareholder in the Pentywyn ironworks in south Wales, as well as one of the directors of the Monmouthshire Iron Company who built an ironworks and new town near Ebbw Vale. Although these ventures were badly affected by a slump, Lethbridge was

determined to open iron mines on his Chargot Estate and, in 1839, had three trial pits dug at Chargot Wood, Goosemoor and Withiel Hill. Lethbridge was soon aware of the problems of transporting the ore to the coast for shipping to south Wales. After unsuccessful negotiations with a neighbour about the building of a tramway to Watchet, Lethbridge built his own (rather primitive) furnace near his mine in Chargot Wood. This venture came to an end with Lethbridge's death in 1849. The potential of the Brendon Hills as an iron ore source was again realised shortly after this. Ebenezer Rogers, a Welshman, formed the Brendon Hills Mining Company in 1852 and struck a rich lode on Brendon Hill, the beginning of the Raleigh's Cross mine. Rogers was bought out by the larger Ebbw Vale Company in 1853, and the Brendon Hills Iron Ore Company was formed. This company obtained mineral rights in the Brendons and across the Quarme Valley to Eisen Hill (Jones 1997;1998).

In the latter part of the 19th century there were workings at many sites in the Brendons and on Eisen Hill (Fig 5.27), spurred on by technological advances in the manufacture of steel, which meant that the low phosphorous iron ore from the Brendons was in great demand. The appointment of Morgan Morgans as mines captain in 1858 came at a time of expansion of mining on the Brendons. The problem of transporting the iron ore was solved by an ambitious railway that linked the main areas of mining at Raleigh's Cross mine and Gupworthy to the coast at Watchet via an incline – the whole known as the West Somerset Mineral Railway (WSMR). The section from Watchet to Roadwater and Comberow was complete in 1857, and in 1859 the incline was opened. The line extended as far west as Gupworthy by 1864, but although an extension of the railway across the Quarme Valley to Eisen Hill was planned, it was never constructed. The cost of transporting the ore by road to Minehead must have contributed to the closure of these shafts in 1877 (Bye and Lovell 1977).

Brendon Hill, now a lonely windswept spot, became the focus for the mining community. Within a few hundred yards of the top of the incline were the two most productive mines – Carnarvon and Raleigh's Cross – a goods yard and stores, two limekilns, a station, a chapel and rows of terraced cottages for the miners and their families (Figs 5.29 and 5.31).

Figure 5.28
The engine house at Burrow Farm is the only one of its kind to survive on the Brendon Hills, where iron ore was intensively mined in the late 19th century.
(AA99/06790)
(© Crown copyright.NMR)

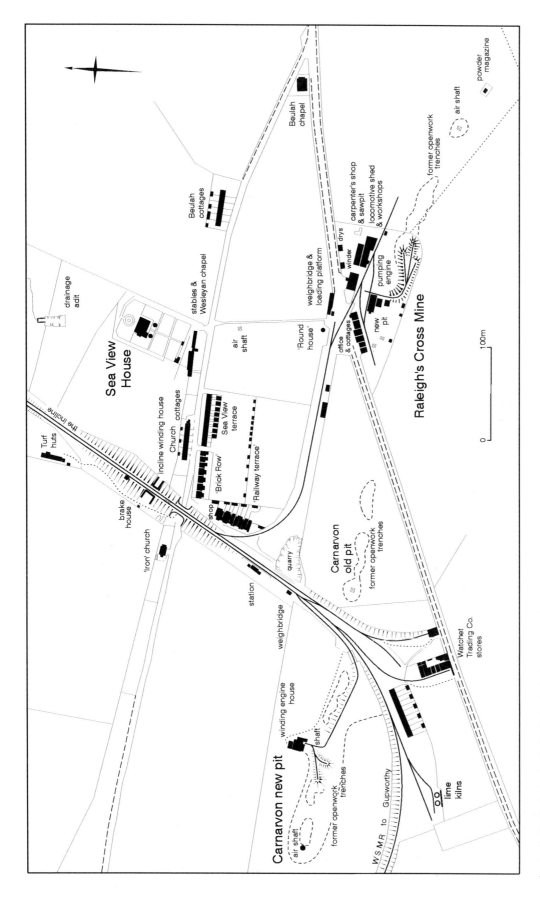

Figure 5.29
Brendon Hill village
c 1870: the busy hub of the
Brendon Hills iron mining
district. The head of the
incline lies close to two of
the most productive mines
– Carnarvon Pit and
Raleigh's Cross – and a
thriving community of
miners and their families
lived in cottages scattered
across this now deserted
area. (After Jones 1998,
facing p15)

Figure 5.30
This air photograph show
how little remains of the
19th century mines on the
Brendon Hills. The course
of the WSMR winds along
the summit, cutting the
fields in two. Burrow Farm
engine house lies in the
foreground.
(NMR 18282/02)
(© Crown copyright. NMR)

The discovery of a process enabling steel to be made from phosphoric ores, together with imports of cheap open-cast mined ores from Spain, meant that the iron ore from the Brendon Hills lost its competitive advantage. The Ebbw Vale Company pulled out of the venture and a notice to surrender was given in 1882. The WSMR was closed in 1898, then re-opened in 1907 to serve a short-lived attempt to work Colton Pits and Timwood, but mining came to an end after a few years and the railway was closed in 1910.

The archaeological remains of this hectic episode on the eastern edge of Exmoor are well known and documented. The story of the WSMR and the mines is told in *The West Somerset Mineral Railway and the story of the Brendon Hills Iron Mines* (Sellick 1970). The National Park Authority, who now own the incline, have co-ordinated the Brendon Hills Industrial Survey, which has recorded the remains of mine buildings, machinery and the incline in some detail (Jones 1998). Today the remains of the mines, the buildings that housed the machinery and the communities who lived at Brendon Hill and Gupworthy are scanty. Most of the shafts are infilled and lie in enclosed fields. The course of the WSMR is a striking feature in the Brendon Hills landscape (Fig 5.30). Buildings have been demolished and spoil heaps levelled as the areas were reclaimed for agriculture in the 20th century. In 1875 the new owner of the Chargot Estates insisted that the Ebbw Vale Company reinstated the land to its former condition. All of the mine buildings were demolished and the spoil heaps reduced in size by covering the building ruins. This was done at Langham Hill, Smoky Bottom and at all the sites in Bearland Wood. The engine house at Burrow Farm is the only one still standing (Fig 5.28). That at Kennisham Hill was demolished as late as 1978. The engine, together with its granite plinth, was originally brought from one of the Cornish mines. The granite base, now removed to the car park, is a poignant reminder of the enterprise. Only buildings that provided a useful function escaped: hence the contrast between the station at Brendon Hill (Fig 5.31), which was used as a house until very recently, and those at Northbrook and Comberow where only a search of the undergrowth will reveal the platform and foundations of the station house.

Iron ore prospecting on the former Royal Forest

John Knight, who bought the Royal Forest of Exmoor in 1818, was an ironmaster from a Shropshire family. A year after this purchase, Knight set about acquiring the mineral rights for the former Royal Forest, previously reserved for the Crown. John Knight's only venture was an unsuccessful quest for copper ore at Wheal Eliza, close to his Simonsbath home. In a story that parallels that of the Brendon Hills to the east, however, iron ore was mined from the central part of Knight's Exmoor estates in the latter part of the 19th century. The transport problem, so neatly solved by the WSMR, was never resolved in the former Royal Forest.

Frederic, John Knight's son, was drawn to search for iron ore on his Exmoor estates by the success of the Brendon Hill mines. He took advice from the Brendon Hill Iron Ore Company, and shafts were sunk at Blue Gate, Hangley Cleave, Burcombe and Picked Stones in 1854. After a favourable geological report, Knight began negotiations with the Dowlais Iron Company of Merthyr Tydfil. The transport problem was to be solved by the construction of a railway from Simonsbath to Porlock, with the Dowlais Iron Company providing rails and machinery for the inclined planes, and Knight constructing the trackbed. Mining was undertaken by the Company in the Cornham Ford area in 1855 and 1856, but after some initial success results were disappointing and they finally stopped work on Exmoor in 1858. Another firm, Schneider and Hannay, obtained a lease for much of the rest of the former Royal Forest in 1856. They worked Blue Gate, but, to Knight's disappointment, gave notice to quit mining on the Forest at the end of 1856, as they considered there was no ore to take profitably. Knight granted

Figure 5.31
The little station at Brendon Hill was used as a house until very recently. All of the stations on the WSMR were built to this design, but most now lie in ruins. (Hazel Riley, English Heritage)

a lease to the Plymouth Iron Company in 1857, including most of Honeymead, Picked Stones and parts of Winstichen and Warren Farms. After disappointing results at Picked Stones and Exe Cleave, the Plymouth Iron Company withdrew from the Forest in 1859. A final attempt to work the former Royal Forest for iron was undertaken in the beginning of the 20th century, when the Exmoor Mining Syndicate worked at Burcombe, Picked Stones and Blue Gate from 1910 to 1914. Transporting the ore remained costly – it was taken either to South Molton or Dulverton station by traction engine (Burton 1989; Jones 1997; Orwin *et al* 1997).

The remains of many of these mining trials and operations are still visible on the former Royal Forest, mainly to the south of Simonsbath (Fig 5.27). Spoil heaps and the foundations of miner's cottages and a smithy evoke a time when Cornham Ford housed a small community. The workings at Hangley Cleave show how the 19th-century workings concentrated on the area of earlier workings. A 19th-century adit and linear spoil heap lie at the base of an earlier east–west openwork, which followed the lode at the surface. A 19th-century trial trench lies to the east (Figs 5.32 and 5.33). The proposed Simonsbath-Porlock railway was never completed: it appears that most of the trackbed was constructed – it can be traced as an earthwork along much of its course – but rails were not laid (Fig 5.26).

The Heasley Mill mining area
The area around North Molton on the south-western edge of Exmoor has been a mining area since the 14th century, when the king's copper mine is mentioned. This is probably a reference to Bampfylde mine, straddling the Mole Valley, north of Heasley Mill. Copper was also mined at Higher Mines Wood – farther up the valley and also known as the Britannia mine – and iron ore came from New Florence in Radworthy Cleave, east of Heasley Mill.

Although the mining remains at Bampfylde mostly date from the later mining activity, there are extensive documentary sources for the mine from the 17th and 18th centuries. These include the Barnstaple Port Books, which record copper ore exports from 1696 to 1720, and the North Molton

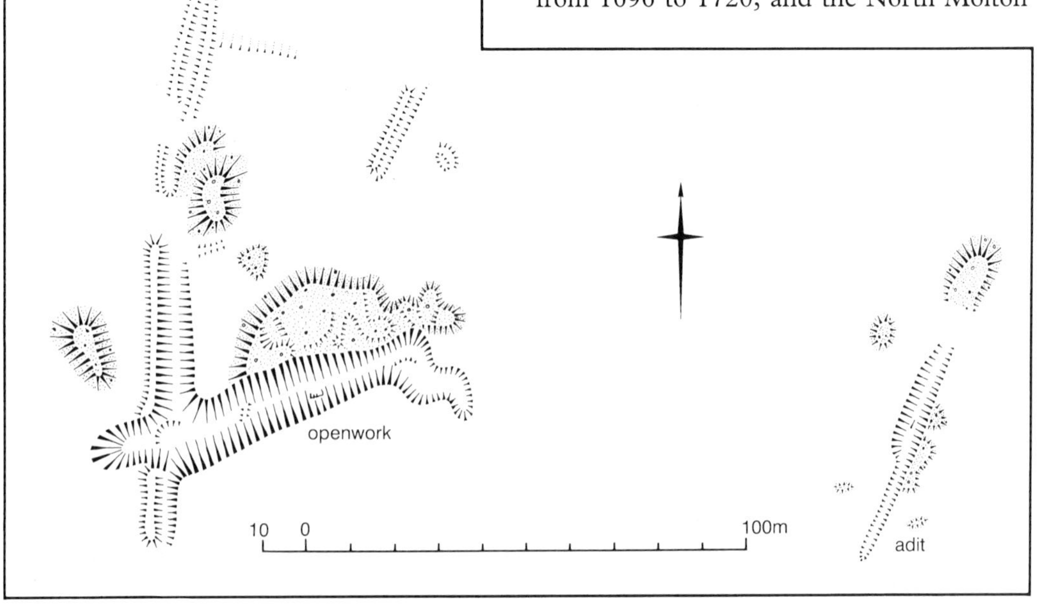

Figure 5.32
Earthwork survey of Hangley Cleave iron mine. A 19th-century adit and spoil heap lies at the base of an earlier openwork, following an east–west lode at the surface.

Figure 5.33
Using GPS to record the
remains of iron mining at
Hangley Cleave. (Hazel
Riley, English Heritage)

parish registers, which give a picture of life at the mine. Many Cornish families moved to the area at this time, attracted by relatively good wages, but the mine worked only intermittently in the later part of the 18th century. In 1809 John Williams, a Cornishman, began work at Higher Mines Wood, which continued to produce copper until about 1840. A period of uncertainty at Bampfylde ended in 1856, with the creation of the Bampfylde Mining Company and the appointment of James Pope as mines captain. Copper was produced until *c* 1870, with iron ore keeping the miners in work from 1873 until 1879 when the mine was closed. The demand for iron ore at this time led to the opening of the Florence (later New Florence) mine, where easily worked iron ore deposits were taken from the valley sides. The mine was worked from 1871 until 1892. The high cost of transport was again a problem, solved here in 1874 by the construction of a tramroad from the mine to the railway near South Molton station. The mine was investigated during World War II, when UK mineral sources were sought: a troop of Canadian Royal Engineers pumped out some of the workings but found no deposits worth exploiting (Dixon 1983; 1997).

The best preserved of these sites is at Bampfylde where both extraction and processing features can be seen (Fig 5.34).

The remains of shafts, spoil dumps, wheel pits and the water courses that powered the waterwheels are strung out along both sides of the Mole Valley. Some of the earlier workings on the South and Bampfylde lodes can be seen on the western side of the valley, while the 'Musick' shaft on the east dates from the 18th century. The leats that fed the 19th-century waterwheels run into the site from the north, and the mine office and mine captain's house lie close to the confluence of the River Mole and a tributary stream. The most impressive building is the crusher/winder house, built in 1855 (Fig 5.35). A crusher for processing copper ore was mounted in the house to the east of the wheel pit; a winder, on pillars to the west of the wheel pit, wound in the 'Engine' shaft. The waste from dressing the copper ore lies in huge linear spoil dumps to the north of the crusher house (Claughton 1997b).

Limekilns and stone quarries

Limeburning and limekilns

Lime has been used both in mortar and for agricultural improvement since the Roman period. Limestone (calcium carbonate) is burnt or calcined to form lime (also known as quicklime). This form of lime can then be used for lime mortar, or spread over fields where soils are too acidic for arable cultivation. Early types of kiln were temporary structures and only lasted for a single firing.

Figure 5.34
Bampfylde mine: earthwork
survey of the central
mining complex. Addi-
tional interpretative infor-
mation from Claughton
1997b.

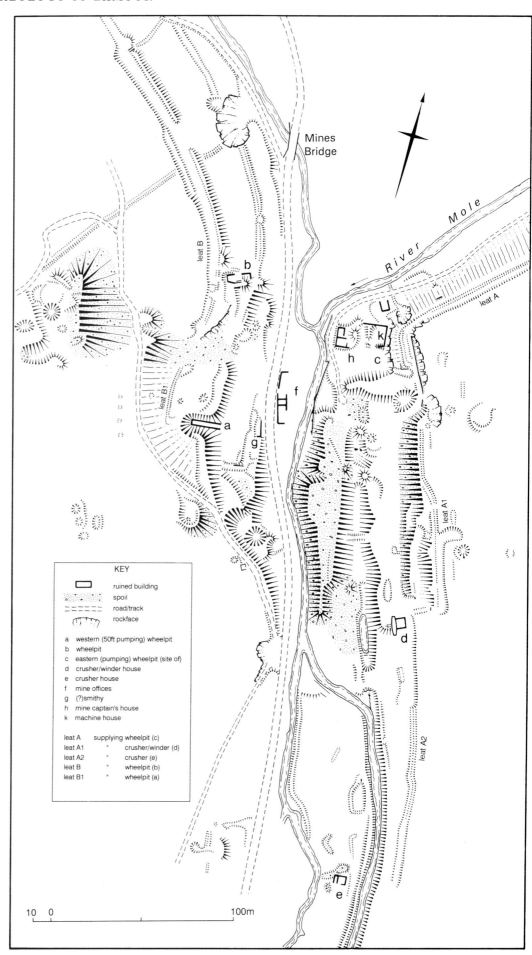

KEY

☐	ruined building
⋮	spoil
– – –	road/track
⌣⌣⌣	rockface

a western (50ft pumping) wheelpit
b wheelpit
c eastern (pumping) wheelpit (site of)
d crusher/winder house
e crusher house
f mine offices
g (?)smithy
h mine captain's house
k machine house

leat A   supplying wheelpit (c)
leat A1   "   crusher/winder (d)
leat A2   "   crusher (e)
leat B   "   wheelpit (b)
leat B1   "   wheelpit (a)

As demand for lime grew in the 18th century, more permanent structures were built, which made continuous firing of the kiln possible. These kilns share three main features: a combustion chamber – the bowl or pot – a draw hole at the base of the bowl, and some form of access to the top of the bowl. Limestone and culm – a mixture of coal and coal dust – was loaded into the bowl. The kiln was fired and the burnt lime was drawn off via the draw hole at the base. The bowl was kept loaded from the top, so that the kiln could be used continuously. Because of this, the whole structure, and in particular the bowl, had to be strong and substantial – hence the survival of so many to the present day (Williams 1989).

The remains of 48 limekilns are extant within the National Park; several others are known of from documentary sources but no longer exist (Holley 1997). Their distribution on Exmoor reflects two things: the underlying geology and the expense of transporting such bulky materials as limestone and coal (Fig 5.36). Ten limekilns lie at the coast, either in harbours – such as those at Porlock Weir or Lynmouth or on the shingle beaches where boats could pull

Figure 5.35
The crusher/winder house at Bampfylde mine is one of the few mine buildings on Exmoor to survive as more than a tumble down ruin. (AA96/6168)
(© Crown copyright.NMR)

Figure 5.36
Exmoor: distribution of limekilns. (Based on an Ordnance Survey map, with permission. © Crown copyright. All rights reserved)

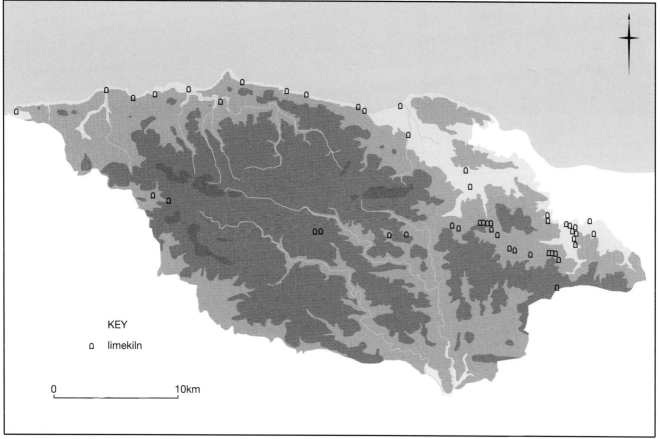

KEY

◻ limekiln

0 ————— 10km

Figure 5.38 (facing page)
Glenthorne: survey of the
limekiln and ancillary
buildings.

up and offload their cargoes – at Bossington beach, Glenthorne and Embelle Woods (Figs 5.37 and 5.38). Most of the remaining limekilns are strung out along the narrow bands of thin limestones of the Middle and Upper Devonian Ilfracombe Beds, which outcrop across the central spine of Exmoor. These include the Leigh Barton, Roadwater and Rodhuish limestones. The Budleigh Salterton Pebble Beds, which contain a significant proportion of limestone, were also exploited where they occur on the eastern edge of the moor. Striking exceptions to this distribution are the limekilns at Brendon Hill, built close to the WSMR, which transported both limestone and coal. The majority of the limekilns on Exmoor date from the late 18th or 19th century.

Most of Exmoor's limekilns are rectangular in plan, with a single draw hole. Circular kilns, such as those on the coast at Heddon's Mouth and Lynmouth tend to have two or more draw holes. The limekilns are generally built into an embankment or cliff. Only the kiln on Bossington beach is freestanding. They are built with local stone – beach cobbles where expedient – the bowl is made of hard stone or brick to withstand the constant heat (Fig 5.37). Those kilns that are not sited directly below a quarry, have an access ramp for loading the bowl with limestone and fuel. Other structures associated with limekilns include the limestone quarries, storage areas and sheds, and transportation. The complex at Glenthorne includes a rectangular kiln with a half arched access tunnel as well as an ordinary draw hole, three ancillary buildings that housed the lime burners upstairs and their boats, tools, fuel and lime downstairs, fronted by a quay built of beach cobbles (Fig 5.38).

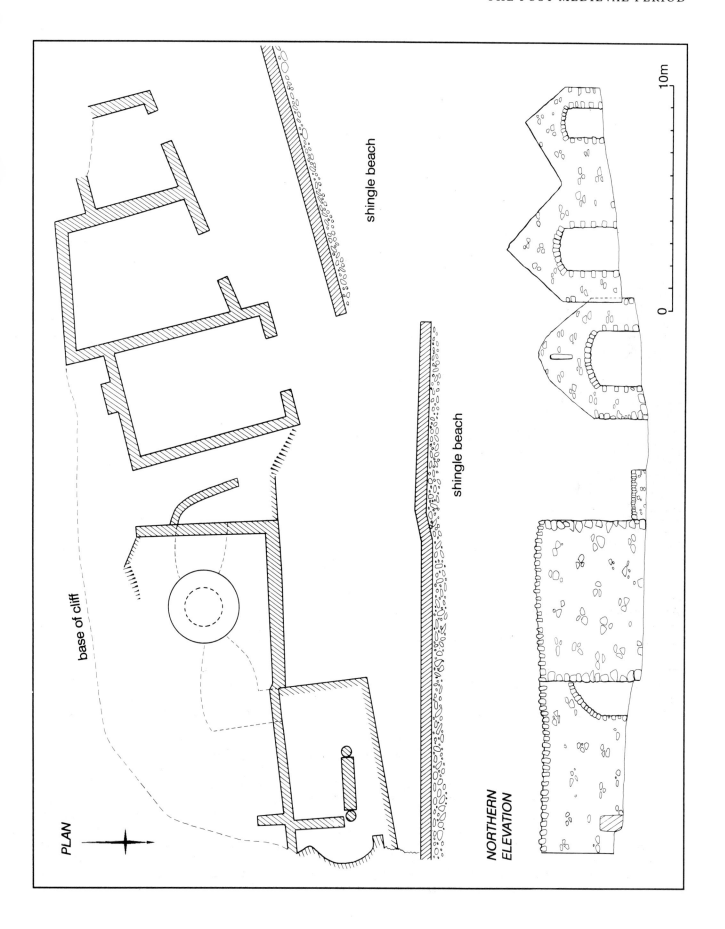

PLAN

base of cliff

shingle beach

shingle beach

NORTHERN
ELEVATION

10m

0

Building stone

There are many examples of small quarries that provided material for local building and roofing scattered across Exmoor, but the interest lies in the farms, cottages and churches themselves (Fig 5.39). The hard grey slates used in St Petrock's church, Parracombe, contrast with the burgundy sandstone found around Porlock and Dunster. Local slate is used in the farm buildings at Leigh Barton and at Treborough most of the houses in the tiny hamlet are hung with slates from the nearby quarry. Industrial buildings also use locally available materials, such as the limekilns at Treborough quarry and on Bossington Beach (Figs 5.39 and 5.37). Beach pebbles were also used to build a series of pillboxes on the beach at Porlock (Chapter 6).

Treborough slate quarries

The Treborough slate quarries, owned for many generations by the Trevelyan family of Nettlecombe Court, exploited a narrow but deep vein of slate of the Devonian Morte Series, which outcrops on the steep slopes below the village of Treborough. Sir Hugh Luttrell ordered 2,000 slate tiles for Dunster Castle in 1426 – records show that the cost of carriage to the castle from Treborough was double that of the slates themselves. A lease of 1674 mentions a "quarry of tylings" and Treborough slates were used to repair the roof of the church at Luccombe after it had blown off in the great storm of 1734 – the boys of the parish were paid 6d to gather up the fallen tiles. More intensive working at the quarry dates from the 19th century; a price list of 1898 gives the main products as: roofing tiles, chimney tops, hearth and shelving stones; steps; staddle stones; window sills; cisterns and headstones (Fig 5.40). Further working took place from 1914 to 1938, when the quarry was finally closed (Allen and Giddens 1983). The existing remains mostly date from the 19th- and 20th-century quarrying. Two deep quarry pits with massive spoil heaps can be seen on an air photograph, taken in 1964 before the east pit was infilled (Fig 5.41). Slate dressing was also carried out on the site, and a waterwheel powered a slate mill for stone cutting. Limestone occurs close to the slate vein and four limekilns lie by the side of the road, which passes through the quarry complex.

Figure 5.39 (facing page) The use of local stone in Exmoor's vernacular architecture gives a pleasing variety to the buildings. St Petrock's church (top left) (AA96/6221); East Luccombe Farm (top right) (BB99/10349); Leigh Barton Farm (middle left) (AA99/06853); Treborough Farm (middle right) (AA00/0372); Treborough limekilns (bottom left) (AA99/07835); pillbox, Porlock (bottom right) (AA97/1456). (© Crown copyright.NMR and © English Heritage)

Figure 5.40 St Peter's churchyard, Treborough: slate gravestone of Isaac Chedzoy, quarry worker. (AA99/07929)

Figure 5.41 Treborough slate quarries: the Ordnance Survey map of 1902 shows the extent of the 19th-century quarries. Now the pits are filled with rubble and overgrown. (Reproduced from the 1902 Ordnance Survey map, Somerset XLVII SE).

Landscape Study 17 Newland limestone quarry

The complex of quarries and limekilns at Newland, near Exford, is a good example of how important the thin beds of limestone, which occur across the central portion of Exmoor, were to the agricultural improvers of the late 18th and 19th centuries (Fig 5.42). The western quarry and three small limekilns were worked from before 1800 until *c* 1868. John Knight, after a fruitless search for workable limestone on his estates, bought Newland quarry in 1832 – previously lime had been transported from the coastal kilns at Combe Martin for Knight's agricultural schemes. He expanded the quarry and by the time John Knight was succeeded by his son Frederic in 1851, Francis Comer and two of his sons, living at nearby Newland Cottage, were all working as lime burners (Warren 1977; Burton 1997).

The eastern quarry was owned and worked by John Comer. Work began sometime about 1850 and by about 1880 it became clear that this deep quarry pit needed some sophisticated engineering to provide power for both hauling the rock out of the quarry and draining the pit itself. A waterwheel 25ft (7.6m) in diameter and 3ft (0.9m) wide was installed in a deep wheelpit to the south of the quarry. It was fed via a leat taken off Pennycombe Water and provided power via a cable to turn a winding drum at the head of the quarry pit. From here the incline down to the quarry was eventually as steep as 1 in 2. Before the installation of the wheel, tubs were hauled out using a hand winch. The quarry pit became so deep that constant drainage was required. A flat-rod system carried power from the same waterwheel to a T-bob mechanism, which transferred power to a pump sited down a deep shaft that connected to the quarry workings. The building that housed this mechanism – the T-bob house – together with an adjacent smithy still stand at the top of the water-filled quarry pit (Fig 5.43).

Figure 5.42
Newland limestone quarry in 1889. (Reproduced from the 1889 Ordnance Survey map, Somerset XLV.11)

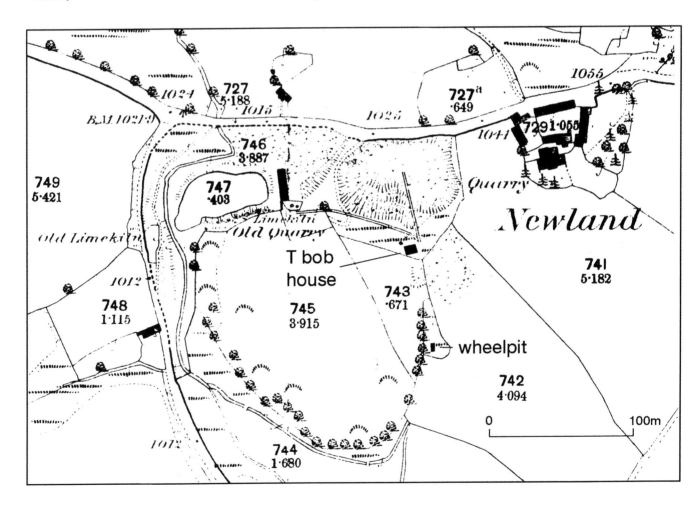

Figure 5.43
The T-bob house at Newland quarry housed the mechanism that hauled the tubs full of limestone out of the deep quarry pit, just behind the stone wall. The winch in the foreground was used for this purpose before the T-bob machinery was installed. (AA00/0362)

At the top of the incline the tracks kinked sharply to convey the tubs of limestone to the limekilns, which were sited on the edge of the now disused western quarry. Next door to the kilns are the lime store and cart shed. Isaac Clarke, owner of the limeworks from 1856–1903, also owned a boat that brought the culm used for firing the kilns from South Wales into Porlock Harbour. At this time a cart load of lime cost about ten shillings. The limeworks remained in use until 1914, when an underground stream broke into the workings and flooded them – fortunately at night.

A story is told in Exford of a casual labourer at the quarry who disappeared. When the kilns were next cleared out the steel toe-caps of his boots were found – the unfortunate chap had fallen in. The story goes that this particular load of lime was used to replaster Withypool chapel in order to give the labourer a Christian burial.

Harbours and holidays

The rugged beauty of Exmoor's coast has caught the imagination of writers and artists since Coleridge and Wordsworth tramped the moors from the Quantocks to Porlock and Lynmouth in the late 18th century. Towering cliffs and limited access to the shore means that the National Park contains within its boundaries only two coastal settlements of note: Lynmouth and Porlock, the latter having its harbour at Porlock Weir. Just outside the western and eastern edges of the park lie Combe Martin and Minehead – the latter an important port in the 17th century. As the fishing industry declined in the 18th and 19th centuries, its place was taken by tourism: a new class of leisured gentlefolk travelled to the area, eager to experience the romantic landscapes of Exmoor and its coast. With the coming of the railways in the 19th century, Exmoor was opened up to yet more travellers, this time with sun and seaside holidays in mind. Hotels, rows of villas and esplanades were built at many small towns on the English coast – even Woody Bay had a pier.

The fishing industry

Fish and shellfish have been an important local resource since people first lived near Exmoor's coast (Chapter 2). As well as offshore fishing, the predominantly shingle nature of the foreshore around Minehead, Porlock Bay and Lynmouth offered opportunities for different methods of taking the fish, with many pools, gullies and stone weirs constructed across the foreshore (Fig 5.44). This area between high and low water has long been recognised and exploited, with documentary references from as early as the 14th and 15th centuries. At Porlock the right to fish the foreshore belonged to the Lord of the Manor, at Lynmouth the foreshore rights were owned by Forde Abbey in Dorset (Gilman 1978; Chanter 1906).

The Bristol Channel has been a busy shipping route since at least the 11th century, with coastal traders and offshore fishing vessels using its ports and small harbours. There was trade with south Wales and southern Ireland, and by the end of the 15th century large vessels fished hundreds of miles off the Exmoor coast, past Ireland and out into the Atlantic. In the early part of the 17th century, large shoals of herring established themselves in the Bristol Channel and for the next two hundred years the small ports and harbours of the north Devon and west Somerset coast prospered because of this.

Figure 5.44
The wide rocky expanse of Minehead Bay provided the ideal environment for fish weirs, pools and gullies to trap fish on the ebb tide.
(NMR 18281/20)
(© Crown copyright. NMR)

Figure 5.45 (facing, top)
This air photograph was taken when an exceptionally low tide exposed several fish weirs on Gore Point, Porlock Weir.
(NMR 18280/17)
(© Crown copyright. NMR)

Figure 5.46 (facing, bottom)
Porlock Weir: fish weirs east of the harbour.
(NMR 18280/24)
(© Crown copyright. NMR)

Red herring houses for drying the fish were built at Porlock Weir and Lynmouth – so called because of their colour after processing. Lynmouth contained many of these fish cellars and curing houses, built close to the shore on both sides of the River Lyn. They were vulnerable to storm damage and none, apparently, has survived. By the beginning of the 19th century the numbers of herring caught had fallen dramatically; numbers of local craft fell and the remaining larger vessels operated from the large ports (Gilman 1978; 1999).

Fish weirs

The archaeological remains of Exmoor's foreshore fisheries survive in the form of the fish weirs, constructed on the foreshore to take advantage of the tidal range of the Bristol Channel. The weirs, built of large beach cobbles, are V-shaped, with the point of the V facing seawards. Nets or baskets were fixed to the seaward end, which was an open channel, to catch fish as the tide ebbed and the weir emptied. Whitebait were commonly caught in Lynmouth's fish weirs in the early 20th century and at Minehead one of the harbour weirs is still in use. The use of fish weirs in the Severn Estuary dates back to medieval times, where some wooden structures have been dated by dendrochronology and radiocarbon methods to perhaps as early as the 9th century AD (Godbold and Turner 1994). The weirs were often controlled by monastic institutions (Bond 1988). Although the weirs on Exmoor's coast have not been dated, the documentary evidence for the leasing of foreshore rights suggests that the foreshore fisheries date from the medieval period through to the 20th century.

Fifteen stone fish weirs survive on Exmoor's coast. An isolated example west of Glenthorne supplied salmon for the big house. At Lynmouth, the remains of two fish weirs survive, one converted to the town's swimming pool. Several fine fish weirs also survive at Porlock Weir. The most spectacular are on Gore Point, where they are ranged along a rocky promontory (Fig 5.45). A large weir lies to the east of the harbour, it has been re-built at least three times (Fig 5.46). This is probably the site of an oyster perch, used in the 19th century by the Pollard brothers, when Porlock Bay was famous for its oysters. The oysters were dredged up out in the Bay, then kept in bags in the weir until needed – an example of an older feature being put to good use.

Figure 5.47
This romantic view of the
Valley of Rocks was
composed in the mid-19th
century. (By courtesy of
Tom Mayberry)

Exmoor as a tourist destination

At the end of the 18th century Exmoor was still a remote and isolated place. It took 15 hours to journey from London to Exeter, but a further 12 hours to cover the 39 miles from Exeter to Barnstaple. This was due to the appalling condition of the roads. Robert Southey, writing in 1799, noted that the Valley of Rocks, Lynmouth, 'would attract many more visitors if the roads were passable by carriages' (quoted in Travis 1994, 138) (Fig 5.47).

The wealthy, thwarted by the Napoleonic wars in their Grand Tours of the continent, sought the picturesque in this country. A few intrepid travellers visited the Exmoor coast in the late 18th century. Coleridge and the Wordsworths were early visitors, tramping the 30 miles from their homes in the Quantocks to Porlock and Lynmouth. The scenery around Culbone inspired Coleridge's Osorio and Kubla Khan; the Rhyme of the Ancient Mariner was composed on a walk over the Brendons from Watchet to Dulverton. The Exmoor coast was also a place for radicals to hide. In 1812 Shelley resided at Lynmouth, where he wrote Queen Mab and distributed his pamphlets by sea and fire balloon (Mayberry 1992; Holmes 1974). Blackmore's *Lorna Doone* brought many visitors to the remote Doone Village by Badgworthy

Water – now recognised as a deserted medieval settlement (Chapter 4).

Although the coastal towns were linked by a steamer service in 1822, Exmoor remained relatively isolated until the advent of rail links in the late 19th century. Minehead station was opened in 1874, and the town became a base for day trippers to Exmoor's beauty-spots, as well as a resort in its own right. Lynmouth was linked to the main line at Barnstaple in 1898, by which time it boasted several hotels and the cliff railway. Dulverton, on the southern edge of the moor, was served by Brushford station. Its fine Victorian hotel was a good base for those wishing to indulge in the traditional Exmoor pursuit of hunting, following the revival of the Devon and Somerset staghounds in 1855.

Two places on Exmoor's rocky western coast were singled out for development. In 1885 the speculator Colonel Lake bought the Martinhoe Estates with a view to developing Woody Bay as a tourist resort, complete with pier, hotels, a cliff railway and branchline to the Barnstaple – Lynmouth railway. The pier, receiving steamers in 1897, was battered by the storms of 1899 and 1900, and broke up. Lake was revealed as a charlatan and went bankrupt. Holdstone Down, which rises to more than 300m, lies on the coast between Heddon's Mouth and Combe Martin. In the late 19th century a Mr Hawkins from Surrey decided to develop the area for select residential use. He purchased 235 acres of the Down from the Inclosure Commissioners and 143 plots and a network of roads were planned. The scheme met with little interest – possibly because of the steep and rocky descent to the shore. The optimistically entitled 'Beach Road' was never built and only two of the plots are occupied today.

The post-medieval landscape

The tranquillity of Exmoor is now part of its special attraction. The remains of its rich and diverse industrial heritage, however, are written across the landscape. Water was harnessed as a source of power. It drove the machines, which pumped out the deep shafts at Bampfylde mine and processed the metal ores won from the ground. Numerous isolated hamlets and farms had their own water wheels. In the small towns of Dulverton and Dunster cloth manufacture relied on the fast flowing streams and rivers. The poor acidic soils of central Exmoor were always lime-hungry. Limekilns are scattered across Exmoor, placed either close to the restricted outcrops of limestone, or at the coast, ready to exchange limestone from south Wales for iron ore from the Brendon Hills and the former Royal Forest of Exmoor. It was at this time that the problems of transporting such bulky material as iron ore and limestone were at their most acute. Ambitious railways and tramways were planned and, in some cases, built. Iron ore was moved from the moor to the coast and, in the case of limestone, the process was reversed.

Landscape Study 18 Coastal industries at Porlock Weir

The little harbour at Porlock Weir has been the port of Porlock since that town became landlocked sometime in the earlier part of the medieval period. Early in the 19th century ambitious schemes were afoot to mine iron ore in the former Royal Forest of Exmoor, then owned by the Knight family. A railway right across the moor was planned. It was to run from Simonsbath in the very heart of the former Royal Forest of Exmoor to Porlock Weir. Here, a new harbour was planned to cope with the expected expansion in trade. None of this came to pass. Negotiations with landowners began and the track bed was constructed across some of the route (Fig 5.26), but no railway was ever built. Porlock Weir remained a small harbour but by the end of the 19th century it was a busy place. Early photographs show the products traded: piles of limestone were unloaded direct from boats onto the beach; coal onto the dockside, with piles of bricks and tiles from the works by the harbour waiting to be shipped out. The nearby woods of Embelle and Culbone were exploited. Pit props and chemical wood – green oak from which alcohol was distilled – were exported to south Wales. Bark was also stripped from the scrub oak to use in the tanyard at Porlock, with hides and leather transported via Porlock Weir. Ship-building was carried out at the harbour. Herrings were a mainstay of the economy, sold locally or delivered around the villages. Surplus fish were salted in barrels or even sent to Bossington where they were used on the fields as fertiliser. Oysters from Porlock Bay were also a valued product. Until the beginning of the 20th century, the tiny harbour had its own fish market.

Behind the harbour lies the tiny hamlet of Worthy (Fig 5.48). A limekiln is tucked into the cliff edge, ready to receive the loads of culm and limestone from south Wales. The processed lime was taken up to the fields on the gentler ground beyond the coast. Foreshore fisheries took advantage of the ebbing tide to take a catch. In the early 19th century the Lovelace family built a splendid, ornate house on the cliff edge. A complicated series of paths and tunnels spiralled around the steep grounds, eventually leading down to a boathouse on the shore. The house has been demolished, the garden paths and terraces are used only by pheasants, and the once delightful boat-house is a rocky ruin.

Above the wooded cliffs is a fertile strip of land that has been exploited by a group of successful farms. They are well placed to take advantage of the maritime climate that dominates here and the other improvements that were taking place on Exmoor. One of these is Silcombe, standing at the head of a remote combe with extensive and dramatic views out of the Bristol Channel. Most of the farm buildings date from the 1860s and reflect the improving influence of the Lovelace family. They replaced an earlier, less regular, farmstead that was largely swept away or rebuilt.

*Figure 5.48 (facing page)
Worthy: unloading
limestone and coal on the
beach in the 19th century.
Overland transport on
Exmoor was a problem,
particularly in the 19th
century as industrialisation
progressed, and trade links
developed across the Bristol
Channel to south Wales.
(© Copyright Jane Brayne)*

*Figure 5.49
Silcombe: the impressive
bank barn built in the
1860s shows the influence
of the wealthy Lovelace
estate and the expected
yield from the estate's
improved farms.
(AA00/0946)*

The Lovelace rebuilding of Silcombe was achieved in a series of building campaigns, but the overall plan was clear from the beginning. It began with the provision of a substantial bank barn built in 1864 to provide a large threshing barn and shippon. Another building from the earlier farmstead, which incorporated the earlier house, was substantially rebuilt to provide a shippon and hayloft. Still another building incorporated stables and open-fronted sheds, and might have included other functions such as implement storage, a root house and chaff house. The present house was built in 1866, presumably when the earlier one was converted to agricultural use. More buildings outside the foldyard have since been removed but were probably pigsties, poultry houses or shelter sheds.

The provision of the very large threshing barn and shippon demonstrates that in the 1860s the farm was in mixed use, growing cereal crops and rearing cattle. There was some dairy production and the keeping of pigs and poultry. The scale of the barn, the provision of two threshing floors and a substantial granary shows, however, that the farm was intended to produce a high proportion of cereal crops, probably including a significant amount of corn for sale as well as grain to supplement livestock feed.

The Lovelace's investment at Silcombe demonstrates confidence in agricultural production there (Fig 5.49). It was well placed to take advantage of the other developments on Exmoor. The lime, burnt in the kilns on the beaches below, fuelled by the charcoal from the coastal woodlands, was destined to be spread on the fields at Silcombe to grow high yields of corn. The harvest would be garnered into the large bank barn with its double threshing floors, the centrepiece of the farmstead.

6
The 20th century

The field archaeology of the 20th century

The 20th century has been a period of continuing change on Exmoor, in a sense completing the process that occurred in the 19th century. Farms were abandoned and agricultural improvements continued. The two global conflicts brought many changes in the form of increased demands on agriculture and the use of the moor for military training. In the second half of the century there has been a period of management, conservation and discovery. The National Park was created in 1954, and for many of its early years the historic environment was not squarely addressed. As we have seen, amateur archaeologists carried on finding new sites and writing about their discoveries (Chapter 1). It was not until the 1980s, however, that a flurry of more extensive recording work was begun, and this has continued up until the present.

Settlement desertion

In the early years of the century a number of isolated farms failed, because of their extreme, marginal locations. This was the continuation of the process of amalgamation that had taken place in the preceding one hundred years. An example of such a recent desertion is Shortacombe, near North Molton. The ruins of this farm stand on a spur overlooking the upper reaches of the Mole valley. All that remains are a disused barn and areas of stone and rubble, yet its fortunes and decline can be charted through the 1800s towards its eventual demise at the beginning of the 20th century (Fig 6.1). The tithe map of 1840 shows two ranges of buildings set on either side of a square yard. By 1890 there were three ranges and tree-planting belts to provide shelter for the farmstead. By 1905 more buildings had been added. Sometime after this the farm was abandoned, because on the most recent map only a single building remains on the site.

In the 19th century there was a period of apparent prosperity for Shortacombe, the maps showing the periodic addition of farm buildings. Its decline was abrupt, however; the reasons for this are not clear, but its isolated location and the poor state of agriculture in the 1890s must have been a contributing factor.

Mike Jones tells of visiting Spangate, a remote hill farm on the slopes of Dunkery. The visit was to update the electoral register. When Mike finally penetrated the overgrown and deeply hollowed lane, he found the ruins of the farm. The inhabitants had moved away and the buildings were collapsing. Spangate is but one example of a common phenomenon. Such recent abandonments evoke strong feelings. Furniture, iron bedsteads and personal possessions lie around among the ruins and in the surrounding hedges. Perhaps the farmer can tell us that his father was born in the house, which is now only a heap of stones. Powerful though these places are, we should remember that they are a single chapter in a long process of settlement change. After all, Exmoor is littered with abandoned farms, whether the farmhouses and cottages of the 19th and 20th centuries or the enclosures of the Iron Age or the isolated hut circles and fields of the Bronze Age. They represent the constant adjustment of the settlement pattern to meet changing needs and environmental conditions. This is the central theme of Exmoor's story. Places such as Shortacombe and Spangate are also the final chapter in that story. For the modern value of property and Exmoor's role as a place of recreation ensure that property on the moor is now too valuable an asset to be allowed to sink back into the earth from which it was built. The settlement pattern has become largely static, although the function of buildings will inevitably continue to change.

The two global conflicts caused a resurgence in agriculture based on the need to produce more food. Large parts of Exmoor

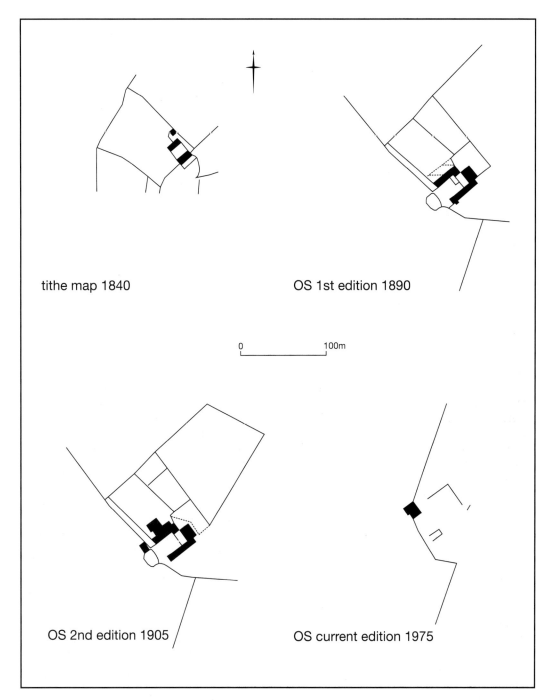

tithe map 1840

OS 1st edition 1890

0   100m

OS 2nd edition 1905

OS current edition 1975

Figure 6.1
Shortacombe: the develop-
ment of the farmstead
during the 19th century
and its abandonment in the
early years of the 20th
century, as shown by the
tithe map of 1840 and the
Ordnance Survey maps of
1890, 1905, and 1975.
North Molton tithe map
reproduced by courtesy of
the Devon Record Office.
(Based on an Ordnance
Survey map, with permis-
sion. © Crown copyright.
All rights reserved)

were pressed into arable cultivation. In the years after World War II this pressure continued, in a climate where domestic food production was a matter of necessity as well as one of national pride. The advent of fully mechanised farming at this time was to reduce the number of people required to work the land, but on Exmoor the continuing importance of livestock farming lessened the impact of such changes. Nevertheless, in the 20th century there has been a steady decline in the number

of people employed on the land, and Exmoor has been part of that general trend.

The industrial exploitation of Exmoor, as we have seen, came to a halt at the end of the 19th century. Renewed interest in the early years of the 20th century, before The Great War, however, caused some of Exmoor's mines to be re-opened. These attempts were dogged by misfortune and a lack of funds (Chapter 5). Examples are Blue Gate, Cornham and Picked Stones, although similar ventures were begun across Exmoor and the Brendon Hills.

By 1912 Rogers Shaft at Bluegate had been reopened, and a tramway constructed to take the ore from the shaft head to the road, from whence it was conveyed to South Molton by traction engine. The tramway trackbed is still visible running across the workings dug in the 1850s. The presence of a large body of ore was proved here, but transport and pumping costs were eventually to prove prohibitive so that all work stopped in 1913. At Picked Stones a tramway was installed in 1912 and this was connected to

the mine by an incline the following year. Transportation was again an obstacle and production ceased in July 1914.

This was not the end of the story, for the beginning of World War II led to another reassessment of some of Exmoor's mineral reserves. At New Florence Mine, soldiers of the Canadian army explored the workings to assess whether it was worth re-opening them. They were judged to be unviable and so came to an end nearly 2,000 years of iron exploitation on Exmoor.

Figure 6.2
This air photograph of Bossington Hill, taken in 1946, shows the remains of a triangular track where tanks drove while firing at a moving target. (RAF: 1069/UK/1655 3017) (© Crown copyright 1946/MOD. Reproduced with the permission of the Controller of Her Majesty's Stationery Office)

Figure 6.3
This World War II pillbox,
built of beach pebbles,
stands on the shingle ridge
behind Porlock Bay and
looks out over the Bristol
Channel. It was part of a
network of coastal defences
built to defend the Vale of
Porlock from seaborne
invasion. (AA97/1458)
(© Crown copyright.NMR)

The field archaeology of World War II

During World War II many of England's remote areas were requisitioned for military use. Exmoor was no exception, and much of the former Royal Forest was occupied for infantry and artillery training. Other activities went on, such as the development and trialling of rocket technology. A tented camp was created on Treborough Common for American GIs. In addition outlying areas such as Molland Common, Anstey Common, Holdstone Down and North Hill were requisitioned for training purposes. On Holdstone Down the remains of a tank turret and a number of scoops in the ground surface are all that remain of an episode of artillery training. The memories of big guns being stationed here and firing into the former Royal Forest leave no trace in the landscape.

An extensive tank training ground was established on North Hill, Selworthy Beacon and Bossington Hill. A concrete approach road, 6km long, was built from Minehead to the western end of Bossington Hill to service the area. Accommodation and engineering complexes were built at the eastern end of the ranges, while farther west, farms were evacuated and three target railways were built each with a corresponding triangular tank circuit. The tanks would be driven around these circuits, while the target would be conveyed from one end of the railway to the other. They were designed to simulate battle conditions for tank warfare. The remains of the circuits, target railways and associated buildings can still be seen. A large number of other structures were built, most appear to be observation posts – some were associated with the target railways – many were built to observe other parts of the training grounds. Some structures appear to be gun emplacements probably for artillery practice. Earthwork obstacles were built for tank training and the whole landscape was transformed into a series of training devices to prepare the allied tank crews for the invasion of Europe (Fig 6.2). The only standing World War II building on North Hill is the transmitter/receiver block of a radar station of the coast defence chain home low (CD/CHL) type. It is a rare and well-preserved example.

The Exmoor training grounds were part of a much wider system of training facilities across north Devon and west Somerset. There were practice invasion beaches at Woolacombe with man-made sand dunes, concrete landing craft at Braunton Burrows, and a coastal firing range at Doniford, in use since the 1920s (Wasley 1994; Hawkins 1996).

Defensive installations were constructed on a minor scale across Exmoor. The coast was defended by a network of pillboxes at Porlock Bay many of which still survive (Fig 6.3). Pillboxes were also built inland at Raleigh's Cross and Vale (Roadwater). In Treborough quarry and at Felon's Oak were underground explosives stores for use by secret groups of the home guard. Anti-glider ditches were dug on Martinhoe Common, and a small gun battery was built on Countisbury Hill. At Blackpits a searchlight was installed with a group of Nissen huts, supposedly to aid aircraft navigation. On Stent Hill, near Culbone, a group of brick buildings are all that remain of an installation whose purpose was to confuse enemy navigation.

This complex was supported by a group of Nissen huts beside the toll road in Culbone Woods, and defended by an anti-aircraft battery nearby. The Nissen hut bases and platforms for anti-aircraft guns lie close to the barrows and stone row of the Neolithic and Bronze Age, a poignant reminder of the richness of Exmoor's history.

A number of aircraft crashed on Exmoor during World War II. These were crashes due either to navigational error or poor weather conditions. Although they usually leave no trace in the landscape, on Martinhoe Common a section of rebuilt hedge bank is accounted for locally by a plane that crashed through it; a similar example exists above Lower Sherdon.

Landscape Study 19 The Exmoor firing ranges

During World War II the north-eastern part of the former Royal Forest was requisitioned for training purposes. The area was closed to the public and access was only permitted at certain times for those shep-

herding livestock. The main activity carried out was artillery practice, and for this purpose guns were often positioned outside the former Royal Forest – on North Molton Ridge or Holdstone Down for examples –

and the shells fired over the intervening countryside into the ranges. The targets varied, but included the farms of Tom's Hill and Larkbarrow, constructed by the Knight family in the 1860s. Both were destroyed and remain only as evocative ruins today (Fig 6.4).

The physical traces of the army's time here can be found in the landscape, but these slight survivals do not reflect the intensity of wartime activity. The remains are varied and include the bases of several Nissen huts forming a camp near Slocombeslade. At Elsworthy an observation post, made of timber and corrugated iron, is set into the hillside overlooking the impact area at Larkbarrow. The deeply rutted surface of the moor around Tippacott Ridge shows where the military vehicles gained access to the ranges. Numerous small pits, dug outs and mortar positions were constructed in the remote combes. Several of the prehistoric monuments are marked with Antiquity Stars – metal stars set on tall iron posts – which were put up by the army to enable the gunnery crews to distinguish between archaeological monuments and targets.

Examples survive on a cairn near Drybridge Combe and at Alderman's Barrow.

On Brendon Common there is a memorial to Colonel Maclaren who commanded the chemical weapons troops of the Royal Engineers. He was killed there while demonstrating a device. The weapon in question was probably a 5-inch rocket, which had been developed and trialled on Exmoor as the delivery system for chemical weapons. Although the 5-inch rocket was never used to convey chemical weapons it played a significant part in the D-day landings where multiple rocket launchers were deployed as a beach barrage weapon.

Close by are the remains of a concrete and brick structure surrounded by a network of concrete posts. The function of this complex is uncertain, but it might have been built for the trials of the rocket launcher. The Royal Engineers blew up the building after the war. Once at the heart of secrecy and witness to technological developments, Brendon Common is now a place of tranquil beauty, with only the Maclaren monument and a few isolated concrete posts showing what once took place there (Fig 6.5).

Figure 6.5
Brendon Common: a network of concrete posts surround a demolished building, probably used during weapons testing on the ranges (AA96/6213)
(© Crown copyright. NMR)

Figure 6.4 (facing page) Larkbarrow Farm was used as a target for artillery practice during World War II. The ranges of the farmyard and its beech shelter belt can be seen. The field to the left of the farm is pock-marked with shell holes.
(NMR 15608/21)
(© Crown copyright. NMR)

Managing Exmoor's past for the future: the role of the Exmoor National Park Authority

by Veryan Heal, former Principal Conservation Officer, Historic Environment, Exmoor National Park Authority

The legacy of thousands of years of human activity in the landscape is vulnerable and irreplaceable, at risk from current land use by farming, forestry, development and recreation. The decisions we make and the actions we take can destroy in minutes the inheritance of millennia. Its future is in our hands. On Exmoor, the National Park Authority (ENPA) has a leading role to play in securing that future.

Exmoor was designated a National Park in 1954, under the provisions of the 1949 Wildlife and Access to the Countryside Act, with the primary purpose of preserving and enhancing its 'natural beauty'. It was not until the Environment Act (1995) was passed that the human dimension of the landscape was explicitly recognised, when the phrase 'cultural heritage' was included. This has helped to focus more attention on the historic environment of Exmoor. In 1997 all the English National Parks became free-standing Authorities, independent of the County Councils, though within the framework of local government.

From its establishment in 1954 until August 1991 the National Park had no specialist staff dedicated to the historic environment and relied heavily upon the archaeology and historic buildings advisory services of Devon and Somerset County Councils. In addition, the Exmoor Archaeology Advisory Group was set up in the 1980s and met quarterly to provide advice for the National Park Officer. In 1999 the meetings of the Group were replaced by an archaeological forum, at which those engaged in work on Exmoor, for the Authority or as partners, present and discuss their findings and ideas.

In 1991 ENPA established the post of archaeologist, followed in 1996 by the post of Historic Buildings Officer, both with considerable financial support from English Heritage. This Historic Environment Team provides curatorial cover for Exmoor and is located, with other environmental specialists, in the Park Management Department at Dulverton. The Department provides the National Park Officer with advice on the management of the land owned by the Park and on development control and policy. Its staff give advice to the public about the care and conservation of the historic and natural environment.

The Exmoor National Park Authority and the historic environment

By comparison with other areas of the South West, Exmoor has received relatively little attention from antiquarians and early 20th-century archaeologists. The area has had only a slight reputation for its historic environment and was regarded as something of an untouched wilderness by many and rather a black hole by most of the archaeological world. Exmoor's location in the outback of two counties, its little-known and relatively slight antiquarian records and the lack of concerted focus on the area had militated against recognition of its real wealth. A small number of discerning writers, however, had drawn attention to Exmoor's potential and some had ventured into the field, but the records of fieldwork and archaeological registers was patchy and sparse (Chapter 1).

Chanter and Worth, writing in 1906, bemoaned the destruction of Exmoor's stone monuments and cairns by farmers, road menders and hedgers. Their view was that 'whatever antiquarian work is to be done... must be quickly done, and in any event the district affords a fruitful and little-worked field for operations' (Chanter and Worth 1906, 552). Nearly 90 years elapsed before the appointment of an archaeological curator for Exmoor and the establishment of this survey addressed that need.

The stone monuments of Exmoor have been, perhaps, the exceptional attraction for antiquarians and archaeologists, indeed the stone settings are considered by many to be unique. The RCHME stone monuments survey (Quinnell and Dunn 1992) is a considerable and valuable achievement, providing accurate information on the location, form and condition of the sites.

The combined experience of that survey, a pilot project carried out in the 1980s and an air photographic transcription of the whole of the National Park made the case for a major survey of Exmoor. Shortly afterwards, the RCHME's archaeological survey of Exmoor from which this publication stems, was begun (Chapter 1).

Figure 6.6
Porlock Marsh 1999: the
recent breach in the shingle
ridge is gradually turning
Porlock Marsh into a
salt-marsh. The earthworks
of the 18th-century duck
decoy are clearly visible
(foreground).
(NMR 18530/13)

This project has been of incalculable benefit to the understanding of Exmoor and the well-being of the physical evidence for its past, it has also provided a sound database for the ENPA.

Chanter and Worth were also ahead of their time in recognising, despite the depredations, that the importance of Exmoor was for its generally high level of preservation: 'Especially is it interesting, as showing how much must have been lost elsewhere in the county, as the tide of agriculture flowed' (1906, 552). Nearly a century later the national Monuments at Risk Survey (MARS) reported: 'National Parks stand out as exceptionally important for the future because of the relatively slow destruction rates suffered in recent decades and the high level of areal survival represented' (Darvill and Fulton 1998, 215). It is clear from all the recent work that the quality of preservation is outstanding, on the moor, in woodland and even in improved ground. This means that fieldwork, geophysical survey, sampling and excavation might yield high quality results.

Much of the work on the historic environment of Exmoor has so far, quite intentionally, concentrated on building up the record for the area by survey and recording. Some projects have delved deeper, such as the survey of Porlock Marsh in 1995, the recording of the West Somerset Mineral Railway complex, the Greater Exmoor Early Iron-working Project and the National Trust Vernacular Buildings Survey of the Holnicote Estate.

Palaeoenvironmental work

Exmoor has good potential for palaeoenvironmental survey and sampling, building on the small amount of past work in this field (Straker and Crabtree 1995). Current work has produced Neolithic dates for trees engulfed by peat at between 350m and 400m OD and other work has shown considerable depths of peat in valley contexts spanning millennia (R Fyfe, personal communication). There are many locations at which buried soils, or structures buried by peat formation, could be fruitfully examined. It is intended to continue a programme of investigation of these and other suitable deposits, in order to build a fuller picture of the environmental context of human activity on Exmoor and the impact of that activity on the natural world.

Porlock Marsh lies behind a pebble ridge separating it from the foreshore of Porlock Bay (Fig 6.6) (Chapter 2). An imminent threat of marine inundation was recognised in 1994. This meant that the surface archaeology and the buried deposits of the marsh would be likely to become flooded and inaccessible for survey or investigation. The area is of archaeological importance not only for its visible archaeology, but also for the deep deposits that have built up beneath a landscape of fields intersected by drainage ditches carrying the water of the marsh out to the sea. These deposits held high potential for palaeoenvironmental sampling and possible cultural remains.

The threat was such that funding was obtained from English Heritage for an evaluation of both the visible archaeology and Marsh deposits in advance of the anticipated flooding. During early 1995 the fieldwork was carried out, using a powered auger for the core sampling, and in 1996 the breaching of the ridge occurred.

The results of the sampling and analysis of fossil pollen and other palaeoenvironmental information show a long record of vegetation development and coastal change, dating from nearly 10,000 years ago. Within this, there is evidence that might point to human activity and land use, causing changes in the environment apparent after c 7,000 years ago (Canti *et al* 1995). Monitoring has been carried out since the sea breached the shingle ridge. This has revealed palaeochannels, ditches and posts extending beneath and seaward of the former ridge. In one channel the partial remains of an aurochs were discovered, excavated and radiocarbon-dated to the Bronze Age (McDonnell 1998), making this arthritic elderly male one of the latest examples known from Britain.

Surveys for management

The ENPA is carrying out a programme of surveys for management of its own estate: nearly 5,000 hectares of open moor, woods and improved land. The surveys, completed by consultants and the RCHME, provide location information and an assessment of the condition and threats to the historic environment of our own holdings. Farms in the ENPA Farm Conservation Scheme have also been surveyed. These surveys, some part-funded by English Heritage, have been carried out on the moor and in woodland and help to inform management, as well as adding to the record. In some locations the archaeological record has been increased by nearly 500%.

In 1992 the discovery of a late prehistoric enclosure in a larch plantation at Timberscombe Wood (Fig 6.7) led to its purchase by the ENPA, in order to manage it in the interests of the site. The trees were cleared using horses to take out the timber, and the monument will remain in a clearing while the surrounding broadleaf woodland regenerates.

Woodland surveys were carried out during the 1990s by the ENPA and the National Trust. The preliminary survey of Horner Wood, near Porlock, revealed not only the wealth of woodland archaeology, but also the potential for finding large unrecorded sites. In the margins of Horner Wood on Ley Hill a presumed late prehistoric enclosure and a well preserved deserted medieval settlement were recorded for the first time (Chapter 4). Subsequent excavation on the deserted medieval settlement has produced radio-

Figure 6.7
The recently discovered prehistoric enclosure at Timberscombe.
(NMR 18241/31)
(© Crown copyright.NMR)

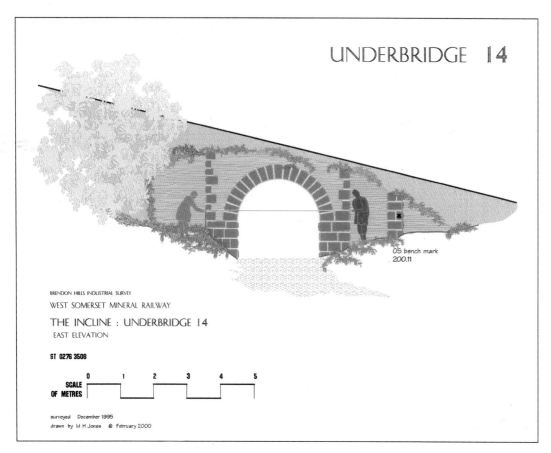

UNDERBRIDGE 14

BRENDON HILLS INDUSTRIAL SURVEY
WEST SOMERSET MINERAL RAILWAY

THE INCLINE : UNDERBRIDGE 14
EAST ELEVATION

ST 0276 3508

SCALE OF METRES 0 1 2 3 4 5

surveyed December 1995
drawn by M H Jones © February 2000

OS bench mark 200.11

Figure 6.8
The incline, underbridge No.14: part of the detailed recording work carried out for ENPA by Mike Jones. (By courtesy of Exmoor National Park Authority and M Jones) (© Copyright ENPA)

carbon dates of the late 13th to 14th century. These sites demonstrate the quality of preservation of archaeological remains in woodland. The date obtained from the deserted buildings on Ley Hill overlaps with the date produced by dendrochronology for a cruck construction cottage on another part of the Holnicote Estate, which was dated to 1316 (Richardson 1999, and personal communication).

The Brendon Hill mines and mineral railway are one of the outstanding archaeological features of Exmoor, and with help from English Heritage and the Rural Development Commission, the ENPA has been able to commission a survey of the extant remains. The incline at Brendon Hill, the centrepiece of the West Somerset Mineral Railway, was subsequently purchased by the ENPA. The survey is drawing to its conclusion and represents a major contribution to our appreciation of the historic landscape (Fig 6.8). This work will inform the long-term management of, and access to, the complex.

Conservation

There have been opportunities to establish schemes for the better conservation and management of both archaeological sites and historic buildings. In partnership with English Heritage, ENPA has been carrying out works of repair, consolidation and protection of nationally important monuments. The RCHME survey has produced detailed plans of many of these monuments. A long-running aspect of the scheme has been an erosion monitoring exercise, designed to record rates of erosion or recovery at selected monuments. In 1996 the Conservation Areas Partnership Scheme was established, which ran until 1999. This focused on the proper repair of traditional farms and farmsteads, whose buildings are repositories of a great deal of the social, economic and technological history of Exmoor.

The National Trust's Vernacular Buildings Survey of the Holnicote Estate

This project reaffirms the continuity between the archaeological traces of deserted buildings and those still standing today. Through meticulous observation and recording the survey has produced a building-by-building record of domestic houses, ancillary buildings and farmsteads of the estate. This has revealed the great age of some, overlapping the dates for deserted medieval settlements, the remarkable preservation of historic fabric behind apparently more recent exteriors, particularly notable at Selworthy Green, (Fig 6.9) and the sheer wealth of the historic building resource on Exmoor.

Although much of our vernacular architecture appears unremarkable or undistinguished, it holds important evidence for the way of life and technology of our Exmoor forebears, which is far more informative than the chocolate box exterior might lead us to believe. Further study of the character and antiquity of the buildings of Exmoor is a high priority for future work leading towards the understanding and management of Exmoor's historic environment.

The Greater Exmoor Early Ironworking Project

The mining of iron ore on Exmoor is well documented during the 19th century and this has been studied both in the former Royal Forest and on the Brendon Hills (Jones 1997) (Chapter 5), but the early history of mining on Exmoor had been neglected. The Greater Exmoor Early Ironworking Project, jointly funded by the ENPA and the National Trust, set out to establish the nature and date of iron mining and smelting. A number of new smelting sites have been discovered. Radiocarbon dates show that some of these sites are Romano-British, one is early medieval and others date from the medieval and post-medieval periods (Juleff 2000). With enthusiastic assistance from the Exmoor Mines Research Group and the Tiverton Archaeological Group, the project continues to investigate and sample very well preserved sites and collate the data, setting a new standard for the investigation of iron-working sites.

Collaboration and partnership

Towards the end of the 20th century there has been a flurry of projects on Exmoor. Some of them have made invaluable contributions to our understanding of the wider picture, and some have illuminated particular details. For the future, it is important that the improved information on the historic environment, which flows from this recent work, is integrated in the development of management and planning policies. The new information will enable themes for research and investigation to be identified and prioritised. A database for both

archaeology and historic buildings, compatible with the Authority's other databases, is under development, and will enable the historic environment to be better linked to planning, land use and recreation issues.

The role of the authority's archaeologist has been to attract others to work on Exmoor, to establish productive partnerships with the national agencies and local groups, and to identify and prioritise themes of research and management, while seizing opportunities that have arisen. During the 1990s archaeological activity has increased on Exmoor and with it public awareness of the rich historic landscape.

One of the first major archaeological events to be held by the ENPA was a symposium in 1992, published as Exmoor's Industrial Archaeology (Atkinson (ed) 1997). This occasion brought together a range of active participants in the subject and led to the formation of the Exmoor Mines Research Group (EMRG). This was the forerunner of a number of partnerships. Exmoor has been the forum for fruitful co-operation between national and regional bodies, university departments, private consultants and local groups. English Heritage (EH); the Royal Commission on the Historical Monuments of England (RCHME); the National Trust (NT); the Exmoor Mines Research Group (EMRG), the Rural Development Agency (RDA), local groups and landowners have all played a significant part. The Authority depends upon establishing co-operative relationships in order to pursue and achieve its purposes and we have seen both benefits to the field archaeology and enhancement of its appreciation and enjoyment by the local community and wider public as a result. In managing and interpreting the historic landscape it is very important to avoid artificial divisions between archaeological sites and historic buildings and the existence of an integrated historic environment team is an important guard against this. With the help of EH the Authority has been able to establish such a team.

The widening and deepening of our understanding of Exmoor's historic environment and the opportunities for enjoyment and education that can be created from this understanding must be the targets for the future. The richness of Exmoor's past is an integral part of its present wealth and we must continue to work together to ensure that our successors inherit and enjoy no less valuable a legacy.

Understanding Exmoor's historic landscape?

When standing on the remote moorland ridge of The Chains you might use the word 'wilderness' to describe what you see. Look again and you can make out the silhouette of a skyline barrow; a little farther afield a clump of rushes hide a prehistoric stone setting. Not far from where you stand a 19th-century field bank turns below the crest of the hill; on it is a solitary beech tree bent by the prevailing wind, the remnant of a long-dead hedge. So even here in this remote and barren landscape there is the evidence of human endeavour spanning 4500 years, if we take the time to see it.

Perhaps the feeling of wilderness is enhanced by Exmoor's isolation. The thin spread of farms makes the landscape seem more remote than it really is, yet even the far flung sheltered combes and spurs show the signs of abandoned farms and enclosures or the traces of old fields. Nearly all of the ancient oak woodlands contain pollarded and coppiced trees, boundaries, and charcoal burning platforms. Even the rocky beaches have a scatter of fish weirs, bearing witness to centuries of activity. As we have seen, these traces form the underlying strand in the landscape that helps us chart its development.

The remains of the more ancient past provide a huge challenge to students of the historic environment, for they manifest themselves in a subtle and understated way. As Hazel Eardley-Wilmot remarks, past generations 'quietly melted into the landscape' (1983, 69). At White Ladder, for example, the prehistoric stone row comes and goes as the peat swells and shrinks with the seasons. Other prehistoric stone monuments are equally hard to find and are very vulnerable. Even the most innocent of agencies – such as a sheep rubbing against them – will eventually lead them to topple over and become forgotten.

The language of the ancient landscape is often difficult to comprehend. There is a lack of dating evidence from Exmoor, so that we currently rely on the broadest of chronological frameworks. The purpose of some of the monuments, such as stone settings, is unknown. Their occurrence with other monuments such as small cairns has been noted, but what does it represent? We are still a long way from seeing how this ancient landscape worked.

Recent periods continue to defy our understanding. On Winsford Hill and the other commons around the former Royal Forest, low banks and ridge and furrow show us how ambitious those medieval farmers were. Massive areas of apparently untouched moorland bear the scars of the medieval plough and were once tracts of fields. What were the processes that led to this enclosure of the commons; who controlled and organised it? These are not just academic questions, neither are they

easily or unequivocally answered; they are fundamental issues in resolving how Exmoor has evolved. They are relevant to everyone who lives and works on Exmoor today, the inheritors and custodians of that landscape.

The recent upsurge in archaeological work has emphasised the richness and diversity of Exmoor's remains. Fieldwork has produced new revelations: from the spectacular enclosure at Timberscombe to the well preserved deserted medieval settlement at Ley Hill. No doubt more discoveries such as these are waiting to happen, not only on the moor itself, but also in the woodlands that surround it.

Many of Exmoor's monuments are remarkably well preserved, due to the relatively low intensity of agricultural operations, compared to other parts of Devon and Somerset. Examples of this are the survival of the fragile prehistoric stone settings and the discovery of very slight Bronze Age house platforms within 19th-century enclosure fields. Even among Exmoor's historic buildings recent work by the National Trust has demonstrated that earlier buildings survive in later structures. The discovery of sites is only the beginning of the process of understanding what they represent and how we should best conserve them for the future. The survival of such high quality information should provide a valuable resource for further study and research into the historic environment.

Some sites are clearly significant although they currently defy our understanding. An example is on Horner's Neck (Fig 6.10) where the earthwork remains of a group of buildings occupy a giddy and isolated position overlooking the precipitous slopes of the Lyn Gorge. Superficially the building remains are similar to an abandoned farmstead, but their position is very extreme, and no farm is documented here. A small-scale excavation by Exeter University failed to reveal any dating evidence that one would expect from a late medieval or post-medieval farm. So might the buildings on Horner's Neck mark an earlier complex, the size of the buildings suggesting that the site was of high status? Whatever its true purpose, it is a unique survival.

Recent work has repeatedly changed the way we view the past. The work on early iron working by ENPA and the National Trust is enabling us to glimpse the importance of Exmoor's iron ore reserves in the late prehistoric period – it is beginning to change the way in which we see the late prehistoric landscape. The very recent past has its own contribution to make. The remains of chemical weapons technology on Brendon Common and the World War II tank training range on North Hill, are important and rare survivals.

Figure 6.11
Woodbarrow Hangings:
barrows on the sky-line
are a familiar part of
Exmoor's landscape.
(AA00/0961)

Exmoor's archaeological remains are a testimony to how busy the landscape has been. They bear witness to a continual struggle to adapt and survive sometimes in harsh conditions. Often they hint at the importance of places at particular periods. The massive promontory work on Wind Hill, Countisbury, still dominates the modern landscape and hints at the former importance of the place. It is no coincidence that it overlooks Lynmouth – one of the few landing places on this otherwise inhospitable coast.

All of these sites, of whatever period, are important in their own right. Taken as individual monuments, each one plays a part in adding to our knowledge of Exmoor's past. When they are put together they begin to show us how our ancestors exploited and used the landscape and formed what we see today. They also contribute to our understanding of the wider landscape of Devon and Somerset. Indeed some are considered to be nationally important.

It is impossible to separate Exmoor's archaeological remains from the landscape we see today. A sweeping Exmoor skyline is dominated by the Bronze Age barrows strung out along it – they are part of the topography (Fig 6.11). In the same way if, when caught in a moor mist, you encounter a ridge top barrow, you feel that the monument has always been there – it owns the landscape, and you are the fleeting intruder. During recent years we have seen how rich Exmoor's historic landscape is. As this work progresses we become better equipped to ask the right questions of the past. In many cases the answers to those questions still elude us, but understanding the past and the developing sequence it represents is a lengthy and slow process. This book is a stage in that journey. By characterising and illustrating the rich diversity of Exmoor's field archaeology it seeks to foster more investigation and analysis, so that we can better understand the people who have formed the Exmoor of today. But most of all it is a celebration of Exmoor's subtle historic landscape.

Appendix 1
Site gazetteer

The sites located on the distribution maps are listed below with their National Grid Reference and NMR number. The detailed survey records for each site are available from the NMR at Swindon via this number. Many of the sites in this list are on privately owned land and permission for access should be sought.

Stone rows

(Fig 2.11)

Cheriton Ridge
SS 7517 4379
SS 74 SE 90

Culbone
SS 8343 4738
SS 84 NW 20

Furzehill
SS 7382 4396
SS 74 SW 90

Madacombe
SS 8313 4258
SS 84 SW 125

Porlock Common
SS 8456 4465
SS 84 SW 82

Thornworthy Little Common
SS 7128 4387
SS 74 SW 85

White Ladder
SS 7323 3722
SS 73 NW 20

Wilmersham Common
SS 8567 4195
SS 84 SE 18

Stone circles

(Fig 2.11)

Porlock Allotment
SS 8451 4466
SS 84 SW 10

Withypool
SS 8383 3430
SS 83 SW 1

Stone settings

(Fig 2.11) (Roman numerals are those given in Quinnell and Dunn 1992)

Almsworthy Common
SS 8430 4171
SS 84 SW 3

Badgworthy Lees
SS 7848 4468
SS 74 SE 23

Beckham Hill
SS 8063 4238
SS 84 SW 18

Brendon Two Gates
SS 7659 4363
SS 74 SE 13

The Chains Valley
SS 7491 4177
SS 74 SW 2

Chapman Barrows
SS 6979 4333
SS 64 SE 2

Cheriton Ridge
SS 7481 4337
SS 74 SW 141

Cheriton Ridge
SS 7501 4439
SS 74 SE 142

Cheriton Ridge I
SS 7499 4437
SS 74 SW 92

Cheriton Ridge II
SS 7489 4428
SS 74 SW 40

Cheriton Ridge IV
SS 7541 4330
SS 74 SE 15

Clannon Ball
SS 7591 4364
SS 74 SE 18

Codsend Moors
SS 8828 4114
SS 84 SE 20

East Pinford
SS 7966 4273
SS 74 SE 7

Furzehill Common
SS 7332 4450
SS 74 SW 33

Furzehill Common I
SS 7348 4391
SS 74 SW 59

Furzehill Common II
SS 7373 4424
SS 74 SW 32

Furzehill Common V
SS 7389 4470
SS 74 SW 35

Halscombe
SS 7699 3838
SS 73 NE 36

Hoaroak
SS 7496 4264
SS 74 SW 9

Hoaroak
SS 7397 4378
SS 74 SW 34

Hoaroak Hill
SS 7444 4394
SS 74 SW 105

Hoccombe Combe
SS 7866 4441
SS 74 SE 6

Hoccombe Hill I
SS 7809 4344
SS 74 SE 86

Hoccombe Hill II
SS 7706 4368
SS 74 SE 27

Hoccombe North
SS 8312 4387
SS 84 SW 48

Horsen
SS 7906 3736
SS 73 NE 11

Kittuck
SS 8207 4388
SS 84 SW 47

Lanacombe
SS 7799 4256
SS 74 SE 150

Lanacombe
SS 7801 4261
SS 74 SE 108

Lanacombe I
SS 7811 4272
SS 74 SE 49

Lanacombe II
SS 7841 4288
SS 74 SE 50

Lanacombe III
SS 7861 4301
SS 74 SE 51

Lanacombe IV
SS 7864 4316
SS 74 SE 88

Long Chains Combe North
SS 7456 4235
SS 74 SW 94

Long Chains Combe South
SS 7438 4209
SS 74 SW 95

Longstone Barrow
SS 7077 4252
SS 74 SW 47

Manor Allotment
SS 8018 4369
SS 84 SW 135

Molland Common
SS 8145 3105
SS 83 SW 58

Pig Hill I
SS 7562 4443
SS 74 SE 85

Pig Hill II
SS 7584 4488
SS 74 SE 87

Porlock Allotment I
SS 8336 4378
SS 84 SW 27

Porlock Allotment II
SS 8409 4435
SS 84 SW 81

Squallacombe I
SS 7381 3822
SS 73 NW 18

Squallacombe II
SS 7361 3800
SS 73 NW 32

Swap Hill
SS 8055 4260
SS 84 SW 39

Thorn Hill
SS 7279 4343
SS 74 SW 3

Tom's Hill
SS 8017 4328
SS 84 SW 1

Trout Hill I
SS 7941 4322
SS 74 SE 1

Trout Hill II
SS 7956 4313
SS 74 SE 5

Trout Hill III
SS 7939 4288
SS 74 SE 89

Westermill
SS 8224 4093
SS 84 SW 14

Wilmersham Common
SS 8600 4206
SS 84 SE 93

Winaway
SS 7226 4376
SS 74 SW 1

Withycombe Ridge
SS 7906 4452
SS 74 SE 82

Wood Barrow
SS 7148 4232
SS 74 SW 49

Woodbarrow Hangings
SS 7151 4283
SS 74 SW 15

Solitary and paired stones

(Fig 2.11)

Badgworthy Hill
SS 7860 4355
SS 74 SE 145

Badgworthy Lees
SS 7859 4464
SS 74 SE 97

Badgworthy Lees
SS 7877 4466
SS 74 SE 96

Bill Hill
SS 7231 4080
SS 74 SW 88

Black Barrow
SS 8301 4417
SS 84 SW 127

Clannon Ball
SS 7580 4366
SS 74 SE 99

East Pinford
SS 8051 4266
SS 84 SW 136

Five Barrows
SS 7293 3693
SS 73 NW 4

Furzehill Common
SS 7395 4421
SS 74 SW 96

Heale Down
SS 6538 4645
SS 64 NE 15

Hoar Moor
SS 8586 4075
SS 84 SE 40
Hoar Moor
SS 8621 4106
SS 84 SE 39

Hoccombe Hill
SS 7704 4389
SS 74 SE 100

Horcombe
SS 7458 3842
SS 73 NW 42

Ilkerton Ridge
SS 7207 4474
SS 74 SW 18

Long Holcombe
SS 7694 3543
SS 73 NE 37

Long Holcombe
SS 7738 3594
SS 73 NE 74

Long Stone, Challacombe
SS 7051 4307
SS 74 SW 10

Lyn Down
SS 7272 4752 &
SS 7272 4753
SS 74 NW 17

Near Blackmoor Gate
SS 6513 4301
SS 64 SE 10

Near Blue Gate
SS 7616 3810
SS 73 NE 54

Porlock Allotment
SS 8403 4470
SS 84 SW 59

Porlock Common
SS 8506 4475
SS 84 SE 108

Shallowford Common
SS 7128 4419
SS 74 SW 137

Shilstone Hill
SS 7625 4578 &
SS 7605 4571
SS 74 NE 45

Sparcombe Water
SS 8208 4116
SS 84 SW 15

Squallacombe
SS 7394 3820
SS 73 NW 33

Thorn Hill
SS 7239 4360
SS 74 SW 97

Trout Hill
SS 7902 4317
SS 74 SE 135

Trout Hill
SS 7943 4294
SS 74 SE 131

Vellacot Lane
SS 6020 4688
SS 64 NW 1

Long Stone, West Anstey
Common
SS 8493 2940
SS 82 NW 9

Whit Stones
SS 8532 4624
SS 84 NE 14

Wilmersham Common
SS 8554 4211
SS 84 SE 53

Winstitchen
SS 7955 3803
SS 73 NE 43

Withypool Common
SS 8278 3435
SS 83 SW 46

Yenworthy Common
SS 7987 4838 &
SS 7988 4836
SS 74 NE 14

Major barrows and barrow groups

(Fig 2.20)

Alderman's Barrow
SS 8367 4233
SS 84 SW 11

Anstey Barrow
SS 8735 2858
SS 82 NE 4

Brockenbarrow Group
SS 668 425
SS 64 SE 4

Chains Barrow
SS 7345 4190
SS 74 SW 4

Challacombe Common
SS 682 429
SS 64 SE 17

Chapman Barrows
SS 695 435
SS 64 SE 19

Cheriton Ridge ring cairn
SS 7456 4477
SS 74 SW 37

Cosgate Hill
SS 791 488
SS 74 NE 3

Culbone Hill
SS 832 474
SS 84 NW 9

Dunkery Beacon
SS 8915 4158
SS 84 SE 14

Five Barrows
SS 731 368
SS 73 NW 5

Haddon Hill
SS 965 286
SS 92 NE 25 &
SS 92 NE 26

Holdstone Down
SS 619 477
SS 64 NW 3

Ilkerton Ridge
SS 719 449
SS 74 SW 17

Longstone Barrow
SS 7073 4277
SS 74 SW 11

Lype Hill
SS 9503 3710
SS 93 NE 1

North Molton Ridge
SS 778 325
SS 73 SE 1

Robin and Joaney
How
SS 908 427
SS 94 SW 2 &
SS 94 SW 3

Rowbarrow
SS 875 415
SS 84 SE 8,
SS 84 SE 10 &
SE 84 SE 89

Selworthy Beacon
SS 924 479
SS 94 NW 102 &
SS 94 NW 111

Setta Barrow
SS 7255 3806
SS 73 NW 1

Trentishoe Down
SS 632 477
SS 64 NW 4

Two Barrows
SS 746 362
SS 73 NW 2

Wambarrows
SS 876 343
SS 83 SE 5

West Anstey Barrow
SS 854 291
SS 82 NE 3

Withycombe
Common
SS 9866 3945
SS 93 NE 4

Wiveliscombe Barrow
ST 0056 3486
ST 03 SW 2

Wood Barrow
SS 7163 4251
SS 74 SW 13

Cists

Clannon Ball
SS 7586 4367
SS 74 SE 91

Langridge Wood
ST 0141 3733
ST 03 NW 9

Hut circles

(Fig 2.32)

Almsworthy Common
SS 8404 4177
SS 84 SW 51

Challacombe Common
SS 6823 4258 &
SS 6819 4259
SS 64 SE 60

Codsend Moors
SS 8689 4064 &
SS 8715 4047
SS 84 SE 37

Codsend Moors
SS 8758 4112 &
SS 8761 4113
SS 84 SE 85

Codsend Moors
SS 8868 4023 &
SS 8871 4047
SS 84 SE 87

East Pinford
SS 7997 4237
SS 74 SE 36

Great Hill
SS 8483 4220,
SS 8508 4215 &
SS 8514 4235
SS 84 SE 41

Hoar Moor
SS 8574 4074
SS 84 SE 34

Holdstone
Down
SS 6233 4813
SS 64 NW 12

Honeycombe Hill
SS 8564 4219
SS 84 SE 90

Honeycombe Hill
SS 8594 4238
SS 84 SE 19

Martinhoe
Common
SS 6702 4698
SS 64 NE 46

Martinhoe
Common
SS 6802 4669,
SS 6792 4673 &
SS 6791 4679
SS 64 NE 34

Parracombe
Common
SS 6932 4497
SS 64 SE 46

Porlock Allotment
SS 8384 4448,
SS 8390 4441 &
SS 8389 4439
SS 84 SW 55

Porlock Allotment
SS 8433 4358 &
SS 8435 4356
SS 84 SW 57

Porlock Allotment
SS 8446 4429
SS 84 SW 143

Porlock Allotment
SS 8446 4431
SS 84 SW 142

South Common
SS 6970 4469 &
SS 6974 4466
SS 64 SE 25

Thorn Hill
SS 7279 4312 &
SS 7287 4314
SS 74 SW 7

Thorn Hill
SS 7280 4357
SS 74 SW 28

Thorn Hill
SS 7287 4374,
SS 7292 4376 &
SS 7289 4375
SS 74 SW 26

Trentishoe Down
SS 6271 4810 &
SS 6270 4811
SS 64 NW 7

Trentishoe Down
SS 6288 4804
SS 64 NW 15

Valley of Rocks
SS 7066 4967 &
SS 7043 4966
SS 74 NW 8

Prehistoric field banks and field clearance cairns

(Fig 2.32)

Beckham
SS 8094 4178
SS 84 SW 35

Bin Combe
SS 9045 4142
SS 94 SW 98

Cheriton Ridge
SS 7477 4333
SS 74 SW 41

Coley Water
SS 8460 4466
SS 84 SW 56

East Pinford
SS 8044 4261
SS 84 SW 38

Holdstone Down
SS 6170 4780
SS 64 NW 44

Holdstone Down
SS 6220 4818
SS 64 NW 12

Lanacombe
SS 7735 4225
SS 74 SE 122

Lanacombe
SS 7841 4284
SS 74 SE 105

Pinford
SS 7986 4263 &
SS 7957 4251 SS 74 SE 38

Porlock Allotment
SS 8369 4397
SS 84 SW 146

Porlock Allotment
SS 8383 4299
SS 84 SW 58

Porlock Allotment
SS 8436 4371
SS 84 SW 29

Porlock Allotment
SS 8443 4437
SS 84 SW 142

Shallowford Common
SS 712 440
SS 74 SW 30

Shallowmead
SS 741 361
SS 73 NW 19

South Common
SS 6972 4455
SS 64 SE 25

South of Shallowford
SS 7111 4389
SS 74 SW 31

Thorn Hill
SS 7290 4374
SS 74 SW 26

Trentishoe Down
SS 6295 4764
SS 64 NW 31

Prehistoric field systems

(Figs 2.32 and 3.1)

Codsend
SS 8875 4034,
SS 8770 4025,
SS 8654 4060 &
SS 8705 4068
SS 84 SE 87,
SS 84 SE 86,
SS 84 SE 84 & SS 84 SE 37

Great Hill
SS 8513 4247
SS 84 SE 41

Hoar Moor
SS 8636 4090
SS 84 SE 91

Honeycombe Hill
SS 8594 4238
SS 84 SE 19

Mansley Combe
SS 8990 4060
SS 84 SE 107

Martinhoe Common
SS 670 469
SS 64 NE 46

Valley of Rocks
SS 7051 4959
SS 74 NW 8

Withycombe Hill
ST 0015 4104
ST 04 SW 18

Hillforts

(Fig 3.1)

Bat's Castle
SS 9881 4213
SS 94 SE 17

Cow Castle
SS 7945 3735
SS 73 NE 3

Grabbist Hill
SS 9830 4367
SS 94 SE 2

Mounsey Castle
SS 8856 2955
SS 82 NE 2

Oldberry Castle
SS 9093 2820
SS 92 NW 4

Shoulsbury Castle
SS 7055 3909
SS 73 NW 6

Wind Hill
SS 7405 4936
SS 74 NW 3

Hill-slope enclosures

(Fig 3.1)

Bagley
SS 8825 4256
SS 84 SE 30

Barham Hill
SS 7026 4592
SS 74 NW 44

Beacon Castle
SS 6646 4601
SS 64 NE 4

Berry Castle, Porlock
SS 8590 4495
SS 84 SE 3

Blackford
SS 8617 4418
SS 84 SE 45

Brewer's Castle
SS 8832 2977
SS 82 NE 1

Bury Castle, Brompton Regis
SS 9385 2698
SS 92 NW 7

Bury Castle, Selworthy
SS 9176 4716
SS 94 NW 2

Codsend (west and east)
SS 8695 4070 &
SS 8876 4039
SS 84 SE 25 &
SS 84 SE 87

Dean Cross
SS 6254 4485
SS 64 SW 41

Doverhay Down
SS 8858 4541
SS 84 NE 13

East Pinford
SS 8022 4256
SS 84 SW 37

Furzebury Brake
SS 9358 4830
SS 94 NW 14

Gallox Hill
SS 9843 4265
SS 94 SE 4

Harwood Brakes
SS 9290 4100
SS 94 SW 38

Higher Dumbledeer
ST 0005 4109
ST 04 SW 70

Higher Holworthy
SS 6870 4433
SS 64 SE 55

Hill Road
SS 9378 4760
SS 94 NW 38

Hollerday Hill
SS 7149 4972
SS 74 NW 78

Horner's Neck
SS 7470 4897
SS 74 NW 86

Kentisbury Down
SS 6427 4330
SS 64 SW 2

Ley Hill
SS 8905 4405
SS 84 SE 104

Longwood
SS 9812 4038
SS 94 SE 27

Lynbridge
SS 7173 4872
SS 74 NW 68

Monkslade Common
SS 9947 3918
SS 93 NE 6

Myrtleberry (north and south)
SS 7428 4877 &
SS 7416 4832
SS 74 NW 14 &
SS 74 NW 15

Penn Allotment
SS 8146 4006
SS 84 SW 140

Porlock Allotment (east and west)
SS 8431 4373 &
8404 4341
SS 84 SW 29 &
SS 84 SW 30

Road Castle
SS 8629 3758
SS 83 NE 5

Roborough Castle
SS 7305 4599
SS 74 NW 13

Rodhuish Common
SS 9989 3922
SS 93 NE 90

Scrip Wood
SS 7531 4896
SS 74 NE 28

South Common
SS 6967 4474 &
SS 6978 4475
SS 64 SE 25

Staddon Hill Camp
SS 8818 3768
SS 83 NE 4

Stock Castle
SS 7183 4690
SS 74 NW 9

Sweetworthy (north)
SS 8906 4254
SS 84 SE 12

Sweetworthy (west and east)
SS 8887 4236 &
SS 8899 4241
SS 84 SE 49 &
SS 84 SE 50

Thurley Combe
SS 8641 4236
SS 84 SE 79

Timberscombe
SS 9572 4139
SS 94 SE 90
Trottsway Cross
SS 9023 3962
SS 93 NW 6

Valley of Rocks
SS 7061 4971 &
SS 7046 4964
SS 74 NW 8

Voley Castle
SS 6556 4623
SS 64 NE 1

Wester Emmets
SS 7431 3755
SS 73 NW 23

Roman military sites

(Fig 3.1)

Martinhoe
SS 6630 4933
SS 64 NE 2

Old Burrow
SS 7880 4934
SS 74 NE 4

Rainsbury
SS 9902 2918
SS 92 NE 59

Early iron-working sites

Blacklake Wood (smelting)
SS 9040 2868
SS 92 NW 36

Colton Pits (extraction)
ST 0535 3484
ST 03 SE 8

Horner Wood (smelting/smithing)
SS 8967 4387
SS 84 SE 106

Invention Woods (smelting)
SS 8972 2936
SS 82 NE 32

Roman Lode (extraction)
SS 753 382
SS 73 NE 10

Sherracombe Ford (smelting)
SS 7200 3665
SS 73 NW 41

Shircombe Slade (smelting)
SS 8912 2935
SS 82 NE 31

Inscribed stones

(Fig 4.1)

Caractacus Stone
SS 8898 3355
SS 83 SE 6

Cavudus Stone (not in situ)
SS 7005 4825
SS 74 NW 5

Culbone Stone
SS 8320 4735
SS 84 NW 15

Castles

(Fig 4.1)

Bury
SS 9385 2698
SS 92 NW 17

Dunster
SS 9911 4344
SS 94 SE 6

Holwell
SS 6697 4460
SS 64 SE 14

Monasteries

(Fig 4.1)

Barlynch
SS 9292 2898
SS 92 NW 6

Dunster
SS 9900 4367
SS 94 SE 1

Deserted medieval settlements

(Fig 4.1)

Badgworthy
SS 7935 4445
SS 74 SE 14

Bramble Combe
SS 9441 4790
SS 94 NW 27

Grexy Combe
SS 9406 4791
SS 94 NW 26

Ley Hill
SS 8917 4500
SS 84 NE 67

Mansley Combe
SS 9029 4059
SS 94 SW 94

Sweetworthy
SS 8877 4242
SS 84 SE 31

Major post-medieval mines

(numbers refer to Fig 5.27)

Bampfylde 6
SS 7390 3268
SS 73 SW 8

Bearland Wood 27
SS 9740 3590
SS 93 NE 58

Betsy 30
SS 9850 3540
SS 93 NE 46

Blackland 17
SS 8410 3680
SS 83 NW 35

Blue Gate 12
SS 7608 3770
SS 73 NE 23

Britannia 7
SS 7451 3369
SS 73 SW 16

Brockwell 20
SS 9280 4290
SS 94 SW 59

Burrow Farm 33
ST 0089 3453
ST 03 SW 20

Carnarvon 34
ST 0204 3429 &
ST 0236 3424
ST 03 SW 24

Colton 36
ST 0535 3484
ST 03 SE 8

Cornham Ford 11
SS 7499 3840
SS 73 NW 24

Girt Down 2
SS 5915 4815 &
SS 6114 4783
SS 54 NE 30 &
SS 64 NW 14

Girt Vale 3
SS 5957 4726
SS 54 NE 28

Gupworthy 26
SS 9670 3530
SS 93 NE 35

Hangley Cleave 10
SS 7440 3650
SS 73 NW 28

Higher Goosemoor 24
SS 955 355
SS 93 NE 50

Honeymead 15
SS 8091 3997
SS 83 NW 20

Ison 21
SS 9100 3700
SS 93 NW 32

Kennisham Hill 25
SS 9630 3610
SS 93 NE 60

Knowle Hill 19
SS 9130 4450
SS 94 SW 49

Lancecombe 23
SS 9435 3586
SS 93 NW 56

Langham Hill 28
SS 9772 3560
SS 93 NE 59

Lothbrook 31
SS 9863 3545
SS 93 NE 47

Luckyard Wood 22
SS 9236 3600
SS 93 NW 36

Marcia 9
SS 7873 3005
SS 73 SE 43

New Florence 8
SS 7520 3215
SS 73 SE 15

Newland 16
SS 8202 3752
SS 83 NW 22

Parracombe 5
SS 6675 4488
SS 64 SE 57

Picked Stones 14
SS 7980 3767
SS 73 NE 27

Smoky Bottom 29
SS 9780 3530
SS 93 NE 39

Timwood 35
ST 0319 3528
ST 03 NW 43

West Challacombe 1
SS 5849 4736
SS 54 NE 18

Wheal Eliza 13
SS 7847 3812
SS 73 NE 8

Wheal Gregory 18
SS 8550 3740
SS 83 NE 40

Wheal Vervale 4
SS 6260 4645
SS 64 NW 43

Withiel Hill 32
SS 992 351
SS 93 NE 48

Limekilns

(Fig 5.36)

Allercott (west, middle and east)
SS 9568 3925,
SS 9611 3922 & SS 9622 3927
SS 93 NE 74,
SS 93 NE 76 & SS 93 NE 75

Beggearn Huish
ST 0463 3941
ST 03 NW 21

Bossington
SS 8912 4832
SS 84 NE 38

Brendon Hill
ST 0199 3415
ST 03 SW 27

Challacombe
SS 6928 4123
SS 64 SE 43

Chargot
SS 9808 3721
SS 93 NE 62

Edbrook
SS 8986 3826
SS 83 NE 79

Embelle Wood
SS 8163 4925
SS 84 NW 29

Glenthorne
SS 8005 4953
SS 84 NW 43

Golden Cleeve
SS 9340 3899
SS 93 NW 65

Golsoncott
ST 0285 3911 &
ST 0292 3908
ST 03 NW 63

Harper's Lane
ST 0348 3800
ST 03 NW 20

Heddon's Mouth
SS 6550 4957
SS 64 NE 8

Higher Rodhuish
ST 0133 3982
ST 03 NW 37

Huish Barton
ST 0499 3836
ST 03 NE 84

Lee Bay
SS 6943 4923
SS 64 NE 10

Lower Court Farm
SS 9979 3675
SS 93 NE 78

Lower Roadwater
ST 0350 3884
ST 03 NW 27

Lynmouth
SS 7218 4965
SS 74 NW 19

Newlands (west and east)
SS 8241 3849 &
SS 8251 3851
SS 83 NW 25 &
SS 83 NW 26

Nurcott (north and south)
SS 9651 3905 &
SS 9657 3887
SS 93 NE 63 &
SS 93 NE 64

Old Close
SS 7054 4084
SS 74 SW 158

Pinns
SS 8840 3822
SS 83 NE 75

Pooltown
SS 9854 3707
SS 93 NE 61

Porlock Weir
SS 8632 4799
SS 84 NE 29

Putham Wood
SS 9395 3875
SS 93 NW 59

Roadwater (west and east)
ST 0326 3909 &
ST 0340 3847
ST 03 NW 26 &
ST 03 NW 68

Rodhuish
ST 0128 3951
ST 03 NW 64

Rodneys
SS 7647 5023
SS 75 SE 8

Southwoods
ST 0202 3649
ST 03 NW 65

Treborough
ST 0187 3681,
ST 0174 3683 &
ST 0168 3683
ST 03 NW 32

Watersmeet
SS 7466 4863
SS 74 NW 29

Well Farm
SS 9490 4205
SS 94 SW 54

Westcott
SS 9709 3823
SS 93 NE 54

West Luccombe
SS 8995 4616
SS 84 NE 43

Wild Pear Beach
SS 5826 4778
SS 54 NE 23

Woodadvent
ST 0359 3756
ST 03 NW 69

Woody Bay
SS 6769 4898
SS 64 NE 9

Wootton Courtenay
SS 9450 4335
SS 94 SW 58

Worthy
SS 8583 4833
SS 84 NE 78

Appendix 2
Radiocarbon dates mentioned in the text

Site: Halscombe Allotment
Type: Buried tree
Date: 4690 ±50 BP
3635–3360 Cal BC (at 2σ)
Ref: V Heal personal communication

Site: Porlock Bay
Type: Aurochs
Date: 3687–3399 Cal BP (at 2σ)
Ref: McDonnell 1998, 1

Site: Shallowmead
Type: Ring Cairn
Date: 3060 ±80 BP
1501 1187 Cal BC (87% probability at 2σ)
Lab Code/Ref No: HAR-2829
Ref: Quinnell 1997, 25–6

Site: Bratton Down
Type: Cairn
Date: 2832 ±42 BP
1111–896 Cal BC (90% probability at 2σ)
Lab Code/Ref No: BM-1148
Ref: Quinnell 1997, 7

Site: Sindercombe
Type: Iron Smelting
Date: 2067 ±44 BP
Cal BC 195– AD 17 (at 95.4 % probability)

Lab Code/Ref No: AA-25941
Ref: *Devon Arch Soc Newsletter* 70 (May 1998), 11

Site: Sherracombe Ford (date 1)
Type: Iron Smelting
Date: 2000 ±50 BP
Cal BC 160–AD 90 (at 95% probability)
Lab Code/Ref No: Beta-98972
Ref: Juleff 1997, 23

Site: Sherracombe Ford (date 2)
Type: Iron Smelting
Date: 2030 ±50 BP
Cal BC 170–AD 75 (at 2σ)
Lab Code/Ref No: Beta-132448
Ref: Juleff 2000, 3

Site: Blacklake Wood
Type: Iron Smelting
Date: 1520 ±60 BP
415–650 Cal AD (at 2σ)
Lab Code/Ref No: Beta-132445
Ref: Juleff 2000, 4

Site: New Invention (A)
Type: Iron Smelting
Date: 680 ±50 BP

1260–1400 Cal AD (at 2σ)
Lab Code/Ref No: Beta-132446
Ref: Juleff 2000, 4

Site: New Invention (B)
Type: Iron Smelting
Date: 720 ±50 BP
1225–1310/1360–1385 Cal AD (at 2σ)
Lab Code/Ref No: Beta-132447
Ref: Juleff 2000, 4

Site: Ley Hill
Type: Deserted Medieval Settlement
Date: 675 ±45 BP
1270–1398 Cal AD (at 2σ)
Ref: Richardson 1999, 56 and personal communication

Site: Horner Wood (date 1)
Type: Iron smithing (and some smelting)
Date: 420 ±40 BP
1425–1515/1590–1620 Cal AD (at 2σ)
Lab Code/Ref No: Beta-133315

Site: Horner Wood (date 2)
Type: Iron smithing (and some smelting)
Date: 300 ±40 BP
1480–1660 Cal AD (at 2σ)
Lab Code/Ref No: Beta-133316
Ref: Juleff 2000, 4

Appendix 3
RCHME Exmoor Project Reports

Large-scale surveys and area survey reports
(available in the NMR)

Best, J 1996 East Pinford and Great Tom's Hill: the field archaeology
Dempsey, J 1997 Staddon Hill Camp, Winsford, Somerset
Fletcher, M 1997 Roman Lode, Burcombe, Exmoor, Somerset
Jamieson, E 1999 The Valley of Rocks, Lynton and Lynmouth, Devon
Riley, H 1996 The prehistoric enclosures and medieval and post-medieval settlements at Bagley and Sweetworthy, Luccombe, Somerset
— 1997 Cow Castle, Exmoor, Somerset
— 1999 Mounsey Castle and Brewer's Castle: two Iron Age enclosures in the Barle Valley, Somerset
Riley, H, and Wilson-North, R 1997 The field archaeology of North Hill
Wild, P 1998 Bury Castle, Selworthy
Wilson-North, R 1996 Badgworthy deserted medieval settlement
— 1996 Lyshwell and Shircombe: deserted farmsteads and field systems
— 1997 Berry Castle, Porlock, Somerset
— 1997 A medieval settlement and prehistoric enclosure at Ley Hill, Luccombe, Somerset
— 1997 Oldberry Castle, Dulverton, Somerset
— 1998 An 18th-century house and park at Withiel Florey
— 1998 Haddon Hill, Brompton Regis, Somerset
— 1999 Old Burrow and Martinhoe: the Roman fortlets on Exmoor
— 1999 The priory of St Nicholas, Barlynch, Brompton Regis, Somerset
Wilson-North, R, and Riley, H 1996 Bury Castle, Brompton Regis, Somerset

— 1998 A rectangular enclosure at Rainsbury, Upton, West Somerset
— 1998 Road Castle, Winsford, Exmoor.

Air photographic transcription reports
(available in the NMR)

APU, 1994 Molland Common, West Exmoor
APU, 1995 Wester Shircombe
Crutchley, S 1999 Withypool Common, East Exmoor
— 2000 Colton Pits, Nettlecombe, Somerset
— 2000 Woodadvent Lane Enclosure, Nettlecombe, Somerset
Dyer, C 1994 Anstey Common, West Exmoor
— 1998 The Brendon Hills Mapping Project.
Winton, H 1999 Challacombe, West Exmoor
— 1999 Parracombe, West Exmoor
— 1999 Winsford Hill, West Somerford

Historic buildings reports
(available in the NMR)

Jones, B V 2000 Cloggs Farm, Withypool, Somerset
— 2000 Horsen Farm, Exmoor, Somerset
— 2000 New Barn, Ashott Barton, Exford, Somerset
— 2000 Outfarm, Marshclose Hill, Hawkridge, Withypool, Somerset
— 2000 Silcombe Farm, Silcombe, Oare, Somerset
— 2000 Weatherslade Farm, Withypool, Somerset

Glossary

aceramic: of a period of time, such as the later Iron Age in Devon, when pottery was not generally used

air photographic transcription: the process of putting information from air photographs onto a map or plan

aurochs *(Bos primigenius)*: ancestor of our domestic cattle, thought to be extinct from Britain by the end of the Bronze Age, but lived on in parts of mainland Europe until early post-medieval period

barbed and tanged flint arrowhead: type of flint tool generally thought to date from the Early Bronze Age

Beaker: type of fine Bronze Age pottery, usually thought of as Early Bronze Age, recent dating work suggests that it has a broad date range between 2600 to 1800 BC

berm: area of level ground between the ditch top and rampart base of an Iron Age hillfort or other earthwork, often associated with the **box rampart** type of construction

box rampart: type of rampart found on Iron Age hillforts, formed with a timber frame, where horizontal struts linked vertical uprights on the front and back of an earthern core; generally earlier in date than the **glacis** type ramparts

causewayed enclosure: enclosure with characteristic interrupted ditches, dating from the Early Neolithic period

cist: stone-lined grave, covered with stone capstone, generally dating to the earlier part of the Bronze Age

clearance cairns: small heaps of stone, cleared from areas in advance of cultivation; can range in date from prehistoric to post-medieval

cordoned urn: type of Bronze Age pottery, generally dated to the Early Bronze Age

counterscarp bank: on an Iron Age hillfort, bank on the outer side of the ditch

discoidal flint knife: type of finely worked flint tool, generally dating from the Late Neolithic period

glacis or dump rampart: rampart constructed by successive dumps of soil, tipped to create a continuous steep slope from the ditch bottom to rampart top; generally later in date than the **box rampart** type

Glastonbury Ware: *see* South-Western Decorated Ware

Greenstone: general term for igneous or metamorphic rock, made into axes and widely traded in Neolithic Britain

henge monument: circular enclosure with characteristic external bank and internal ditch, dating from the later part of the Neolithic period

kerb: wall of upright stone slabs or laid stones placed in a ring around the base of a barrow to retain the mound material

leaf-shaped arrowhead: finely worked flint tool, generally dated to the Early Neolithic period

long barrow: burial monument of the Neolithic period, often containing several interments, and divided into several compartments (a chambered tomb) where suitable building material was available

lynchet: earthwork formed by the down-slope build-up of soil, caused by ploughing on a slope

macehead: perforated stone object, generally thought to be of Late Mesolithic date

megalith: term describing a monument such as a chambered tomb constructed of large stone slabs

microliths: very small flint tools dating from the Mesolithic period

NMR: National Monuments Record, part of English Heritage's national archive, kept at the National Monuments Record Centre, Swindon

outfarm: barn located away from the main farm buildings, with attached foldyard for overwintering cattle

outwork: on hillforts and hill-slope enclosures, linear banks and ditches marking a secondary area adjacent to the main site

palstave: type of bronze axe with flanges and a well-developed stop-ridge, generally dating from the Middle Bronze Age

periglacial: extreme conditions experienced in a region close to a glacier

Pleistocene: geological term applied to the period of time marked by the end of the Tertiary era and the end of the last full glacial environment, when Britain was subject to several glacial and interglacial regimes

palaeoenvironmental data: information about past environments obtained by the study of fossilised plants, pollen and insects

radiocarbon dating: method of dating organic material based on the fact that all living things contain traces of a radioactive isotope of carbon, which decays at a known rate after that organism's death; as the technique has become increasingly refined, so archaeologists have been able to refine traditional chronologies, once only based on typology and extrapolation

ridge and furrow: long, parallel ridges of soil separated by linear depressions, caused by repeated ploughing using a heavy plough; broad ridges (5m spacing) are indicative of the medieval period, narrower gaps suggest post-medieval cultivation

SMR: Sites and Monuments Record: for Exmoor the records are kept at the County Halls for Devon and Somerset, in Exeter and Taunton respectively

South-Western Decorated Ware: type of pottery with incised, curving decoration (also known as Glastonbury Ware), dates from the Middle Iron Age (4th century BC), and continued to be made well into the 1st century BC, perhaps into the Roman period

transverse and triangular arrowheads: type of flint arrowheads, generally thought to date from the later Neolithic period

tree ring: circular area enclosed by a bank and ditch, containing clumps of trees; generally of post-medieval date

univallate: earthworks comprising a single bank and ditch; the usual form of Exmoor's hillforts and hill-slope enclosures

References

Allcroft, H 1908 *Earthwork of England*. London: Macmillan

Allen, N 1990 *Exmoor's Wild Red Deer*. Dulverton: The Exmoor Press

Allen, N, and Giddens, C 1983 'Treborough slate quarry and conservation area'. *Exmoor Review* **24**, 23–9

Astill, G 1992 'Rural settlement: the toft and the croft', *in* Astill, G, and Grant, A (eds), *The Countryside of Medieval England*. Oxford: Basil Blackwell, 36–61

Aston, M 1983 'Deserted farmsteads on Exmoor and the Lay Subsidy of 1327 in West Somerset'. *Somerset Archaeol Natur Hist* **127**, 71–104

— 1988 'Settlement patterns and forms', *in* Aston, M (ed) *Aspects of the Medieval Landscape of Somerset*. Taunton: Somerset County Council, 67–81

— 1993 *Monasteries*. London: Batsford

Aston, M, *et al* (eds) 1989 *The Rural Settlements of Medieval England*. Oxford: Basil Blackwell

Atkinson, M (ed) 1997 *Exmoor's Industrial Archaeology*. Dulverton: Exmoor Books

Aubrey, J 1626–1697 *Monumenta Britannica* (facsim edn Little, Brown and Co 1980)

Baker, S 1993 *Survival of the Fittest: A Natural History of the Exmoor Pony*. Dulverton: Exmoor Books

Barton, N 1997 *Stone Age Britain*. London: Batsford/English Heritage

Beer, K E, and Scrivener R C 1982 'Metalliferous mineralisation', *in* Durrance, E M, and Laming, D J C (eds), *The Geology of Devon*. Exeter: University of Exeter, 117–47

Bettey, J H 1989 *The Suppression of the Monasteries in the West Country*. Gloucester: Alan Sutton

Binding, H nd *Discovering Dunster: A History and Guide*. Dulverton: The Exmoor Press

Blackmore, R D 1994 *Lorna Doone: A Romance of Exmoor*. London: Penguin

Bond, C J 1988 'Monastic Fisheries', *in* Aston M (ed), *Medieval Fish, Fisheries and Fishponds in England*. Oxford: Brit Achaeol Rep **182I**, 69–112.

Bourne, H 1991 *Living on Exmoor*. Dulverton: Exmoor Books

Boyd Dawkins, W 1872 'Ancient geography of the west of England'. *Somerset Archaeol Natur Hist* **18**, 26–33

Brown, R A 1989 *Castles from the Air*. Cambridge: Cambridge University Press

Burl, A 1993 *From Carnac to Callanish: The Prehistoric Stone Rows and Avenues of Britain, Ireland and Brittany*. New Haven and London: Yale University Press

Burton, R A 1989 *The Heritage of Exmoor*. Barnstaple: R A Burton

Burton, R 1997 'A brief history of Newland lime quarries, Exford'. *Bull Somerset Indust Archaeol Soc* **75**, 6–9

Butler, J 1997 *Dartmoor Atlas of Antiquities, 5: The Second Millennium* BC. Tiverton: Devon Books

Bye, R A, and Lovell, T H 1977 'A proposed extension of the West Somerset Mineral Railway to Eisen Hill'. *J Somerset Archaeol Soc* **2**, 24–6

Cameron, K 1979 'The meaning and significance of Old English *walh* in English place-names'. *Engl Place-Name Soc J* **12**, 1–53

Canti, M, *et al* 1995 *Archaeological and palaeoenvironmental evaluation of Porlock Bay and Marsh*. Archaeology in the Severn Estuary 6, 49–69

Chadwyck Healey, C E H 1901 *History of Part of West Somerset*. London: Henry Sotheran and Co

Chanter, J F 1906 'The parishes of Lynton and Countisbury, I'. *Rep Trans Devonshire Assoc* **38**, 113–68

Chanter, J F, and Worth, R H 1905 'The rude stone monuments of Exmoor and its borders, part I'. *Rep Trans Devonshire Assoc* **37**, 375–97

— 1906 'The rude stone monuments of Exmoor and its borders, part II'. *Rep Trans Devonshire Assoc* **38**, 538–52

Cherry, B, and Pevsner, N 1989 *The Buildings of England*: Devon, 2 edn. London: Penguin

Christie, P M 1988 'A barrow cemetery on Davidstow Moor, Cornwall: Wartime excavations by C K Croft Andrew'. *Cornish Archaeol* **27**, 27–170

Claughton, P 1997a 'Lead and silver mining', *in* Atkinson, M (ed), *Exmoor's Industrial Archaeology*. Dulverton: Exmoor Books, 73–102

— 1997b 'On gold at North Molton'. *Exmoor Mines Research Group Newsletter* **10**, 2–7

Collinson, J 1791 *The History and Antiquities of the County of Somerset* (facsim edn Allan Sutton 1983)

Cook, H 1994 'Field-scale water management in southern England to AD 1900'. *Landscape History* **16**, 53–66

Costen, M 1992 *The Origins of Somerset*. Manchester: Manchester University Press

Crossley, D 1990 *Post-Medieval Archaeology in Britain*. Leicester: Leicester University Press

Cunliffe, B 1991 *Iron Age Communities in Britain*, 3 edn. Routledge: London and New York

— 1993 *Danebury*. London: Batsford/English Heritage

— 1995 *Iron Age Britain*. London: Batsford/English Heritage

Darvill, T, and Fulton, A 1998 MARS: *The Monuments at Risk Survey of England 1995, Main Report*. Bournemouth and London: School of Conservation Sciences, Bournemouth University and English Heritage

Dines, H G 1956 *The Metalliferous Mining Region of the South West, II*. London: HMSO

Dixon, D 1983 Mining and Community in the Parishes of North Molton, South Molton, Molland and Twitchen, Devonshire. Unpublished M Phil thesis, University of Southampton

— 1997 'Copper and gold mining in the Exmoor area', *in* Atkinson, M (ed), *Exmoor's Industrial Archaeology*. Dulverton: Exmoor Books, 41–72

Dunn, C J 1997 Ham Hill, Somerset. RCHME survey report

Dunning, R W 1987 *A History of Somerset*, 2 edn. Bridgwater: Somerset County Library

— 1995 *Somerset Castles*. Tiverton: Somerset Books

Eardley-Wilmot, H 1983 *Ancient Exmoor*. Dulverton: The Exmoor Press

— 1990 *Yesterday's Exmoor*. Dulverton: Exmoor Books

Edmonds, E, *et al* 1975 *British Regional Geology: South-west England*. London: HMSO

Eeles, F C 1928 *Somerset Churches near Dulverton*. Taunton: Barnicott and Pearce

— 1945 *The Church of St George, Dunster*, 5 edn. London: Press and Publications Board of the Church Assembly

Elworthy, F T 1896 'An ancient British interment'. *Somerset Archaeol Natur Hist* **42**, 56–66

Essex, S 1995 'Woodland in the Exmoor National Park', *in* Binding, H (ed), *The Changing Face of Exmoor*. Dulverton: Exmoor Books, 68–83

Farmer, D H 1978 *The Oxford Dictionary of Saints*. Oxford: The Clarendon Press

Fenton, R 1811 *A Tour in Quest of Genealogy through several parts of Wales, Somersetshire and Wiltshire in a series of Letters to a Friend in Dublin*. London: Sherwood, Neely and Jones

Field, D 1999 'Bury the dead in a sacred landscape'. *Brit Archaeol* **43**, 6–7

Fleming, A 1988 *The Dartmoor Reaves*. London: Batsford/English Heritage

Forde-Johnston, J 1976 *Hillforts of the Iron Age in England and Wales*. Liverpool: Liverpool University Press

Fox, A 1952 'Hill-slope forts and related earthworks in south-west England and South Wales'. *Archaeol J* **109**, 1–22

— 1961 'The Iron Age bowl from Rose Ash, north Devon'. *Antiq J* **41**, 186–98

Fox, A, and Ravenhill, W L D 1966 'Early Roman outposts on the north Devon coast: Old Burrow and Martinhoe'. *Proc Devon Archaeol Soc* **24**, 1–39

Fox, H S A 1983 Contraction: desertion and dwindling of dispersed settlements in a Devon parish. *Medieval Village Res Group Ann Rep* **31**, 40–42

Francis, P D 1986 'A record of vegetational and land use change from upland peat deposits on Exmoor: Part 1 Background and fieldwork'. *Somerset Archaeol Natur Hist* **130**, 1–9

Francis, P D, and Slater, D S 1990 'A record of vegetational and land use change from upland peat deposits on Exmoor: Part 2 Hoar Moor'. *Somerset Archaeol Natur Hist* **134**, 1–25

— 'A record of vegetational and land use change from upland peat deposits on Exmoor: Part 3 Codsend Moors'. *Somerset Archaeol Natur Hist* **136**, 9–28

Francis, P T H 1984 A survey and description of the 'catch meadow' irrigation systems found in the Exmoor region of West Somerset. Unpublished BA dissertation, University of Durham

Gerrard, S 1997 *Dartmoor: Landscapes Through Time*. London: Batsford/English Heritage

Gibson, A 1992 'The excavation of an Iron Age settlement at Gold Park, Dartmoor'. *Proc Devon Archaeol Soc* **59**, 19–47

Gilman, J M 1978 'The Exmoor Fishing industry'. *Exmoor Review* **19**, 31–7

— 1999 *Exmoor's Maritime Heritage*. Dulverton: Exmoor Books

Godbold, S, and Turner, R C 1994 'Medieval fishtraps in the Severn Estuary'. *Medieval Archaeol* **38**, 19–54

Gover, J E B, *et al* 1969 *The Place-names of Devon, I*. Cambridge: Cambridge University Press

— 1973 *The Place-names of Devon, II*. Cambridge: Cambridge University Press

Gray, H St G 1906 'The stone circle on Withypool Hill, Exmoor'. *Somerset Archaeol Natur Hist* **52**, 42–50

— 1928 'The Porlock stone circle, Exmoor'. *Somerset Archaeol Natur Hist* **74**, 71–7

— 1931a 'Rude stone monuments of Exmoor (Somerset portion), part III'. *Somerset Archaeol Natur Hist* **77**, 78–82

— 1931b 'Bronze implements found in the parish of Old Cleeve, Somerset'. *Somerset Archaeol Natur Hist* **77**, 136–7

Gray, H St G, and Tapp, W M 1912 'A survey of Old Burrow Camp, Exmoor'. *Rep Trans Devonshire Assoc* **44**, 703–17

Greene, J P 1992 *Medieval Monasteries*. Leicester: Leicester University Press

Griffith, F M 1985 'A nemeton in Devon?'. *Antiquity* **59**, 121–4

— 'Changing perceptions of the context of prehistoric Dartmoor'. *Proc Devon Archaeol Soc* **52**, 85–99

— 1997 'Developments in the study of Roman military sites in south-west England', *in* Groenman-van Waateringe, W, *et al* (eds), *Roman Frontier Studies 1995*. Oxford: Oxbow Monograph 91, 361–7

Griffith, F M, and Weddell, P 1996 'Ironworking in the Blackdown Hills: results of recent survey', *in* P Newman (ed), *The Archaeology of Mining and Metallurgy in South-West Britain*. Peak District Mines Hist Soc Hist Metallurgy Soc Special Publ, 27–34

Grinsell, L V 1958 'Evidence of Roman ironworking on Exmoor'. Somerset and Dorset Notes and Queries 27, 192–3

— 1969 'Somerset barrows: Part 1 west and south'. *Somerset Archaeol Natur Hist* **113**, 1–43

— 1970a *The Archaeology of Exmoor*. Newton Abbot: David and Charles

— 1970b 'The barrows of north Devon'. *Proc Devon Archaeol Soc* **28**, 95–129

— 1984 *Barrows in England and Wales*. Princes Risborough: Shire Publications

Hallam, O 1978 'Vegetation and land use on Exmoor'. *Somerset Archaeol Natur Hist* **122**, 37–51

Halliday, U J 1995 *Glenthorne: A Most Romantic Place*. Dulverton: Exmoor Books

Hancock, F 1905 *Dunster Church and Priory*. Taunton: Barnicott and Pearce

Hawkins, M 1996 *Somerset at War 1939–1945*. Bridgwater: Hawk Editions

Helbaek, H 1952 'Early crops in southern England'. *Proc Prehistoric Soc* **18**, 194–233

Henderson, C G, and Weddell, P J 1994 'Medieval settlements on Dartmoor and in west Devon: the evidence from excavations'. *Proc Devon Archaeol Soc* **52**, 119–40

Higham, R 1979 The castles of medieval Devon. Unpublished PhD thesis, University of Exeter

Higham, R, and Hamlin, A 1990 'Bampton Castle: history and archaeology'. *Proc Devon Archaeol Soc* **48**, 101–10

Holley, S 1997 An investigation of limekilns on Exmoor for the purposes of conservation. Unpublished BSc dissertation, University of Bournemouth

Holmes, R 1974 *Shelley The Pursuit* . London: Weidenfeld and Nicolson

Hoskins, W G 1992 *Devon*, 2 edn. Tiverton: Devon Books

Johnson, N, and Rose, P 1982 'Defended settlement in Cornwall, an illustrated discussion' in Miles, D (ed), *The Romano-British Countryside*. Oxford: Brit Archaeol Rep **103**, 151–208

— 1994 *Bodmin Moor: An Archaeological Survey, I: The Human Landscape to c 1800*. London: English Heritage and RCHME

Jones, M H 1997 'Iron mining' in Atkinson, M (ed), *Exmoor's Industrial Archaeology*. Dulverton: Exmoor Books, 14–40

— 1998 Notes on some of the Brendon Hills Iron Mines and the West Somerset Mineral Railway. Unpublished report

Juleff, G 1997 Earlier Iron-working on Exmoor: preliminary survey. Exmoor National Park Association and National Trust survey report

— 2000 'New radiocarbon dates for iron-working sites on Exmoor'. *HMS News, Newsletter of the Historical Metallurgy Society* **44**, 3–4

Kinnes, I, *et al* 1991 'Radiocarbon dating and British Beakers: the British Museum programme'. *Scot Archaeol Rev* **8**, 35–68

Lyte, H C M 1909 *A History of Dunster and of the Families of Mohun and Luttrell*. London: St Catherine Press

MacDermot, E T 1973 *A History of the Forest of Exmoor*. Newton Abbot: David and Charles

McDonnell, R J 1985a Archaeological Survey on Exmoor: An Interim Report. Historic Buildings and Monuments Commission for England survey report

— 1985b Recommendations for the management of archaeological sites in the Exmoor National Park at Warren, Pinford, Tom's Hill and Hayes Allotment. Western Archaeological Trust survey report

— 1998 *Porlock Bay Aurochs*. Exmoor National Park Authority excavation report

Mayberry, T 1992 *Coleridge and Wordsworth in the West Country*. Stroud: Allan Sutton

McOmish, D, *et al* 2001 *The Field Archaeology of the Salisbury Plain Training Area*. Swindon: English Heritage

Merryfield, D L, and Moore, P D 1974 'Prehistoric human activity and blanket peat initiation on Exmoor'. *Nature* **250**, 439–41

Miles, H 1975 'Barrows on the St Austell granite, Cornwall'. *Cornish Archaeol* **14**, 5–82
— 1976 'Flint scatters and prehistoric settlement in Devon'. *Proc Devon Archaeol Soc* **34**, 3–16
Miles, R 1972 *The Trees and Woods of Exmoor*. Dulverton: The Exmoor Press

Norman, C 1982 'Mesolithic hunter-gatherers 9000–4000 BC', in Aston, M, and Burrow, I C G (eds), *The Archaeology of Somerset*. Taunton: Somerset County Council, 15–21

Orme, N 1984 'A school note-book from Barlinch Priory'. *Somerset Archaeol Natur Hist* **128**, 55–63
— 1990 'More pages from a Barlinch schoolbook'. *Somerset Archaeol Natur Hist* **134**, 183–5
Orwin, C S 1929 *The Reclamation of Exmoor Forest*. Oxford: Oxford University Press
Orwin, C S, and Sellick, R 1970 *The Reclamation of Exmoor Forest*, 2 edn. Newton Abbot: David and Charles
Orwin, C S, *et al* 1997 *The Reclamation of Exmoor Forest*, 3 edn. Dulverton: Exmoor Books

Page, J L W 1893 *An Exploration of Exmoor and the Hill Country of West Somerset*, 3 edn. London: Seeley and Co
Pearce, S M 1978 *The Kingdom of Dumnonia: Studies in History and Tradition in South-western Britain*. Padstow: Lodenek Press
— 1981 *The Archaeology of South West Britain*. London: Collins
— 1983 *The Bronze Age Metalwork of South Western Britain* . Oxford: Brit Archaeol Rep **120**
Pevsner, N 1989 *The Buildings of England: South and West Somerset*. London: Penguin
Phelps, W 1836 *The History and Antiquities of Somersetshire*. London: J B Nichols and Son
Platt, C 1982 *The Castle in Medieval England and Wales*. London: Secker and Warburg
Polwhele, R 1793 *Historical Views of Devonshire*

Quinnell, H 1988 'The local character of the Devon Bronze Age and its interpretation in the 1980s'. *Proc Devon Archaeol Soc* **46**, 1–14
— 1994a 'New perspectives on upland monuments: Dartmoor in earlier prehistory'. *Proc Devon Archaeol Soc* **52**, 49–62
— 1994b 'Becoming marginal? Dartmoor in later prehistory'. *Proc Devon Archaeol Soc* **52**, 75–83
— 1997 'Excavations of an Exmoor barrow and ring cairn'. *Proc Devon Archaeol Soc* **55**, 1–39
Quinnell, N V, and Dunn C J 1992 Lithic Monuments within the Exmoor National Park: a New Survey for Management Purposes. RCHME survey report

Richardson, I 1999 'Ley Hill deserted medieval settlement, Horner Wood'. *The National Trust Ann Archaeol Rev* **7**, 56
Riley, H 1996 The prehistoric enclosures and medieval and post medieval settlements at Bagley and Sweetworthy. RCHME survey report
Roe, D A 1968 *A Gazetteer of British Lower and Middle Palaeolithic Sites*. London: Counc Brit Archaeol Res Rep **8**
Rowley, T 1997 *Norman England: An Archaeological Perspective on the Norman Conquest*. London: Batsford/English Heritage

Savage, J 1830 *History of the Hundred of Carhampton*. Bristol: William Strong
SCRO *c*1750 Plan of Dunster church and priory. Somerset County Record Office, Taunton DD/L 1/10/35a
Sellick, R 1970 *The West Somerset Mineral Railway and the Story of the Brendon Hills Iron Mines* (2 edn). Newton Abbot: David and Charles

Silvester, R J 1979 'The relationship of first millennium settlement to the upland areas of the south west'. *Proc Devon Archaeol Soc* **37**, 176–90
Silvester, R J, and Quinnell, N V 1993 'Unfinished hillforts on the Devon moors'. *Proc Devon Archaeol Soc* **51**, 17–31
Sinclair, G 1972 *The Vegetation of Exmoor*. Dulverton: The Exmoor Press
Stevens, D 1985 'A Somerset Coroner's Roll'. *Notes Queries Somerset Dorset* **31**, 451–72
Straker, V, and Crabtree, K 1995 'Palaeoenvironmental studies on Exmoor: past research and future potential', in Binding, H (ed), *The Changing Face of Exmoor*. Dulverton: Exmoor Books, 43–51

Thorn, C, and Thorn, F (eds) 1980 *Domesday Book: Somerset*. Chichester: Phillimore
— 1985 *Domesday Book: Devon*. Chichester: Phillimore
Todd, M 1984 'Excavations at Hembury, Devon, 1980–83: a summary report'. *Antiq J* **64**, 251–68
— 1987 *The South-west to AD 1000*. London and New York: Longman
— 1998 'A hill-slope enclosure at Rudge, Morchard Bishop'. *Proc Devon Archaeol Soc* **56**, 133–52
Travis, J 1994 'The rise of the Devon seaside resorts, 1750–1900', in Duffy, M, *et al* (eds), *The New Maritime History of Devon*, I. Exeter: University of Exeter, 136–44
Turner, J 1990 'Ring cairns, stone circles and related monuments on Dartmoor'. *Proc Devon Archaeol Soc* **48**, 27–86

VCH Devon I 1906 *The Victoria History of the County of Devon*, I. London: Constable
VCH Somerset II 1911 *The Victoria History of the County of Somerset*, II. London: Constable

Warren, D 1977 'Newland quarry'. *J Somerset Indust Achaeol Soc* **2**, 36–9
Wasley, G 1994 *Devon at War 1939–1945*. Tiverton: Devon Books
Watney, V J 1928 *The Wallop Family*, I. Oxford: John Johnson
Weaver, F W 1908 'Barlinch Priory'. *Somerset Archaeol Natur Hist* **54**, 79–106
Whybrow, C 1967 'Some multivallate hillforts on Exmoor and in north Devon'. *Proc Devon Archaeol Soc* **25**, 1–18
— 1970 Antiquary's Exmoor: *A Regional Study of Ancient Man*. Dulverton: The Exmoor Press
Williams, R 1989 *Limekilns and Limeburning*. Princes Risborough: Shire Publications
Wilson-North, R 1996 Badgworthy deserted medieval settlement. RCHME survey report
Woollcombe, H 1839 Some Account of the Fortified Hills in the County of Devon, whether British, Roman, Anglo-Saxon or Danish, with plans of many of them. Manuscript in Devon and Exeter Institution Library
Worth, R H 1879 'First report of the barrow committee'. *Rep Trans Devonshire Assoc* **11**, 146–60
— 1905 'Twenty-fourth report of the barrow committee'. *Rep Trans Devonshire Assoc* **37**, 87–95
— 1906 'Twenty-fifth report of the barrow committee'. *Rep Trans Devonshire Assoc* **38**, 57–66
— 1907 'Twenty-sixth report of the barrow committee'. *Rep Trans Devonshire Assoc* **39**, 82–3
— 1913 'Thirty-second report of the barrow committee'. *Rep Trans Devonshire Assoc* **45**, 91–2
Wymer, J J 1981 'The Palaeolithic', in Simmons, and Tooley (eds), *The Environment in British Prehistory*. London: Duckworth, 49–81

Index